RESEARCHING SCHOOL-BASED TEACHER EDUCATION

Researching School-Based Teacher Education

Edited by
DAVID BLAKE
VINCENT HANLEY
MIKE JENNINGS
MICHELE LLOYD

Avebury

Aldershot • Brookfield USA • Hong Kong • Singapore • Sydney

Published by
Avebury
Ashgate Publishing Limited
Gower House
Croft Road
Aldershot
Hants GU11 3HR
England

Ashgate Publishing Company
Old Post Road
Brookfield
Vermont 05036
USA

British Library Cataloguing in Publication Data

Researching School-Based Teacher Education
    I. Blake, David
    370.71

    ISBN 1 85972 000 5

Library of Congress Catalog Card Number: 95-77823

Printed and bound by Athenæum Press Ltd.,
Gateshead, Tyne & Wear.

Contents

Part 4. Conclusion

List of tables and figures

Tables

Figures

Acknowledgements

Our thanks to Andrea Wells of the Chichester Institute of Higher Education for preparing the text for publication.

Part 1
INTRODUCTION

1 The policy context for school-based teacher education

David Blake

Policy development

Government policy on teacher education, presented in *Teaching Quality* (DES 1983) and followed by Circular 3/84 (DES 1984), led to the establishment of the Council for the Accreditation of Teacher Education (CATE) in 1984. CATE then introduced a new process of individual course scrutiny against published criteria. Revised criteria were published in 1989 (DES 1989b) and led to a reconstituted CATE from January 1990. In 1989 government policy initiatives established the licensed teacher and articled teacher schemes, starting up in 1989 and 1990 respectively (DES 1989a).

At the North of England Conference (January 1992) the Secretary of State, Kenneth Clarke, announced his intention of pressing ahead with the introduction of more school-based teacher training (DES 1992a). He argued that schools should play 'the key influential role in a much closer partnership between the school and the teacher training institutions' (para. 20) and that college-based parts of teacher training should be 'fully relevant to classroom practice' (para. 21). The idea of the new partnership was one in which 'the school and its teachers are in the lead in the whole of the training process, from the initial design of a course right through to the assessment of the performance of the individual student' (para. 22). It was announced that the Postgraduate Certificate in Education (PGCE) secondary route would be the first to be reformed, with four fifths of the course school-based (para. 33). As responsibility for training shifted to the schools, so, it was argued, would the resources for that training (para. 39). As for primary training, the Secretary of State said he would review 'whether standard Bachelor of Education (B.Ed) courses needed to be as long as four years' and consult on the proposition that 'the minimum amount of school-based work in four year courses should be ... the equivalent of at least one academic year' (para. 40).

Also in January 1992, Her Majesty's Inspectorate (HMI) published their report on *School-based Initial Training in England and Wales* (HMI 1991). The conclusion was clear:-

> The success of school-based training depends on the quality of the relationship between the training institution and the school, the significant involvement of teachers in the planning, supervision and assessment of the students' training and the active involvement of tutors in supporting the students' work in schools. p.3 (iv)

But a significant number of practical problems was also pointed to, especially the multiple calls on teachers' time and the proposition that the primary purpose of schools is 'to teach pupils, not train students' (p.4). It was concluded that a 'measured increase in the school-based element in initial training under the right conditions would pay important dividends' (p.5).

The Department of Education and Science (DES) consultation document (DES 1992b), *Reform of Initial Teacher Training* (January 1992) specified that four fifths of the secondary PGCE and one quarter of the secondary B.Ed should be school-based, postulated future performance indicators for the selection of partner schools, outlined 27 teacher competences and detailed the way in which institutional accreditation would work. Circular 9/92 (June 1992) modified the initial proposals to 24 weeks school-based work in the secondary PGCE and 32 weeks in the secondary B.Ed (DFE 1992).

New primary criteria (DFE 1993d) pursued the theme of developing partnerships between schools and higher education ('schools should play a much larger and more influential role in course design and delivery, in partnership as appropriate with higher education institutions', DFE 1993d : 5). The criteria opened up the possibility of a three-year, six-subject B.Ed, identified the possibility of courses for specialists, semi-specialists and generalists, and required more attention to be paid to the core curriculum. Not included in the new criteria was the proposal which had appeared in the Secretary of State's earlier draft circular (DFE 1993a) for a new, non-graduate, one-year course for mature students with experience of working with children who wished to specialise in teaching nursery and infant pupils up to the end of Key Stage 1. This was the so-called 'Mums Army' proposal, withdrawn in the face of vociferous opposition from all parts of the education service.

In September 1993 *The Government's Proposals for the Reform of Initial Teacher Training* were published in a blue book (DFE 1993b). The

2

key proposal was the abolition of CATE and the establishment of a new quango, the Teacher Training Agency (TTA), with responsibility for the control and funding of all courses of initial teacher training. Consisting of eight to 12 members appointed by the Secretary of State, it was proposed that the TTA would take responsibility for teacher training from 1995-6. Teacher education would be removed from involvement with the Higher Education Funding Council. New criteria for the accreditation of training courses would be established, with the intention of increasing the part played by schools in controlling and organising training. The Secretary of State, John Patten, was said to favour a reduction in the length of B.Ed courses from four to three years and those institutions which reduced average course length were to be rewarded. The intention of the proposals was to reduce the involvement of higher education in the training of teachers and to transfer more responsibility and funding to schools. In the Queen's Speech to Parliament on 18 November 1993 it was announced that legislation would be brought forward to establish the TTA. The Education Bill was published in November 1993 (DFE 1993e), further increasing the proposed powers of the TTA. Heated discussions took place in both the House of Lords and the Commons over the powers of the agency, especially with regard to school-centred training, but the 1994 Education Act substantially confirmed the blue book's proposals.

Nineteen ninety three also saw the inauguration of wholly school-centred teacher training within the School-Centred Initial Teacher Training (SCITT) scheme. Under SCITT arrangements a fee was paid direct to the school for each student. There was no compulsion to use training provided by higher education, nor to provide a course of training leading to the Postgraduate Certificate in Education (PGCE). The aim of the scheme was 'to give consortia of schools an opportunity to design, organise and provide school-centred ITT courses for graduates, leading to qualified teacher status' (DFE 1993c). In 1994 an increase in the number of school consortia and City Technology Colleges (CTC) Trust consortia offering school-centred training was announced. In total 450 places were available, 30 in primary schools (TASC 1994).

The direction of government policy is clear and consistent. It may be seen as a parallel development to changes in the school system put into place by the Education Reform Act in 1988, indeed as a logical underpinning of that reform. One strand is the provision of a market in initial teacher education, where services may be bought by the consumers from training institutions. Such a market was explicitly created in the training arrangements for the licensed teacher route (DES 1989a), and an extension of it was clearly a part of the rationale for putting schools 'in the lead' in the proposals outlined at the

North of England Conference in January 1992. The SCITT scheme represents a further development of the creation of a market. How far this market philosophy will be carried is as yet unclear, but already a substantial shift of resources from higher education institutions to schools is under way, leading to a new relationship between producers and consumers in the training process. A key element in the development of a market is the availability of a range of competing products, hence the emphasis in creating a diverse set of teacher training routes.

A second strand, also paralleled in arrangements for schools in the Education Reform Act, is the relationship between central government and local provision. For, although there is much emphasis on local autonomy in the arrangements between schools and training institutions, there is also a strong element of central control. It is clear that there is to be continuing supervision of teacher education from the centre through reformulated training and accreditation criteria controlled by the TTA. A further element of central control is retained through the power of inspection. As the furore about new arrangements for school inspections unfolded in 1992, and HMI numbers and responsibilities were transferred to Office for Standards in Education (OFSTED), HMI responsibilities for the inspection of teacher education were unchanged.

A third strand is the drive to make training more school-based. The move was anticipated in the licensed and articled teacher routes. What is underway now is the adaptation of the perceived benefits of school-basedness in those routes to the PGCE and B.Ed. The expected benefits are that practising teachers will have more influence on training, that there will be more emphasis on classroom skills and there will be less of the theory said to bedevil institutions providing teacher education. The implication is that college-based training was not fully relevant to classroom practice.

Research in progress

The chapters which follow (with the exception of chapters 6, 10 and 14) were presented at the national conference on Researching School-Based Teacher Education held at the Chichester Institute of Higher Education (formerly the West Sussex Institute of Higher Education) in July 1994. The purpose of the conference was to bring together people with an interest in research on teacher education policy and practice so that a clear view might be secured about work in progress. There was a widely shared view that policy development in teacher education had been little influenced by research and

4

evaluation. The response to the conference was enthusiastic both with regard to the number of research studies reported and the number of people who attended to discuss the participants' contributions.

The first group of papers, those collected in Part 2 of the book, are concerned with issues and processes in school-based teacher education. In brief these concern: the terminology and concepts surrounding school-based training; the nature of professional competences; students' knowledge base; mentoring skills; the nature of the encounters students in school-based schemes have with the people providing them with professional support; the management of school-based training; the future role of higher education in teacher preparation; the kind of support students receive on their induction into school-based training schemes; the implications for school-based training in England and Wales of developments in school-based training in France, and value conflicts which can arise in school-based teacher training.

Lambert and Totterdell (Chapter 2) review the conceptual framework of the University of London Institute of Education's PGCE for intending secondary teachers. Their conceptual analysis addresses ideas about partnership, theory and practice and ways of working to become a teacher. They see this as occurring within learning communities in school and HE. The notion of partnership has led to a central focus on teachers' behaviour and work in both Institute and school-based course elements. The course aims to produce reflective professionals who engage in systematic research and development.

Baumfield and Leat (Chapter 3) focus on the nature of teaching competence. They analyse mentors' comments on PGCE students on their final school experience in order to evaluate the language and concepts used. In assessing students' teaching they found no divergence between the qualities highlighted by school and HE personnel. They argue that the development of partnership models of teacher preparation offers exciting possibilities for creative dialogue.

Banks (Chapter 4) reports on the findings of a research project tracking a sample of technology students undertaking the Open University's part-time PGCE. The paper locates the pedagogical content knowledge of these mature students and explores how it is reconstructed during school-based work. The nature of beginning teachers' knowledge base is especially interesting in the case of mature students with diverse backgrounds and experience.

Dann (Chapter 5) explores processes involved in the changing role of primary class teachers from teaching practice supervisors to mentors on Keele's primary PGCE. Beginning with a pilot study of six schools in 1992, the scheme was extended to 27 schools, with forty-seven mentors, in 1993.

5

Dann reviews procedures for mentor selection before discussing five key issues: pre-mentoring perceptions; distinctions between mentoring and supervision; relationships between mentors and students (associates in Keele's terminology); time management; and the new role being developed within the teaching profession. She found that the experience of transition to mentoring carried mixed emotions. There were positive benefits for students but increased demands on teachers which they were not always able to respond to because of inadequate resources.

Constable, Norton and Hubbard (Chapter 6) shed light on an important element of the everyday life experience of a student teacher. Data were gathered systematically about the professional encounters between students and their school tutors in initial training at the University of Sunderland. The data were collected by means of a self-report inventory and interviews and reveal who students talked to about their teaching experiences, what they talked about, where and when these conversations took place, who initiated them, how long each encounter lasted and how many encounters were had. Three main emerging issues were the economies of time as a resource; school variation and the development of competences.

Martin (Chapter 7) relates management theory to the process of change in teacher education. His theme is that the process of centrally driven change is making implementation highly problematic for schools and HE. In terms of the roles of HE personnel there has been role ambiguity and a recurring process of redefinition is described. He evaluates the impact of change on individuals and the sense of loss which can result from hasty and ill-thought through change processes.

Kerr (Chapter 8) focuses on the process of induction and support for students in school in the context of the PGCE partnership scheme at Leicester University. He reports on an evaluation of the quality of the school-based component of the course. Whilst there are encouraging elements in students' experiences, Kerr points to the dangers of increased variability in students' experiences in school. He also believes it is possible to discern a rhetoric-reality gap in the way in which some schools conceptualise and support students' reflective practice. In sum there may be a significant gap between desirable elements of ITE and what increased school-basing can achieve given the pressure of ITE involvement in addition to all the other demands on schools.

Cotton's paper (Chapter 9) introduces an interesting comparative dimension by reviewing arrangements for primary teacher training in France. She focuses on the role of the 'maîtres formateurs', carefully selected teachers who take on the role of supervising students in school. The French system demands substantial university-based training for the 'maîtres' before they undertake their role in teacher training. As well as working with students in school, the maîtres formateurs contribute to sessions in the university, especially those concerned with preparation for teaching practice.

Blake, Hanley, Jennings and Lloyd (Chapter 10) explore the value assumptions underlying the vocabulary of new training forms, identify the values which official criteria describing high quality training imply and discuss the potential value conflicts facing schools and HE in developing new partnership schemes. They draw on their empirical work to illustrate the kinds of value conflict which can arise in school-based training.

The second group of papers, collected in Part 3 of the book, comprises institutional case studies of school-based teacher education in practice. Themes emerging from these case studies include: planning for partnership and partnership in action; planning a map of professional competences; the changing roles of personnel involved in school-based training; conceptualising theory and practice in a school-based programme; mentoring from a school perspective; a school's approach to the management of time within a new school and higher education partnership; a comparison of school and higher education administered PGCE programmes; and initial evaluations of pilot PGCEs operating under circular 9/92.

Ellis (Chapter 11) gives an account of the principles underlying the planning of partnership at Cardiff Institute of Higher Education under Welsh Office Circular 63/93. He argues that a mentoring system will be central, that schools will be involved in course design and that a systematic staff development programme will be necessary for both HE and school staff in anticipation of their new roles. The idea of basing partnership on a limited number of primary training schools is evaluated.

Maloney and Powell (Chapter 12) compare training arrangements for PGCE secondary students at Kingston University under traditional and new partnership arrangements, as viewed by students and tutors. Issues which arise are the difficulty of ensuring parity of student experience in 'new' partnership schools and the need for excellent communication between HE and schools about the development of the various professional support programmes. The research threw up alarming variations in the support students received not only in different schools but within the same school and, to an extent, in the same department.

Cain and Kickham's paper (Chapter 13) reviews a process of collaborative planning at La Sainte Union College of Higher Education to identify statements of professional competence and professional qualities. The planning involved HE tutors, teachers and students in training. Their paper shows the detailed planning which a competency-based profile demands, and the benefits which can accrue from a team approach.

Blake, Hanley, Jennings and Lloyd (Chapter 14) focus on changing roles and expectations within a PGCE course operating under Circular 9/92 at the Chichester Institute of Higher Education. They found a general welcome for partnership from students, teachers and tutors. Students tended to identify with schools and to comply with school expectations. HE tutors were regarded as less significant, portrayed as visitors to the scene of the action. Most significant were subject mentors whose support students sought. Mentors and professional tutors were enthusiastic about their new roles but wanted more time for them. They both argued strongly in favour of complementary roles within a partnership model. College tutors views were variable. Link tutors, in general, found much to praise in the new arrangements. Subject tutors felt ground had been lost and considered their role to be marginal.

Egan's paper (Chapter 15) is concerned with PGCE secondary students' views of their training as Art and Design and Physical Education teachers at Cardiff Institute of Higher Education. Particular attention is paid to the relationship between theory and practice. The expertise of teacher educators, it is argued, is distinct from that of teachers working with students in school and is especially valuable in addressing the theoretical and the practical. The danger of losing well-established forms of informal collaborative work in schools, with teachers, tutors and students working together, are illustrated by reference to Cardiff's Artist in Residence and Instructional Teacher Practice initiatives. Egan believes that establishing separate, albeit complementary, domains for teachers and teacher educators in training programmes will lead to fragmentation and a diminished teacher preparation programme.

Dormer (Chapter 16) reports a case study of mentorship in action in a pilot school-based scheme operating under Circular 9/92 at Exmouth Community College. She argues that successful mentoring requires a systematic intellectual framework to support it. Emphasis is placed on mentoring by a number of supportive professionals, rather than the mentor as an individual. If there is to be effective teacher education there needs to be an integration of theory and practice. This will only happen where there is enough time for people to contribute commitment to shared principles of learning and effective communication between school and HE personnel.

Arrowsmith (Chapter 17) develops arguments about the benefits for schools when they become involved in ITT. He identifies the management of teachers' time as the key management challenge in engaging in ITT and reviews Chenderit School's approach. He applies criteria derived from school

8

effectiveness and school improvement literature to justify the investment of staff time. The success of partnership from the school's perspective depends to a large extent on an alignment of the values of the school and of ITT. An overall conclusion is that because of such an alignment of values there is a reduction in the significance of the financial arrangements for the success of the partnership in favour of a range of school improvement factors.

Goodyear, Abbott, Evans and Pritchard (Chapter 18) report on a University of Warwick research project which compares the relative effectiveness of training delivered in consortia of schools with responsibility for administering the training with courses which represent partnerships between schools and HE. The two models are referred to as SAPs (School Administered Programmes) and HEAPs (Higher Education Administered Programmes).

Moxham's paper (Chapter 19) reviews Nene College's 1993-4 pilot PGCE primary course, a main innovative feature of which was the transfer of funding to participating schools to pay for the supervision of school-based training. She found that each school tutor received, on average, half a day's supply cover to supervise students in school. Confusions arose where expectations about funding procedures and personnel roles were not mutual. The need for teacher tutors to be well-briefed and trained was identified. All participants wanted a continued role with HE tutors in a complementary and symbiotic partnership.

Howard (Chapter 20) reports on a study of St. Mary's College's secondary PGCE operating under Circular 9/92. Mentoring is viewed as a form of adult education in the work-place. The context is one of external imposition and compulsory change. A largely negative response to the new form of training is reported from schools. A significant number of staff in the schools in Howard's sample was finding the demands of school-based training unmanageable.

Glover and Hudson's paper (Chapter 21) reports an evaluation study of the first year of Worcester College of Higher Education's school-based secondary PGCE. New management procedures had been introduced and new roles for teachers in schools and HE tutors had been introduced. They found variation in the readiness of schools to take on new training roles. A particular HE problem was the loss of the role of subject tutor within the generic role of professional link tutor. A revision of the new course which involved a reversion to the roles of the 'old' PGCE was set in train and to some extent led to limitations on the realisation of the new course as it had been conceived. Thus there was limited achievement of change in the first year of operation of the new PGCE.

The move towards school-based forms of teacher education has been ideologically and politically driven. Imposed from above, with little genuine consultation, the benefits of school-basing may sometimes have been obscured by the government's dogmatic attacks on higher education's stake in teacher education. It has been difficult to engage in rational debate, not least because of the lack of government interest in evidence and research. Yet, to their credit, most teacher educators, in both school and higher education, have recognised the value of systematic inquiry into the new forms of teacher education. They have recognised that developments in school-based initial teacher education raise complex issues which merit careful investigation. Teacher education policy over the past decade has been characterised by too much sloganising and too little thought. The chapters in this volume are intended to redress the balance.

Part 2
ISSUES AND PROCESSES

2 Crossing academic communities: Clarifying the conceptual landscape in initial teacher education

David Lambert and Michael Totterdell

Introduction

The aim of this chapter is to outline the nature of the conceptual work undertaken over recent years in relation to the evolving PGCE course for intending secondary teachers at the University of London Institute of Education (ULIE). Initial teacher education is experiencing the throes of rapid and under-resourced change and, at the moment when partnership training becomes mandatory for secondary courses (DFE Circular 9/92: September 1994), the condition of this crucially important component of the education service is in a fragile state. We agree with Wilkin and Sankey (1994) that the government has precipitated this by the imposition of what appears to be a new order, defined by regulation, in which the balance of time and responsibility has shifted to schools and teachers. However, as Wilkin and Sankey continue their analysis, they are able to make a very strong case that the main elements of this 'revolution' in training were already being introduced by the profession itself. This certainly was the case with the ULIE partnership, which is described in the following section; it is a description of the conceptual underpinning of this intrinsically motivated change which forms the main part of this chapter.

The fact that we see developments more within an evolutionary rather than revolutionary model, does nothing to reduce the chronic instability of a system of training which is not yet the beneficiary of a clear theoretical framework to guide development. In addition, this shift in responsibility for training is being perceived as an additional burden on schools whose main priority is to educate children, not to provide for the initiation of would-be-entrants to the profession. The government has perceived a crisis in education which it rather belatedly has chosen to blame on the existing teacher training system; its response has been to urge a more practically based system and

13

marginalise, even eradicate, the Higher Education (HE) contribution. We, along with our partner schools, see this as facile and dangerous. In part our concern is that this mote may be a harbinger for a return to the simplistic perspective that teaching is set of technical skills to be applied to both students and content. In part it reflects our joint commitment to creating and sustaining a different framework for thinking about learning to teach; one that acknowledges the complexity of the teaching-learning dynamic and examines the social and political realities of education. And yet we are equally convinced of the necessity to answer this challenge with arguments far more persuasive than those that rely solely on the received wisdom of the past. Included here are those assertions which slip easily off the tongue such as the need for teachers to become 'reflective practitioners' and which, though clearly depicting something desirable, are difficult to crystallise or grasp and which may acquire the appearance and status of an irritating slogan to many beginning teachers.

We need, then, to move forward with more critical honesty than has often been evident in the past and identify what precisely it is that post-graduate initial training can and should provide. In our view, the first stage in this process, in advance of any substantial empirical work, is an attempt to clear some of the conceptual undergrowth. We recognise that one cannot have a concept of a particular, and that concepts are ideas or 'more precisely the abstraction that represents or signifies the unifying principle of various distinct particulars' (Barrow and Milburn 1990: 61). In seeking to engage in conceptual analysis we are not so much offering definitions as an elaboration of the proper grounds for considering that something has a certain characteristic or falls appropriately under a particular rubric. If successful, this elaboration should lead to a scheme of evidence and thus has considerable epistemic importance.

In other words, by couching our description of a shared experience of educational development in conceptual categories our intention is to undertake an interpretative task in identifying and clarifying what it is initial teacher education is about. In so doing we wish to begin to outline a theoretical framework that will accommodate both constructively and creatively the centre-led shifts in HEI-school relations. We attempt to do this in a spirit of continuity and change:

> It is important in the highly politicised climate of training today that continuities with the past are recognised. To do so gives a sense of direction in the current maelstrom that is teacher training, and helps to restore to some degree at least a sense of professional autonomy in the

face of the control that is currently being exercised. The need for collaboration now and in the future between the two partners of school and training institution was never greater . . . . Only if schools and training institutions each contribute their expertise to the professional preparation of teachers will teaching remain a profession; but also only if that is the case will that preparation remain professionally adequate. (Wilkin and Sankey 1994: 19).

We intend to flesh out this statement and, in doing so, point to the way the Institute has interpreted the role of partnership in the training process, concentrating on the fundamental facets of our work. Prominent amongst these is the role which partnership should play in challenging the widespread mind-set which encourages a damaging separation of theory and practice in educational thinking and activity. The challenge is to design a course which articulates a shared responsibility for the preparation and formation of tomorrow's teachers, and the safeguarding of standards. We believe that this is best accomplished by identifying and propagating distinctive, post-graduate ways of working in a range of equally distinctive contexts (see Figure 2.1). At the same time we should explicitly acknowledge that both schools and HE are responsible for generating and nurturing the intellectual dimension of being (becoming) a teacher. We like to think of our developing partnership model as one contained within a broader notion of evolving learning communities: beginning teachers straddling the different, yet symbolically related, academic communities of school and HE can, we feel, be a significant agent in the development of schools 'improving from within' (Barth 1990). Indeed, given the growing recognition of the central importance of school culture, school improvement, raising achievement and promoting effective teaching, we are confident that the partnership model can act as a powerful catalyst within schools in support of the processes of positive change and consequently of educational enrichment (Hillman and Stoll 1994). Furthermore, we readily acknowledge that partnership has increasingly demanded that we make explicit reference to the context of teachers' behaviour and work - both inside and outside the classroom - in those elements of the course which remain Institute-based (cf. Talbert et al 1993).

15

TEACHERS

CLASSROOMS --- SCHOOLS --- SCHOOL CLUSTERS --- AREA

TUTORS

Figure 2.1: The axes of partnership in training

The horizontal scale of experience shows the contexts. The vertical scale indicates distinctive modes of support for the beginning teacher.

Background

The Institute's Partnership in Training PGCE, (ULIE 1994a) developed from a residential conference for tutors and teachers in 1990 which was called specifically to examine current and future PGCE course structures and designs. The conference acknowledge and addressed the following clear messages being signalled in evaluations by students and schools of the existing course:

1.   the separate parts worked well enough, but the course needed to be a more coherent and cohesive experience for all involved;

2.   there needed to be a more active partnership in the training between the Institute and the schools and colleges involved specifically in professional studies, but also more generally;

3.   students found that working in larger groupings in schools and colleges was better than working in isolation.

A pilot phase of the new scheme was run in Camden during 1991-92. This was evaluated (Harland 1992) before being adapted to cover the whole of Greater London, five geographical Areas. During its pilot and transitional years (1991-1994) the Institute tutors were able to work with a team of Professional Studies Tutors, who were largely seconded teachers from partner schools. These were enormously influential in planning, delivering and evaluating the PGCE course, which resulted in the present scheme, Partnership in Training (ULIE 1994a), launched in September 1994 by the

Institute and approximately 180 partner schools.

Each of the five Areas comprises groupings (clusters) of schools and colleges that provide a wide range of educational and socio-economic environments - public schools, further education and sixth-form colleges, grant maintained, voluntary aided, and denominational schools, grammar, county and urban comprehensive schools - and each Area takes about 140-180 students, the number required to ensure a proper spread of subjects across the curriculum. Each Area has a co-ordinator who is responsible to a Senior Tutor. The Area co-ordinator oversees the work of the tutor team drawn primarily from school staff (the School Tutor) and complemented by Institute staff (the Institute Tutor). The course consists of three elements:

1. Curriculum Subject Studies - courses of subject based work with up to two days of each week at the Institute and one day in schools and colleges. Subject work is the major responsibility of the appropriate Institute Tutor working in conjunction with the Subject Supervisor (often the Head of Department) in school.

2. Block Teaching Practice - six weeks in November and December of Term 1 and eight weeks in February/March of Term 2. This is under the supervision of the appropriate Subject Supervisor (normally the Head of Department) and is moderated by the School Tutor and appropriate Institute Tutor.

3. Professional Studies - a course which focuses on 'whole school' issues and professional development, intended to take absolute beginners through to the level of competent, reflective qualified teachers. Much of this component takes place in the school clusters in each of the five Areas, though there is also a significant research-led contribution from the Institute and Institute Tutors.

The overall aim of the course is development of those competent, reflective qualified teachers through the creation of a genuine partnership in initial training between schools and the Institute. This is also to ensure that beginning teachers rapidly acquire a sense of belonging to a broader profession and come to understand the implications of this in their professional development. The principal objectives are to ensure a variety of teaching and learning experiences; to encourage beginning teachers to develop effective ways of working with children and each other; and to develop confident, thoughtful, knowledgeable, and expert teachers in one or two areas.

17

They also need high professional standards. As the course handbook puts it, 'Our beginning teachers must be responsible and responsive new-professionals, competent in practice and having a sound theoretical underpinning for their day-to-day work.' (ULIE 1994b)

Finally, it is worthwhile recording that the Institute has avoided using the term mentor in its documentation out of concern that its connotation might be too narrowly related to the work-place. The beginning teacher works with four professionals, listed below:

1. Institute Tutor (curriculum)
2. Institute Tutor (professional studies)
3. School Tutor (professional studies)
4. Subject Supervisor (curriculum)

All Institute Tutors are curriculum specialists of one sort or another, but have professional studies responsibilities for a mixed group of beginning teachers located in a particular partner school cluster. Subject Supervisors are normally Heads of Department, and the School Tutor is normally a senior member of staff. It is an expectation that School Tutors within a cluster will collaborate and share expertise, and designated Institute Tutors have an additional responsibility to help facilitate such cooperative working practices.

As indicated earlier, the course has been designed within parameters which require beginning teachers to work in certain ways. These are usefully identified by three interdependent yet distinctive course 'foci' which are clearly signalled to all course participants and are explicit on the timetable. It is to this more detailed discussion we can now turn.

As indicated earlier, the course has been designed within parameters which require beginning teachers to work in certain ways. These are usefully identified by three interdependent yet distinctive course 'foci' which are clearly signalled to all course participants and are explicit on the timetable. It is to this more detailed discussion we can now turn.

Course foci for the beginning teacher

The three foci have been developed as an integrative motif for the course programme, and are as follows:

- the teacher as competent practitioner;
- the teacher as reflective professional;

- the teacher as researcher.

These recurring themes run through the whole course, permeating course elements and providing each with a distinctive texture. They also underpin the theme for each term (which designates a particular sphere of information and experience), by providing a supporting tripod of ways of working (see Figure 2.2).

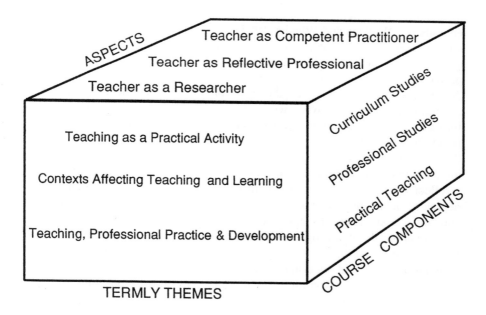

Figure 2.2   The PGCE curriculum cube

The PGCE curriculum is contained inside the box. Choose any one of the three sides as a way into the box and you cut across other concerns. For example, choosing the aspect of the 'Teacher as Reflective Professional' means we must engage with curriculum studies, professional studies and practical teaching. Furthermore, reflective activity will at different times be linked with highly practical and immediate concerns, broader context affecting teaching and learning and future personal and professional development.

It is intended that beginning teachers should adopt persona and concomitant set of attitudes as part of the mode 'learning teacher'. They are not experienced as consecutive stages or phases, but rather as core concerns with which beginning teachers engage and to which they return to/consider attend during successive episodes of the course to a greater or lesser extent.

Teacher as competent practitioner Adopting this persona is fundamental in so far as teaching is a complex form of social practice Teachers are practically-oriented professionals, and competence is appropriately conceived as the process of immersion in and mastery of the best developed practices of teaching. Successful practices are normally developed by beginning teachers indwelling traditions of good practice which represent communities of memory in relation to teachers' repertoire, 'role set' and the practical principles they embody (cf. Watkins and Whalley 1995). By attending to particular situations and contexts - often but not exclusively those associated with classrooms (Lambert and Sankey 1994) - and by applying and refining a set of practical principles, both practical insight and practical knowledge begin to develop. All of this occurs, usually on the basis of making incremental progress in extending the range of 'what works for me' and 'what feels right', through forms of practical reasoning. This is of paramount importance of course, but it is not the whole story.

Teacher as reflective professional Professional training demands more than initiation into a set of practices, even if these are the best available. It requires a reflective element to furnish it with ballast and perspective. It demands a degree of detachment, a standing back from the particularities and immediate situational exigencies to take a broader view and develop a deeper understanding through progressively sophisticated forms of critical reflection. However, even at the initial stage, beginning teachers need to probe the assumptions and deliberate upon the values that lie behind the practices. In other words we see reflection as a conscious (indeed self-conscious and self-critical) activity whereby beginning teachers create an intellectual and attitudinal framework for thinking about learning to teach, by participating in a course which is based upon practical experience and values learning by doing. Such a framework must be robust enough to acknowledge the complexity of the teaching-earning dynamic and accept that teachers' work is often messy and ambiguous.

Perhaps the view of reflective inquiry that best resonates with our own is that of Tom who presents it as 'the arena of the problematic' (Tom 1985: 37); it demands a willingness to ask questions, probe difficult and resistant situations, be aware of broad methodological and attitudinal principles and live with ambiguity. This last point is particularly pertinent in the present context; a common language and a common list of practical concerns is comforting but also beguiling, as Edwards points out:

The predictability and control that the doctrine of technical rationality seemingly offers provides comforting reassurance to educational practitioners faced with constant uncertainty. This need for certainty and control is, however, a major inhibitor of educational change. Thus... there is a need to restore ambiguity to its proper place. (Edwards 1992: 465)

Teacher as researcher Because 'the arena of the problematic' is not necessarily transparent, we have come to view research as an appropriate tool hereby beginning teachers have the opportunity to examine the fabric of teaching and learn to make reasoned decisions about practice. At the simplest level this might take the form of - 'that worked well, why?'. Sometimes (but not invariably) a research dimension is needed to answer this sort of question. At a more complex level beginning teachers may attempt to untangle different kinds of questions or different elements within a question, and to suit the manner of inquiry - observational, analytical, historical, philosophical and so on - to the nature of the particular question being pursued. Furthermore, we feel that this process would encourage our beginning teachers to be more reflective about practice, and we see this orientation as emphasising the knowledge, disposition and analytical skills needed to make good decisions about complex classroom phenomena in relation to the role of teacher, culture, the curriculum and pedagogical practices.

Emerging qualities of 'partners in training': towards a person specification for membership of the learning community

One interesting feature of the emerging partnership in training is a recognition that certain higher order values are central to its ethos, and a growing awareness that course participants derive the optimum benefit from involvement. The following values and characteristics appear to be implicit in the ways of working we have outlined.

1.   Implications for the trainee:

    i)   an attitudinal context or climate of trust;

    ii)   responsiveness and self-responsibility;

    iii)   ability to live with complexity and ambiguity;

iv) conceptual flexibility and finesse so as to think clearly, be selective and generate a variety of optional approaches to teaching problems;

v) interdependence and a sense of belonging to a professional community;

vi) ability to tie together intellectual strengths and social conviction and to maintain civility/benevolence in disputation so that argument/discussion remains constructive;

vii) reflective disposition with regard to self, the practice of teaching and the institution of education.

2. Implications for the trainer:

i) awareness of boundaries and role clarity, skills of consultant and critical friend;

ii) ability to provide appropriate guidance and conceptual familiarity with various disciplines of thought;

iii) ability to provide tutorial support and to facilitate collaborative ways of working in a climate of exchange;

iv) ability to be patient with others' explorations and not demand resolution prematurely;

v) capacity to challenge assumptions and encourage implicit values for explicit consideration;

vi) capability to help beginning teachers clarify their own value base and make judgements about what is worthwhile;

vii) capacity to narrow or broaden the focus as needed;

viii) ability to work towards excellence through encouragement;

ix) ability to be both a 'gadfly' and a 'midwife'.

Partnership: the conduit to professional development?

In our own experience initial teacher education has never intentionally separated theory from practice as if they belonged to two different worlds. Indeed, we might justifiably ask whether in fact they ever did. As long ago as 1906 for example, Professor James Welton postulated that educational theory 'is practice become conscious of itself, and practice is realised theory' (Welton 1906: 17). Although we might question this particular formulation, the interface that Welton recognised is crucial and, at the same time, both obvious and, in actuality, very difficult to grasp. Welton went on to argue that without such theory, the 'mechanical teacher does as he was done by; with him [sic] progress implies change, and change is unwelcome, for he cannot adapt himself to it'. And he added a further important condition: that theory should not be 'an unsubstantial vision spun out of the clouds of an untrammelled imagination . . . a theory of teaching which deserves the name is in the closest possible touch with school work' (Welton 1906: 18).

The Institute PGCE takes forward this kind of thinking and promotes an understanding which posits greater congeniality between theory and practice. It recognises, for example, that theory, or at least theorising, is a distinctive activity, requiring of the teacher particular skills and attitudes. We therefore require of beginning teachers that they work in such a way that the judgements they make about their observations and experiences are informed; furthermore that they are contingent and always at a stage of development (Lambert and Totterdell 1993). Teachers who understand and accept this approach are sceptical of those who offer them a canon of theory to be half digested. They are also, and equally importantly, capable of a critical appraisal of observed practice. In short, 'they have been taught in a way that encourages commitment to continuous professional learning and intellectual renewal throughout their careers' (HMI 1983: 18).

PGCE research and development projects are underpinned by this understanding of the theory-practice interface. Observers have noted that 'in essence these are small scale research inquiries undertaken in cooperation with the staff of the placement school or college' (Grace 1993: 5). They have been welcomed as representing a significant innovation at the initial stage of a process of professional formation and development for beginning teachers and we believe that they provide a basis for achieving a balanced integration between education scholarship and practical application in specific school settings. Gilbert Ryle (1966: 27) declared that 'intelligent practice is not a step-child of theory. On the contrary, theorising is one practice amongst others and itself is intelligently or stupidly conducted'. We agree, and we wish

23

our student teachers to grasp this too as they negotiate (sometimes literally) their way through their research.

It should be emphasised that the research is expressly not an end in itself. Ryle went on to note that in teaching we are not solely interested in a person's capacity to find out the truth for themselves; what is more interesting is their ability to organise and exploit it. And as Barnett has argued, 'genuine learning is a sharing and collective activity, in which we test out what we believe we have learnt in the company of others' (Barnett 1992: 75). In other words, the development of the research is crucial. So far this has usually taken the form of a specially prepared report to the school (often to the School Tutor and interested or involved members of staff). Undoubtedly some schools will have to make adjustments to the way they see their role in training and indeed the role of the student teacher if they are to benefit fully from this kind of activity. This is particularly so, as is sometimes the case, when the beginning teacher is prepared to make suggestions or recommendations. Other schools, possibly those who see themselves as communities of learners welcome the scrutiny of systematic, focused enquiry, especially that conducted by the competent yet inexperienced innocent abroad. This is clearly a potential field for serious empirical investigation itself, but early anecdotal evidence is encouraging. As one inner urban school has reported, specifically on research and development:

- it is refreshing to have a new look at knotty problems;

- it is challenging to have some of our assumptions questioned;

- it can increase our knowledge base and improve our understanding of particular issues;

- it can result in suggestions for improvement.

East Area evaluation meeting, 27.6.94

While feedback from beginning teachers' evaluations is not always uniformly positive, very few seem hostile or negative. 'A very stimulating and nerve racking experience' commented one beginning teacher while another wrote:

R&D' really made me change in a positive light. Having had time [since] previous education, this course was really enlightening, and for

24

the first time I felt I was learning in the best possible sense. It also improved my self-esteem, because my work was actually approved for the first time. I felt I could write well.

Conclusion

The development of confident and ambitious teachers, able and willing to transfer this confidence and ambition to their pupils, and prepared to take on the challenges of the next decade into the twenty-first century, demands a course appropriate to the task. In essence, we are aiming to shape a course which produces reflective professionals. For us this is no mere slogan, for what we mean is nothing less than active learners, learners who are:

- skilled in observation (and sensitive to context);

- skilled in describing what has been observed;

- able to engage in analysis and draw supported generalisations or conclusions;

- able to relate these to their own needs and development as well as to those of others.

Involvement of beginning teachers in research and development and the other course activities or ways of working we have considered, can be looked upon as an 'entitlement'; they give access to certain kinds of skills and experience which are distinct, but clearly linked to developing long-term, competent practice.

We believe that the approaches identified in this paper contribute to a distinctive espousal of 'partnership', for what we are proposing depends on collaborative organisation. Partnership is indeed the conduit. It represents an approach to professional training fashioned out of a genuine bridge-building exercise between school and HE cultures, and one which serves to enhance the quality of the initial and continuing development of teachers.

3   Benchmarking the competences

Vivienne Baumfield and David Leat

As we approach the end of the twentieth century, higher education and the world of work are increasingly being urged to work together to meet social and economic priorities. Training, directed towards the acquisition of skills and competences, and education, directed towards acquisition of knowledge and development of self-critical reflection, are also on a converging and mutually reinforcing path. Sir Bryan Nicholson (in Bines and Watson 1992: viii).

The 9/92 competences demonstrate some long standing difficulties encountered in competence based approaches. In considering the use of the competences in Initial Teacher Training (ITT) a number of questions arise:

1.   What is a competence?

2.   Is it helpful to atomise the teaching process into 27 competences?

3.   Are the competences of equal weight?

4.   What is an acceptable level of performance within a defined competence?

5.   To what extent can we assess consistency of performance using the competences; for example, can allowances be made for the impact of context on performance and is regression within a particular competence possible?

The answer to these questions will be partly determined by one's understanding of learning to be a professional. Competence is a widely used word and one that demonstrates an elasticity of meaning. For some, encouraged by the early work of the National Council for Vocational Qualifications (NCVQ) on vocational qualifications, competence has come to mean a narrow behaviourist approach to learning, where roles are reduced to a checklist of skills to be mastered. The Working Group for the Department of Education Northern Ireland (1993) identified 89 competences for qualifying teachers. They recognised that this did not capture the totality of professional competence, so they incorporated a further list of 16 professional values. For others, successful teaching is defined by the ability to reflect on and learn from experience (Ashcroft and Griffiths 1989). The bulk of existing research on teaching as a profession favours experiential learning and refers to the reflective practitioner. In a recent survey of postgraduate ITT course leaders (Barrett et al 1992) almost 75 per cent described their agreed method of training as the reflective practitioner model. The reflective paradigm has developed from the work of Schon (1983, 1987), but despite all the literature it has spawned there is still a distinct lack of clarity surrounding its operation in teacher education.

Wolf (1994), drawing on considerable experience of vocational education, stresses the need to escape the 'atomistic' trap when assessing the broad skills and unpredictable tasks which characterise the complex work of professionals. Teaching is a sophisticated enterprise, which involves more than the operation of a number of technical skills and thus it defies the technical rationality models that once characterised much of professional education. The notion that teachers learned the theory of teaching in lectures and then went out to put it into practice has been proved wanting. Elliott (1991) makes a convincing argument about professionalism, based on experience across a number of professions. He contends that new professional images, including those for teachers, incorporate the need to collaborate and communicate with clients in identifying and solving their problems, emphasising the holistic understanding of situations and self-reflection as a means of overcoming stereotypical judgements. Furthermore he argues that all worthwhile professional learning is experiential. Teaching is well matched to this analysis: much of teaching can be identified as problem solving and decision making in which people (pupils, parents and other staff) are highly significant.

We do not, at present, have the option of choosing not to use the competences in the assessment of students in ITT. The task is to develop a means of working with the 9/92 framework in a manner which retains the

28

integrity of all concerned: Higher Education Institutions (HEIs), schools and students. The new partnerships in ITT must try to find the 'converging and mutually reinforcing path' alluded to by Nicholson (in Bines and Watson 1992). Zeichner (1990) advocates the development of a broad vision of competence which involves both behavioural and interpretative approaches - the best of both worlds. There is a chance that this view will be realised in what Bines (1992) describes as the emerging post-technocratic model of professional education. The characteristics of this model are the development of competence through experience of, and reflection on, practice in a practicum within which students have access to skilled practitioners who act as coaches. Hyland (1994) in his study of the impact of NVQs and GNVQs on post 16 vocational education has found that on a pragmatic level college tutors have tended to retain a methodology based on experiential learning. It should be remembered that Norris (1991) advocated caution in implying that a competence model is undifferentiated, as some fundamentally different approaches have been conceptualised under this banner. Hyland tentatively suggests that the implementation of GNVQs may offer an opportunity to reassess strategies for learning which will not focus solely on outcomes. Perhaps lessons will be learned from these experiences which can assist our assessment of student teachers.

It may be that the model which seeks to juxtapose competence and reflective practice creates a false dichotomy. On the other hand, we may be dealing with epistemologically distinct theories of professional education which will not permit co-operative effort without fudging the issues. Neither can we ignore the political dimension of the debate about ITT when it is often characterised in rhetoric as a conflict between academics in the HEIs and the practitioners in the real world of schools. Hargreaves (1994) has viewed the advocacy of a reflective practitioner model for ITT by lecturers in HEI as an attempt to relieve them from developing collaborative relations with practising teachers; or, to put the matter in its starkest terms, as a justification of their own existence. He argues that the model encourages in the trainee a highly critical approach to the practices observed during the practicum and retains the induction of the trainee into best practice under the lecturer's guidance. Until the provenance of the terms are clarified it will be difficult to resolve these questions. Recent analysis is seeking to extend understanding beyond a simplistic polarisation of viewpoints. Writers (Avis 1994 and Hargreaves 1994) for example have begun to explore the issue of professionalism in teaching in a way that unfolds the tensions and opportunities the emerging partnership models have disclosed. It would be a mistake to seek premature resolution at the expense of the potential for creativity the present situation offers.

Case Study: Newcastle University PGCE Secondary Course

Methodology

Discussions with partnership schools on the assessment of student teachers began in September 1993. It was agreed that the final report for students would not focus on the 27 individual competences. Whilst one or two mentors expressed a need for a competence checklist, most schools preferred to concentrate on the broader categories of Subject Knowledge, Subject Application, Class Management, Assessment and Recording of Pupils' Progress and Further Professional Development. Copies of the 9/92 competences were issued to each mentor and the Mentoring Booklet contains observation strategies which are linked to the gathering of evidence on particular competences. Individual mentors were given a free hand to use any (or none) of the strategies in their observations of students. The final report would then elicit a prose response outlining student performance within the five broad areas of competence. The objective was to establish a description of an individual student's performance in any particular area. Teachers, on the whole, were anxious to resist a checklist or statement bank route but recognised the need for a means of moderating the performance of students both within subject areas in schools and also across the different schools involved in the partnership. The exercise to establish descriptors for each broad area of competence was seen as a move towards defining boundary criteria for excellent, good, satisfactory and unsatisfactory levels of performance.

Responses on the final report forms have been analysed in the areas of competence and key phrases/descriptors for each category - excellent through to unsatisfactory - distilled. As far as possible the teachers' own words have been recorded verbatim. The statements have now been reflected back to the mentors so that they can discuss the findings and suggest any addition/deletion/promotion/demotion of statements. The degree to which mentors feel it is necessary to change statements will act as a check on undue manipulation by the researchers but may also indicate the effects of a moderating process whereby mentors may wish to revise their views on what constitutes performance at a specified level within a broad category. Responses so far suggest some minor adjustments but no fundamental changes have been proposed.

30

Results

Table 3.1 gives, by way of example, the results of the analysis of teachers' comments on each category for the competence area Subject Application. Table 3.2 gives the comments made in the excellent category for two further competence areas - Further Professional Development and Classroom Management - together with those from a Further Comments heading.

In Subject Application, the excellent student is frequently demonstrating qualities such as energy and commitment. The ability to adapt a growing repertoire of strategies and be flexible is mentioned, pupils needs are considered and their knowledge tapped, there are analytical skills and the student is learning from experience and putting that experience to use. Looking across the categories, many of these qualities are reiterated and others appear, notably their success in forming relationships with both staff and pupils. The following extracts serve as an illustration:

Has taken every opportunity to develop herself professionally. Regularly reviewed her needs and methodically worked to fulfil them.

She was aware of the pupils as individuals and related well to them.... Excellent working relationships with colleagues. She has the ability and sensitivity to integrate into many different areas of school life.

We are exceptionally pleased with how quickly the academic and social diversity within and across classes was recognised and harnessed to help maintain active teaching processes.

A careful, self critical and analytical approach to all she does has meant that she has gained maximum benefit from this teaching practice. She has a tremendous awareness of the whole child and an appropriate philosophy.

Aware of the need to be well prepared for all eventualities.

Interesting ideas and innovative approach have been most illuminating.

Discussion

Certain recurring qualities span the four areas of 9/92 competences analysed:

31

Commitment / Motivation / Proactivity

Perception / Ability to read situations

Ability to form relationships

Flexibility

Analytical skills / Ability to learn from experience.

Inevitably we will encounter problems with words as conveyors of meaning in this discussion; problems compounded by the imprecision of some of the key terms used in the debate about teacher education. Nonetheless we found there was correspondence between teachers' descriptions of student teachers and research findings on superior performance of teachers and other professionals which have supported the reflective practitioner paradigm.

Lawes (1987) found that student teachers' ability to judge pupils' comprehension, interest and ability from watching silent video tape of a class was related to the student's teaching effectiveness, as rated by the tutor and supervising teacher. Turning to overt and visible behaviours of student teachers, Neil (1989) compiled ratings of student teachers at interview and from referees on posture, willingness to meet gaze, calmness of behaviour and gesture characterising enthusiastic speech.

These ratings were compared with ratings during the course by supervising teachers and tutors of control, calmness, enthusiasm and progress. He concluded:

> Ratings of calm, dominant behaviour offers the best predictive value in choosing candidates. These qualities seem to allow student teachers to maintain control, they can then show their enthusiasm for their subject and thus build up positive relationships with classes.

Chandler, Robinson and Noyes (1991) used the construct of the proactive student to correlate against ratings of performance. They described a small minority of students who have high levels of personal commitment and motivation who go beyond the normal expectations of traditional teaching. These teachers are innovative and willing to try things out and these least cautious students were rated more highly than their more cautious contemporaries. From a more theoretical stance Ashcroft and Griffiths (1989), in advancing the cause of the reflective paradigm in teacher education in which critical enquiry is fundamental, argue that values related to open-mindedness, responsibility and wholeheartedness need to be developed. They quote Zeichner (1983): 'rather than just accepting existing traditions or curricula and imitating current practice, the effective teacher is seen as one who reflects on the question of what ought to be done'. There is reinforcement here therefore for the idea that critical characteristics are motivation and adventure, the energy, confidence and commitment to experiment, to try things out and take risks.

Flexibility is another characteristic of some teachers' descriptions of student teachers. John (1991) in a study of student teachers' lesson planning found that during the training year the plans became less formal, more flexible and open ended. Livingston and Borko (1989) compared four student teachers with their supervising teachers and accounted for the differences in quality of teaching between these comparative novices and experts by arguing that the schemata of the novices are less elaborate, interconnected and accessible than those of experts. There is some confirmation of this interpretation from research into problem solving (Chi, Glaser, Rees 1982, DeJong and Ferguson Hessler 1986) which suggests that good problem solvers have more elaborate and better developed schemata, which contain knowledge about subject matter and about useful procedures for approaching problems. One can begin to say that more expert practitioners have more useful knowledge structures. Some student teachers develop these useful structures more quickly than others, allowing them to interpret information bombarding them in lessons more meaningfully and to come to better decisions within lessons. This corresponds to Schon's (1983) concept of reflection-in-action. So the less expert students stick to their plan rigidly, because they cannot generate an alternative. The more expert can develop flexibility because their more complex knowledge structures allow them to imagine alternative pathways within the lesson and make a choice about how to proceed.

Flexibility as a component of expertise is further reinforced by Leinhardt's (1988) research on Maths teachers. She concludes that, 'expertise does not refer to doing things the 'right' or 'preferred' way. Expertise is a technical term that refers to working with speed, fluidity, flexibility, situationally encoded informational schemas and mental models that permit larger chunks of information to be accessed and handled'. Much of the knowledge teachers have about teaching is situated within the context of particular classrooms and pupils. Tobin and Frazer (1988) also draw attention to the conscious decision making made possible by superior knowledge. In a qualitative study of exemplary Maths and Science teachers they found that these teachers 'believed that pupils created their own knowledge (a constructivist viewpoint) as a result of active engagement in learning tasks... they had a range of teaching strategies that could be used without a great deal of conscious thought. Those teachers thought and talked about teaching approaches and were receptive to ideas for change'. So some teachers not only have a range of strategies, and with a well formulated theory of learning they know how to adapt and deploy them.

A further significant reference point is provided by the ASSET (Accrediting Social Services Experience and Teaching) programme (1991) developed by Anglia Polytechnic in conjunction with Essex Social Services. Using a variety of inductive approaches the programme developed seven core assessment criteria:

1.   Commitment to Professional Values

demonstrates self awareness and commitment in implementing professional values in practice.

2.   Continuous Professional Learning

demonstrates a commitment to and capacity for reflection on practice, leading to progressive deepening of professional understanding.

3.   Affective Awareness

demonstrates understanding and effective management of emotional responses in relation to others.

4.   Effective Communication

demonstrates ability to communicate effectively.

5.   Executive Effectiveness

demonstrates decisiveness in making difficult judgements in response to complex situations involving responsibility for colleagues and/or clients at risk.

6. Effective Synthesis of a Wide Range of Knowledge

> demonstrates an understanding of the
> relationship between a wide range of
> professional methods, practice, settings
> and conceptual frameworks, and an ability
> to apply this understanding effectively
> through practice.

7. Intellectual Flexibility

> demonstrates general perceptiveness and
> insight and an open-minded awareness of
> alternatives that may require changes in
> decision making and service delivery.

McBer and Company (Spencer 1983), an American consultancy, have researched extensively into professional competence in the USA, using a technique termed behavioural event interviewing (McClelland and Dailey 1973), developed from critical incident method (Flanagan 1954). In a study of State Department Foreign Service Junior Officers, the superior performers were characterised by non verbal empathy (the ability to 'hear' what a foreigner was really saying), speed in learning the political network and positive expectations (a strong belief in the dignity and worth of others, even under stress). Further credence is added to these conclusions by a study of police patrol officers (Elliott 1988) which highlighted, as one of four important qualities, the ability to make a global, holistic assessment of situations.

In these widely differing professional arenas there are some strong similarities which point to some critical characteristics for professionals and which resonate with the descriptive words of the teachers in this study: the ability to perceive information, particularly about people and one's relationship with them; the ability to form effective relationships; motivation; openness to learning; good decision making; and the ability to link information and concepts to gain holistic understanding. Excellent students are very adept at reading situations and people. They are interested in pupils as individuals and are good at decoding their behaviour and sensitive to the messages embedded in that behaviour.

Conclusion

Our aim was to work in partnership to develop a framework of assessment which is inductive and based on the mentors' professional descriptions of students so that we could work with a shared language in our evaluation of student performance. We began with five questions about the use of competences in ITT and we now return to them in the light of our experiences at Newcastle.

1. What is a competence?

We deliberately avoided meeting this difficulty head on but the comments from mentors, particularly in the 'Satisfactory' category, lend some support to the view of competence as potential as well as performance. The 'Good' and 'Excellent' categories seem to be describing students exhibiting greater consistency and reliability whereas the students deemed 'Satisfactory' were erratic but had shown sufficient skill to suggest that improvement would be possible.

2. It is helpful to atomise the teaching process into 27 competences?

The message coming most strongly from Newcastle partnership teachers is one of resistance to fragmentation - hence the insistence on five broad areas. There appears to be a body of opinion which allies itself to the reflective practitioner model of learning to teach. However, there has been an acknowledgement of the value of the competences as a focus for discussion and an exchange of views across the partnership. Other opinions do exist and have sometimes been voiced. This is most noticeable in the context of accountability within the assessment process. When dealing with a potential 'fail' student there is a need to focus more closely on areas of weakness, and documentation may well record comments on a specific competence.

3. Are the competences of equal weight?

Mentors did not expect a consistent profile of competence across all five areas and were happy to pass students who they considered to have weaknesses in some areas.

It was, however, noticeable that mentors did tend to require students to achieve a 'Satisfactory' or better rating in Subject Application and Class Management.

36

4. **What is an acceptable level of performance within a defined competence?**

The lack of focus on individual competences makes it difficult to comment here, except to observe that evidence of potential, however conceived, was sometimes referred to as being acceptable. The scepticism felt by many teachers as to the feasibility of defining levels was one reason advocated for not addressing competences specifically.

5. **To what extent can we assess consistency of performance using the competences - are they context specific and is regression possible?**

Within the context of student entitlement and the moderation of provision across a number of partnership schools this is a crucial question. We had one or two cases involving students who changed schools mid-practice when radically different assessments of a student's ability have been given. If the student is considered to have improved then it is possible to view the discrepancies as reflecting the student's ability to learn from their mistakes. But how do we interpret a perceived decline in competence? It is also possible to detect some evidence from the comments that different expectations of the student have sometimes been a significant factor. The degree of consensus recorded across 114 Final Reports at the 'Excellent' and 'Unsatisfactory' ends of the scale encourages hopes for moderation but some difficult issues remain.

Analysis of teachers' comments has identified statements which do not differ from the opinion of Elliott (1991) that worthwhile professional learning is experiential. It would also be possible to map statements onto learning cycles. This may help to explain why some students are able to learn more from teaching experience and put this learning into practice. Using Kolb's (1984) four stage cycle (experience, reflection, conceptualisation and action) as a framework, the qualities identified in the statements can be seen as potential influences on learning. Some students capture more of their experience because they perceive and decode more from pupils' behaviour, reactions and work in the classroom and are more aware of their own behaviour and its significance. The next two stages are perhaps difficult to disentangle in time but both a willingness to evaluate and a knowledge base with which to interpret are important. Those students with more elaborate and interconnected schemata are more likely to make sense of their experience and to formulate new ideas from which to operate. They are less likely to become defensive and rely on coping strategies. The evidence gathered in the case study is sufficient to enfranchise an attempt to develop such a model but it cannot fully endorse the reflective practitioner paradigm. The statements identify qualities which resonate with those identified in previous research but much still needs to be done to disentangle the overlapping terminology of experiential learning and reflective practice. However, we have found no justification for the view that there is a division between the perceptions of those involved in HEIs and the teachers in school on the qualities which need to be developed in students training to teach. Furthermore, it is a testimony to the creativity of the process of evolving partnerships alluded to earlier that the dialogue began within the framework of the potentially very restrictive 9/92 competences.

The approach we have adopted has produced a pen picture of an excellent student. By allowing mentors the freedom to represent the interplay of competence components in their prose descriptions it has gone some way towards minimising the worst effects of a competence based approach in its attempt to make what is good measurable.

TABLE 3.1: Teachers' comments on subject application

Excellent: Meticulous planning - exercises, activities and practicals tried and tested, so problems foreseen, all resources to hand.

Thoughtful planning - underpinned by research and understanding with innovative and creative activities, uses a variety of strategies, which can be adapted to different contexts.

Planning considers the learning needs of individuals, able to use open ended tasks which allow all pupils to achieve.

Much self generated resource material.

Plans sequence of lessons.

Confident and perceptive enough to allow flexibility once lesson under way.

Pupils stretched and challenged.

Draws upon pupil knowledge and experience.

Analyses strengths and weaknesses of range of styles and strategies and clearly uses experience to inform planning of future lessons.

Good: Carefully planned - materials generally well prepared and organised and NCATs (National Curriculum Attainment Targets) and school policies accommodated.

Discusses and seeks advice in advance.

Lesson plans detailed with clear objectives which are matched by tasks.

Growing awareness of individual needs in planning.

Some lessons stimulating, challenging, relevant, topical.

Presentation clear, articulate and understandable with appropriate use of voice intonation and language.

Develops own materials when necessary.

Resource sheets word processed and well designed.

Uses a variety of teaching styles, strategies and resources (practical, group work, role play, investigation, inquiry, discussion, IT.)

Work pitched appropriately, uses some differentiated resources or extension activities.

Evaluates lessons.

Satisfactory: Adequately planned - Lesson plans sufficient to guide content and timing of lesson.

Clear objectives. (May be insufficiently detailed and some activities not thought through.)

Understandable instructions and explanations.

Some home grown materials.

Some variety in activities and style - willingness to experiment.

Pragmatic rather than challenging, stimulating activities (playing safe).

Aware of the need for differentiation and some attempt made to implement.

Work generally appropriate.

Unsatisfactory: Casual attitude to planning, inadequate thought and detail leading to problems in lesson.

Serious mistakes in prepared materials or understanding of topic.

Lack of variety, particularly overemphasis on teacher talk, lessons predictable and lacking challenge and stimulus.

Poor timing of activities (activities allowed to drag on).

Lack of awareness of the needs of individual pupils and no attempt to differentiate.

Work inappropriate (too high or too low).

No planning of explanation and instructions.

Over reliance on textbooks and school resources.

TABLE 3.2: Teachers' comments in the 'excellent' category in class management / further professional development / further comments

Class management

Forms excellent relationships with the class as a whole and with individuals.

Relates well with pupils across the age / ability range.

Sensitive approach to pupils elicits a very positive response.

Good at learning names and building relationships with pupils at an early stage in the practice.

Praises and encourages pupils and follows school policy on rewards and sanctions.

Encourages, coaxes and involves pupils.

Uses a variety of sanctions and gives praise when appropriate.

Enthusiastic about teaching.

Approachable without losing authority.

Strong presence in the classroom uses the voice well and is clear, calm and enthusiastic.

Combines humour and determination.

Uses own initiative.

Responsive to pupil needs.

Uses a wide variety of teaching strategies to maintain interest and motivation.

Close match between teaching strategy, learning experience and pupil needs.

Devises new ways of maintaining interest and motivating; lessons are challenging and stimulating.

Acute awareness of pupil needs.

Anticipates difficulties before they become a real cause for concern.

Flexibility evident when resources were limited.

High level of preparation and organisation to ensure smooth flow of lesson.

Further professional development

Displays great willingness to participate in all school activities - volunteers and is proactive in seeking such opportunities. Makes an active and responsible contribution to such occasions and thus integrates with many different areas of school life and comes to understand the relationship between school and its community.

A good and full team member in the department, prepared to float and share ideas.

Good communication skills.

Sensitive to the needs and problems of individual pupils.

Seeks advice from a wide range of teaching and other staff.

Careful, self critical and analytical approach to evaluating teaching and pupils' learning such that maximum benefit is gained from practice.

Further comments

Wholly committed and diligent. Formed excellent relationships with staff.

Completely involved herself with the school and extra-curricular activities.

Worked beyond minimum duties.

Willing to grasp every opportunity to gain useful experience.

Reflects on experience in an honest, analytical and positive manner.

Good team player and quick to take up ideas which he will modify if necessary.

Responds well to day-to-day demands of teaching.

Contributed to resources, worked collaboratively, always calm and friendly.

Determined to succeed.

Accepted responsibility and showed initiative.

Relentless in the pursuit of high standards but also able to reassure pupils.

Fully integrated into the school and pleasant to all.

4 Pedagogical content knowledge: What do mature students bring to teaching?

Frank Banks

Introduction

Since the mid-1980s there has been considerable discussion and a growing body of research on the forms of knowledge required by teachers in performing their role (Shulman and Sykes 1986; Shulman 1986; Grossman, Wilson and Shulman 1989; McNamara 1991). Much of this has been initiated by the government's policy review of both teacher education programmes and the consequent re-evaluation of the relationship of college to school based work. The teacher education courses based on the foundation subject of academic study in Education have been subject to change suggested or imposed by governments around the world since the early 1980s (for example in England DES Circulars 3/84, 24/89, 9/92 and DFE 14/93). Such courses originally emphasised general pedagogic skills, knowledge and understanding at the expense of those associated with subjects.

Much research in classrooms has reflected this emphasis on general pedagogy by investigating such issues as, for example, teachers' classroom management, pupil-teacher interactions, pupil groupings and lesson planning, taking the standpoint that the subject content of those lessons is irrelevant. This position tends to devalue a centrally important purpose of a teacher's role; the way that s/he communicates knowledge (and understanding). Therefore, to explore student teachers' initial ideas about the teaching of knowledge and understanding in their subject, a sample of 10 Open University (OU) student technology teachers were interviewed. The interviews took place 14 weeks after the start of their course and following their first school experience.

Subject knowledge, pedagogical content knowledge and curriculum knowledge

The mature OU students bring with them to their initial teacher education course many relevant life experiences, for example, as a parent or as a parent helper in a primary school. These may relate to both an understanding of their subject and also to teaching. For many, their employment background has enabled them to internalise a particular understanding of their curriculum subject which is situated in the reality of the workplace where they put their knowledge to use. This 'knowledge-in-action' may be different to that of a new graduate fresh from college. Similarly, teaching in the workplace has often been the spur for students to become schoolteachers. One PGCE student said:

> Gradually, I've become more and more interested in teaching. This started when we took YTS (Youth Training Scheme) students in the labs, and I was responsible for helping them. I remember some of them had to be taught simple calculations in order to do the job. Then when I had my own two children, I thought yes - this is a career I would really like to follow.

The relationship between the student's subject knowledge and the way the subject perceives how such knowledge is best conveyed to others is the initial research focus of this project. The question Shulman asked of less mature students in the United States became the starting point with the OU's rather older cohort in the United Kingdom.

> How does the successful college student transform his or her expertise in the subject matter into a form that high school students can comprehend? (Shulman 1986)

The different forms of teacher knowledge have been usefully summarised by McNamara (1991: 115) and are adapted here.

Content knowledge

If the aim of teaching is to enhance children's understanding then teachers themselves must have a flexible and sophisticated understanding of subject knowledge in order to achieve this purpose in the classroom. Subject under-

46

standing must be 'flexible and sophisticated' to include the ways in which the subject is conducted by academics within the field, 'to draw relationships within the subject as well as across disciplinary fields and to make connections to the world outside school' (McDiarmid et al 1989: 193).

Teachers' subject knowledge influences the way in which they teach and teachers who know more about subject will be more interesting and adventurous in the ways in which they teach and consequently more effective. Teachers with only a limited knowledge of a subject may avoid teaching difficult or complex aspects of it and teach in a manner which avoids pupil participation and questioning and fails to draw upon children's experience.

Pedagogical content knowledge

At the heart of teaching is the notion of forms of representation, and to a significant degree teaching entails knowing about and understanding ways of representing and formulating subject matter so that it can be understood by children. This in turn requires teachers to have a sophisticated understanding of a subject and its interaction with other subjects. Shulman states:

> Within the category of pedagogical content knowledge I include, for the most regularly taught topics in one's subject area, the most useful forms of representation of those ideas, the most powerful analogies, illustrations, examples, explanations and demonstrations - in a word, the ways of representing and formulating the subject that makes it comprehensible to others. (Shulman 1986)

Curriculum knowledge

Knowledge of subject content is necessary to enable the teacher to evaluate text books, computer software and other teaching aids and mediums of instruction. This appreciation of the use and range of teaching resources and aids *is* 'curriculum knowledge'.

The recent development of technology in the schools of England and Wales has presented particular problems for initial teacher education. A wide interpretation of what constitutes technology in British schools, despite prescription by a national curriculum, means that the subject content knowledge of technology teachers is itself very diverse. Before describing the research and initial findings it is important to consider content knowledge and pedagogical content knowledge in the context of school technology.

Content knowledge in technology

Technology as it is currently being interpreted in schools is a subject designed by committee (McCormick 1990). The national curriculum order attempted to bring together contributions form the subject areas of art and design, business studies (BS), 'craft, design and technology' (CDT), information technology (IT) and home economics (HE). The rationale for this is an assumption that these subjects share a common base of procedural knowledge (knowing how) and could each contribute specific aspects of propositional knowledge (knowing that). Since there is no unambiguous agreement as to what technology is, it begs the question of which subjects or knowledge areas should contribute to it. For example, technology is often linked to science in what is considered by many (particularly politicians) as an 'applied science' which is assumed useful for all as vocational preparation. Naughton defines technology as follows:

> Technology is the application of scientific and other knowledge to practical tasks by organisations that involve people and machines. (Naughton 1988: 12).

Teachers from a craft subject tradition do not share this association with science and would rather wish to draw firmer links with designing and other aesthetic subjects. There is indeed a difference between what is called technology and what is called science in the world outside the classroom. This is put succinctly by Sparkes in the following table:

TABLE 4.1: The goals of science and technology teaching

SCIENCE	TECHNOLOGY
Goal: the pursuit of knowledge and understanding for its own sake. Key scientific processes	Goal: the creation of successful artefacts and systems to meet people's wants and needs. Corresponding technology processes

48

SCIENCE	TECHNOLOGY
Discovery (mainly by controlled experimentation)	Design, invention, production
Analysis, generalisation and the creation of theories	Analysis and synthesis of designs
Reductionism, involving the isolation and definition of distinct concepts	Holism, involving the integration of many competing demands, theories, data and ideas
Making virtually value-free statements	Activities always value-laden
The search for, and theorising about, causes (e.g. gravity, electromagnetism)	The search for, and theorising about, new processes (e.g. control, informatio, circuit theories)
Pursuit of accuracy in modelling	Pursuit of sufficient accuracy in modelling to achieve success
Drawing correct conclusions based on good theories and accurate data	Taking good decisions based on incomplete data and approximate models
Experimental and logical skills	Design, construction, testing, planning, quality assurance, problem-solving, decision-making, interpersonal and communication skills
Using predictions that turn out to be incorrect to falsify or improve the theories or data on which they were based.	Trying to ensure, by subsequent action, that even poor decisions turn out to be successful.

But many (although not all) teachers of technology would wish to concentrate on the above subset of 'Design, construction, testing, planning, quality assurance, problem-solving, decision-making, interpersonal and communication skills' as being quite sufficient for school technology. The content within technology is important here. For example, designing, construction and planning are very different when using resistant materials than is the case with food. As a consequence, 'it is less possible to assume that teachers share an understanding of the nature of technology than in other subjects like science and mathematics' (McCormick 1990: 44).

This lack of common ground as to the nature of the subject extends right to the core of what is considered the distinguishing feature of school technology: the design and technology 'process'. This process was considered so important in national curriculum technology that it provided the basis of the Technology Order and was a natural consequence of a developing 'intellectualisation' of the contributory subjects, away from simple making skills, since the introduction of GCSE. (See Smithers and Robinson 1992 for a discussion of this.)

The National Curriculum has four attainment targets based on the following;

identifying needs and opportunities;

generating and exploring design ideas;

planning and making artefacts, systems and environments;

evaluating processes and products.

The linear model of designing indicated by this sequence was first suggested by the Schools Council in 1974 and has been considered too simplistic by many researchers (Jeffrey 1990; APU 1991). Professional designers do not follow a linear sequence of operations often forced on pupils by teachers as a solution to the practicalities of classroom management or because such process steps need to be done to 'earn marks' in an examination. Rather:

Designing is a distinctive kind of skilled intellectual activity. It draws on some features of, say, scientific or artistic activity, but in many ways it is noticeably different. One of these principle differences is that designing is a 'solution-focused' rather than a 'problem-focused' activity. Designers tend to move fairly quickly to a solution of some kind, rather than spending a long time on trying to understand 'the problem' in encountered in designing are not fixed; they are changeable, depending on the kind of solution the designer has in mind. It is only by posing a solution that the problem can be defined and better understood. Designing is not, therefore, a step-by-step process of analysing the problem and then optimising a solution. It is an iterative process in which both 'problem' and 'solution' are resolved and refined together (Open University 1983: 81-82).

A range of more sophisticated representations of what both professional designers and pupils actually do have been proposed (APU 1991: 20) but the lack of agreement even as to the veracity of these models makes it difficult to be clear about the procedural knowledge teachers should have or what should be taught. The subject content knowledge of teachers in technology then is very varied due to the bringing together of different contributory subjects, and the assumed common 'technological process' has proved to be complex in practice and also context dependent (Hennessy and McCormick 1994). For survival, many teachers' pedagogic strategy is to follow a 'step-by-step' process.

Pedagogical content knowledge in technology

Applebee (1989: 217) notes that 'when we start to teach a new subject, one of the most powerful influences on what we do is our memory of how we were taught'. This is supported by Barnes (1989: 13) who argues that 'shaped by their years as "teacher-watchers", beginning teachers believe that teaching is a matter of telling'. However, the new subject of technology does not have a curriculum history long enough for those involved to have a common and shared 'memory' of how the subject 'should' be taught as may be the case in science or mathematics. Rather in a school's technology faculty there is a collection of different pedagogic styles developed from a distant common ancestor of manual training. The power-coercive strategy which brought together the contributory subjects failed to take account of the different pedagogical content knowledge of the separate subjects and the way that such understandings defined who the teachers felt they were:

> D and T teachers have been that only since September 1990, having previously been CDT (and, before that, woodwork, metalwork of technical drawing) teachers or HE (and, before that, domestic science or needlework or cookery) teachers or BS (and, before that, shorthand

and typing) teachers, and so on. All of them had a confidence and competence associated with particular ways of doing things needing particular familiarity with specialised equipment. And all were surviving with their own support structure (Harrison 1993: 273-275).

The movement from one subject affiliation, identification and competence to a new one has important implications. 'While it is true that teachers ask questions, hold discussions, give explanations, and use metaphors in all subjects, these play out in different ways, with different issues, in different subjects' (McDiarmid et al 1989: 195).

If it is difficult to pin down the content knowledge of technology; a natural consequence is that it is difficult to say what is appropriate pedagogic content knowledge too. However, technology teachers usually have a more tangible product from their lessons and are often, as McDiarmid would put it, 'able to view the subject through the eye of the learner' (McDiarmid et al 1989). In some ways, the teachers conspire with the pupils to concentrate on those aspects of the project, such as making, which is interesting for the pupils and for which the teacher has a fund of useful tips and procedures (Grieve, unpublished).

It is into this uncertain and changing curriculum environment that the Open University mature students bring their pre-conceived notions about what technology in schools should be and what would constitute appropriate pedagogy. If the mentors are uncertain about content knowledge and insecure in the pedagogy they use, what consequences does that have for school-based teacher education?

The study sample

The initial research methodology used semi-structured interview schedules to interview OU PGCE Technology students who compose virtually all the cohort for the 'South' and 'Wales' regions. This will be extended to some of the 'London' region too, giving a group size of 10 students. Agreement to take part in the project was sought from the students, and no student in the chosen geographical areas was excluded from the sample. There were seven men and three women in the sample and most were, or had recently been, in full-time employment. The employment histories of the four students (Students A to D) reported here as exemplars include a marine engineer, mechanical engineer, town planner and silversmith respectively. The students' views were sought in the following areas:

Content knowledge

- those aspects of their educational background and other experiences which they think will be most useful to them as a technology teacher;

- the aspects of technology which they feel most ill-prepared to teach in terms of subject knowledge.

Pedagogical content knowledge

- whether they had been in the position of a 'teacher' and if so how they organised it;

- the ways in which they are learning about teaching technology from their school mentor;

- the way the 'design process' is used in their placement school to help teach technology.

Putting teacher knowledge in context

- taking the example of Environmental Education, what sort of activities would they build into technology projects?

The interviews were conducted in the students' homes. The conversations were recorded and field notes were also taken.

Findings

Content knowledge

Some student teachers have a strong association with the notion of technology as artefacts. They talk about making things and see their role as an explainer of 'how things work'. This is particularly true of those students with an engineering subject background. Others with greater craft or planning knowledge see the processes of technology as being more important. This difference in emphasis is very important as it influences the way in which students approach a number of issues. Student A, for example, has high academic qualifications and sees his job as that of 'explainer' from a strong knowledge base:

> There should be more of the 'Tim Hunkin books' approach. The 'secret life' of the Fax, TV or fridge so that pupils will be interested and want to come into engineering to stop the country going down the tube.

Student C, however, takes a more holistic view of the subject due to her background in problem-solving in teams around issues:

> .... our lecturer in Cardiff was into 'lateral thinking' so he did a lot of 'I'll give you an idea and you project it on and follow it through'. That was quite good because you looked at all aspects. For example, if you say 'I'm going to build a motorway - what implications will it have?' It's like a snowball, it picks up things as it goes. So you have to think in every direction.

Pedagogical content knowledge

Those students with a firm grasp of subject saw the role of their mentor as one of subject illustrator. The student felt that they already knew how to teach but want exemplification of tips. Student B said:

> I went in with ideas like 'I am going to teach how to make a Windmill or God knows what' but they said, 'slow down, you've got to come down a bit'. In looking at worksheets and so on I saw how the thing should be done.

Similarly Student A (an ex-army and navy instructor with a very great experience in 'training' people) said:

> I must say the mentor is so busy it is difficult to find times to talk to him. He showed some good ideas about teaching 'orthographic projection' - pulling out a 3D model [... but ...] many more training aids are needed.

Student D found it difficult, however, to separate out advice about teaching of subject from general teaching strategies shown by her mentor.

> I learnt about letting them put forward ideas they found out for themselves really.

and Student C said of the help from her mentor:

Well in teaching generally I think. My mentor is very calm, very organised. She says you have to be organised before every lesson. The only times things go wrong is when you are not organised.

Putting teacher knowledge in context

Asked to give specific examples of what they would do to teach in a certain technological context say environmental education, these very new (albeit mature) students bring to bear three factors:

- their subject expertise (content knowledge);

- their early notions of appropriate pedagogy;

- their preliminary ideas about the new subject of school technology;

- and what they believe to be its aims.

Student A - a marine engineer:

I would tackle wave power, solar energy or wind power. Perhaps catalytic converters and Diesel vs Petrol engines. I would want to tell them about reusable materials (e.g. 85 per cent of a car is re-used). But I would want to tell them about the problems with such things as Windmills too - noise and disruption of the countryside, with links to geograph.

Student B - a mechanical engineer:

Well, I am very interested in Energy saving. Energy conservation is the up and coming thing. Also pollution. Probably I would do a windmill project - obviously on a model basis - because it is something they can visualise rather than some chimney with gases coming out of it. The can't visualise that except for smoke.

Student C - a town planner:

One thing I had thought about was playgrounds. You could ask them to do a plan layout of a playground and make a model of a roundabout or a swing or something like that - if there wasn't a playground to work on. Anything everyday that they can relate to.

Student D - a silversmith:

It would be ideal to do some research and surveys finding out which areas of the town are untidy. Find out from people where they would put litter bins. It would be a nice opportunity to do things in groups. I think technology is unfortunately very individual much of the time. Perhaps they could produce designs for the bins or maybe a landscaping project - something like that. They could put out their own ideas of what they should do. I think most kids are interested in the environment and it is something they could get really enthusiastic about.

Discussion of results - the relationship between content knowledge and pedagogical content knowledge

Early research in this area saw a clear and some may say common sense distinction between knowledge of content and knowing how to teach that content. 'We all have had a teacher who obviously knew the subject matter but who could not explain it to students' (Grossman et al 1989: 25). Examples from mathematics in particular can show that although a teacher may know how to, say, perform long division s/he may find it very difficult to explain why the procedure works or to represent it properly to a child. The teacher often says 'I know how to do it, but I don't know the ideas behind it'. In the results shown above, however, the clear separation between 'content knowledge' and 'pedagogical content knowledge' is beginning to blur. In learning about what Shulman would call 'powerful analogies, illustrations, examples, explanations and demonstrations' the student teachers are beginning to reconceptualise their own understanding of the subject of technology and of the environmental issues which they will be teaching.

A common experience of many teachers is one of their own deeper understanding as they articulate their ideas to another person. Pedagogical content knowledge feeds back into personal subject knowledge.

McNamara writes:

> A theme which emerges from empirical investigations is that while teachers' subject knowledge and pedagogic content knowledge are important in affecting classroom practice both are modified and influenced by practice and that no clear distinction can be drawn between them (McNamara 1991: 119).

The preliminary results suggest that this is beginning to be the case for these technology teachers. For example, Student A in addressing the noise pollution problems of windmills is beginning to look at technological issues more holistically than is suggested by his technocentric view of artefacts. To teach a wider view embracing a consideration of environmental values, he will also need to consider a greater range of teaching strategies than his current belief that teaching 'is a bit like being on stage really, you need to keep your audience captured'.

The students will be revisited after their second and third school experiences. However, before their third school placement the students are required to analyse a school design and technology project for a number of curriculum features; one of which is the way it addresses the theme of environmental education. In this way it will be possible to compare these students' initial views with their later ideas, which have been moderated by their developing pedagogical content knowledge. Moreover it will be also possible to investigate how their subject understanding of technology and the relationship to school technology is itself changing.

5   Transition to mentoring: Issues in primary initial teacher training

Ruth Dann

Introduction

> The main reason why it is becoming increasingly difficult to train someone adequately for the class-teacher role is that the role itself has become an impossible one to train for (Alexander 1992: 202).

In Alexander's terms those concerned with initial teacher training (ITT) are faced with an immense challenge. This is compounded by the shifting requirements of the training process. The extent to which recent changes in national policy and practice can be seen to reflect political rather than educational concerns poses an added problem for the conceptualisation of emerging trends. Indeed as Smith asserts (1992), so great are the misrepresentations and incidents of propaganda in education, with teacher training being a particular victim, that one needs to wonder whether there is still any point exploring reasoned argument. However, in order to uphold the importance of both rationality and education itself such a pursuit is vital.

Fundamental to the whole concept of mentoring within increasingly school focused ITT is the relationship between theory and practice. More specifically, the way in which these relate to the interrelationship between schools and HEIs in the training of teachers is of crucial concern. Although the movement towards school-based partnership in primary schools is a requirement of circular 14/93 (DFE 1993d), its rationalisation within teacher training programmes needs to be rigorously explored so that developments may be grounded in educational rather than political precepts and priorities. Instead of exemplifying what are often regarded as competing tensions between theory and practice, school-based training offers some potential for creating a new synergy between these two.

The stake which participating teachers have in mentoring will require a conscious sharing of reflective practice. The dynamic relationship hoped to be fostered between the student and mentor is one in which a rich dialogue related to experience, insight, reflection and evaluation needs to be created. If learning is to be anything more for children and teachers than what Edwards and Mercer (1987) call 'ritualled' (that is based only on repetition and limited unapplied experience) then dialogue through which meaning and understanding are communicated is vital. Such a dialogue is essential to the effective sharing of underlying common principles. The opportunities which mentoring offers for this sustained shared experience of a class seems to have valuable potential for teacher training.

Any rationale for mentoring is adequate only within a context in which reality is also explored. Thus the concern is now directed towards teasing out the way in which mentors have perceived and developed their role within the second phase of a new school focused primary PGCE course at the University of Keele.

Research context and strategies

A new initiative was therefore undertaken in 1992 to develop a more school focused primary PGCE course. Six schools showing interest were selected for a pilot phase and 12 students (now called 'associate teachers') were recruited. The six schools were all ones whose staff had seemed keen to develop their existing links with Keele. The teachers involved worked closely with Keele tutors in order to develop the new course. The importance of the school/HEI relationship was seen as crucial to the development of the course.

This pilot phase was extended in phase two (1993-4) to 27 schools (47 mentors) which offered a new challenge to the system of partnership. It is this phase which is explored in this chapter. Those who joined in this second phase were in schools which had been previously linked with Keele through teacher training on the undergraduate concurrent Certificate course.

As part of a course evaluation the perceptions of mentors during the 1993-4 PGCE course were elicited. Part of the concern here was the on-going intention to further develop and refine partnerships with schools and specifically through relationships with individual mentors. However, there was a sense in which the whole context of the year needed to be conceptualised by all parties taking full account of mentors' perspectives. The educational rationale already outlined cannot be recognised by a HEI alone. The very notion of partnership engenders some sense of working together and common agendas. Some attempt to outline these is offered here. The research findings provide a glimpse into a new and developing sphere, one which needs to be the focus of further exploration and inquiry.

A questionnaire was the main vehicle through which mentors' responses and reactions were exposed. This was completed during the final mentor training-session which was on three successive days for the three groups of mentors involved. The questionnaire design was based on the discussions and observations made whilst working closely with 14 mentors and associate teachers in the pilot project, and from issues raised during the mentor meetings. It was composed of a mixture of structured and open ended questions which sought to give opportunity for some elaboration but recognised the need to limit completion time.

The concern in this qualitatively based research is to illuminate and interpret possibilities for eliciting themes from the data. A particular concern is to use research for 'discovery' allowing contextualisation which is seen as a vital aspect of research before the cumulation of theory. As Woods (1987) contends, there is a need within qualitative research to develop themes from which practitioners may construct 'theories and methods of their own ....reflection-in-action' (p.305). Thus the details discussed here may add to the growing bases from which further insights into the theory and practice of mentoring may be gained.

Research findings

The outcomes presented here draw on the questionnaire responses which received a 75 per cent response rate (35 mentors).

Perceptions before mentoring

The way in which mentors perceived their new role and responsibilities prior to embarking on the task of mentoring was an important notion to explore. The mentors were asked to comment on how their expectations of mentoring may have differed from their first experience of mentoring.

Nineteen mentors responded to this question, yielding 22 statements. Three of these stated that they had no expectations at all. It seemed, from informally talking and listening to mentors, that several of them were unable to formalise their expectations into a clear statement so had left out the question. This, together with the retrospective nature of the question may have accounted for the low response rate here. Nevertheless, the issues raised may

61

serve to illustrate the way in which mentors face their task.

Lack of awareness of the increased work load required in mentoring was a matter which was reflected in 27 per cent of the statements. One mentor wrote

I was not aware of the extra work load before agreeing to become a mentor (- not explained by Head). Primary teachers have little or no free time to take on what is expected, when they are already working an overload.

It is indeed difficult to portray the level of commitment and involvement prior to a task. Even for the mentor cited above, the difficulties outlined in relation to overload were accompanied, in other responses, by very positive statements concerning the benefits which his/her associate had gained from the whole experience.

The fun and sense of enjoyment which the mentoring role can give was shown, in 18 per cent of the statements, to be underestimated prior to mentoring. However, this sense of enjoyment was accompanied in all cases by some concerns and problems which were reflected in other responses in the questionnaire. There is certainly some indication from the responses given here that there is a tension between mentoring as rewarding and enhancing to teachers and as a burden, giving an additional workload. One of the mentors highlighted this by stating that it was 'a lot more work, stress and fun than I imagined.'

An important realisation, indicated in 14 per cent of the statements, was the crucial nature of the relationship between the mentor and the associate. Evidently, the experience of mentoring had crystallised the importance of this link and the theme of the relationship of mentors and associates is explored more deeply later in the chapter.

There were several other aspects which the mentors stated had not been anticipated prior to taking on the mentoring task. Each of these accounted for five per cent of the statements. They concern: the lack of awareness relating to the need to assess the associates throughout their attachment; having the opportunity to share their expertise with someone so enthusiastic; realising how much they enjoyed having back their own class to teach; and how hard the mentoring task is to carry out.

The issues raised here relate to the expectations of those embarking on a new challenge within primary education. These expectations, may be significantly different to those of mentor teachers in subsequent years. Once mentoring has been experienced by more teachers, prospective mentors may have already built up expectations based on observations, discussions and reading the increasing amount of material addressing mentoring. The diversity of views expressed from the limited number of mentors illustrated here highlights the variety of perspectives and insights which one role can engender. Accordingly, the perceptions expressed prior to mentoring in this new initiative form only the start of developing perspectives throughout the mentoring experience. Proactive as well as reactive response to these changing and diverse needs is a matter which needs serious and considered response from HEIs.

Distinguishing mentoring from supervision

In order to explore more specifically the role of a mentor, distinctions are called for in relation to any previous experience of supervising students. Twenty seven mentors responded, producing 38 statements, about the way in which mentoring differed from traditional supervision. (Four mentors indicated that they had no previous experiences with students so the question was not applicable to them.) Twenty nine per cent of the statements indicated negative factors related to the task of mentoring. These were comprised of: being time consuming (13 per cent); a big responsibility/burden (11 per cent); and more paper work (5 per cent). However, the remaining comments indicated more positive aspects of their experience. Of particular note were comments related to the associates' greater commitment and more positive attitude (29 per cent), the good relationships formed between mentor and associate (11 per cent) and the benefit to the school resulting from more sustained school contact (8 per cent). Other comments related to mentors' own practices and feelings. Eleven per cent indicated the role to be both positive and rewarding. There were several additional statements, each meriting three per cent of the assertions made: mentors had greater knowledge of the course structure and requirements; reflection on their practice was aided; they had a greater stake in the training process; they were more accountable for their associate's performance and they were more in control in ensuring that pupils got through the work planned during the student's stay. This was because attachment was sustained and normal proceedings were not suspended or restricted for several weeks in order to accommodate a student undergoing a shorter, more traditional style teaching practice.

The breadth of responses elicited here provides an interesting focus for discussion. More than two-thirds of the statements indicated that the changes in their role were favourably regarded, but for a variety of reasons. The greatest factor influencing these comments related to the attitude to and relationship with the associates. This again highlights the very close link between the two which is more evident and more important than in previous supervisory capacities. The crucial role which this seems to play merits some further initial analysis.

The mentor-associate relationship

If dialogue and discussion are to emanate between mentor and associate then there needs to be a forum which allows for the sharing of ideas, discussion of practice, and consideration of possibilities related to the way in which future teaching, curriculum and learning needs are addressed, planned and implemented. The insights offered here give only one side of the relationship, yet acknowledge possible developmental issues.

In one sense the whole notion of partnership at the institutional level, between the HEI and schools, is now extended into the classroom, between the mentor and associate. The change in terminology for the trainee - 'associate teacher' reflects the increased stake which the associate has within the school as the attachment progresses. However, the nature of this partnership is a shifting one. The specifications given by Keele concerning the way in which the associates' progress within this partnership are not directive, but allow for a variety of factors and influences to be accommodated by the mentor. This requires mentors to exercise discretion and sensitivity in their professional judgements regarding the associate's competences and the nature of any support needed. Some concerns were voiced during the year in mentor meetings about the way in which the associate's progress should be paced. In the absence of specific guidelines for what associates should be doing during particular periods in the year some mentors needed reassuring that what they were doing was appropriate. Pacing the partnership was thus a matter in which mentors welcomed support from Keele. This was further reflected in the positive responses received concerning the support sessions offered by Keele throughout the year.

Mentors were asked to respond to one or more of four statements related to the way in which they worked with their associate. Sixty per cent of the responses highlighted that they 'worked well together and the class benefited'. One mentor indicated (in the space left for any additional responses) that 'We had a good rapport right from the start'. There were only two comments which indicated a problem. One of these stated that the associate needed to listen more, whilst the other claimed that the associate did not have a very positive attitude. A further four mentors indicated that their associates were lacking in commitment and enthusiasm (when commenting on

64

the problems of mentoring in another question). This seemed to be more of a problem towards the end of their year when many of the associates had already secured jobs for September or were possibly pre-occupied with interviews and job applications. This certainly concerned some mentors who had to work around associates' legitimate absences and cope with some divided loyalties.

None of the mentors responded to the statement 'My authority was reduced which might cause problems when I have the class back in May'. However, when the mentors were asked in another question about any difficulties encountered as a mentor, two of them stated that re-establishing control in the class on a daily basis had been a concern. This was particularly the case in the early days of the attachment when the pupils were perhaps a little uncertain about the new adult in the class. They were possibly testing the boundaries of their control and discipline when the associates were sometimes unsure of the best strategies to use. Knowing when and how to intervene is thus a vital skill which, although difficult, seemed to work to good effect.

Twenty three per cent agreed with the statement that the 'Associate seemed happy to sit at the side lines until I deliberately passed over more responsibility'. The early stages of the partnership, therefore, needed careful direction from the mentor. The way in which the initial period of observation and familiarity was moved on to greater teaching responsibility evidently seemed to require careful steering in some cases. Additionally, the value of observing and reflecting in the initial stages of the attachment and the requirement to write a school attachment commentary meant that a large teaching load was not to be assumed at this stage. It may be that the mentors felt that the pace of involvement was slow in comparison with that involving traditional placements when students had far less time in which to learn and demonstrate their teaching skills.

Nine per cent of the mentors indicated that they agreed with the statement that they 'found it difficult to let go of the class and take a more marginal role'. This is a particularly pertinent point when considering the amount of time they have to 'share' their class. Relinquishing a large part of their teaching must be quite a sacrifice for many mentors. Whether it is something they will be prepared to do every year will need careful monitoring. One of the comments made by a mentor in response to the question concerning differences between expectations and the reality of mentoring stated 'I didn't think I would be glad on the days they weren't in to have sole responsibility for the class'.

Here looms another potential problem. Teachers who love teaching may not wish to participate in a mentoring scheme each year because of the limited amount of time they will have alone with their class. Accordingly, if new mentors are to be found or there is a rotational basis for mentoring within schools then the implications for training call for urgent attention. Additionally, the on-going nature of the mentoring role already alluded to has serious limitations. The whole nature of school-focused partnership is reliant on the willingness of teachers to assume mentoring responsibilities and the practical details involved. These are probed later in relation to changing conceptions of the profession.

The extent to which mentors felt they influenced their associate's competence in seven key areas of teaching was another aspect of the mentor/associate relationship which was explored. The intention here was to probe whether mentors felt that their role had been influential in developing practice.

TABLE 5.1: The mentors' perspective on their role in developing practice

	Great Influence	Some Influence	Little Influence	No Influence	Blank
Weekly planning	31%	57%	9%	3%	-
Termly planning	43%	51%	`3%	3%	-
Teaching Styles	11%	86%	3%	-	-
Classroom Organisation	23%	69%	3%	3%	-
Control & Behaviour	40%	49% (3%)	11%	-	-
Assessment	6%	74%	17%	3%	-
Matching Needs	26%	63%	6% (3%)	-	3%

(two percentages in brackets indicate that mentors had not assigned their response to only one rating.)

Of particular note in these results is the extensive influence which the mentors seemed to identify. Weekly and daily planning, as well as behaviour and control were seen to be the areas in which the greatest influence was achieved. The 11 per cent claiming they had little influence on control and behaviour may indicate the possible problem already alluded to when the associates have to control the class themselves, using their own strengths and strategies. Thus to some extent there is an element in which the ultimate issues in control and maintaining appropriate behaviour rest with the associates.

Assessment seemed to be the area in which mentors felt that they had least influence. Teachers nationally have voiced their concerns over assessment. Its rather dynamic nature within current changes and reforms has not given a stable context for teachers seeking to identify possible purposes and practices. Many of the mentors indicated that they did not feel confident about helping the associates with assessment, and this was tackled in one of the mentor meetings which was partly used to cover some relevant issues relating to assessment. Possible difficulties had already been anticipated and the session aimed to make the mentors more aware of the tasks the associates would need to carry out and to clarify some aspects of assessment. The support of an HEI is useful here, as also is the sharing of ideas and experiences among mentors.

The responses given seemed to illustrate that the mentors were fairly confident about the way in which they had influenced the development of their associate's teaching competence. This was coupled with the very clear sense in which they felt that sustained school experience was beneficial to the associates. The main issue at stake was the amount of time that mentoring took. The critical nature of this issue merits some further exploration.

Finding the time

As already indicated some mentors had not fully anticipated the amount of work which the mentoring role would require. Their experience had revealed that it was more time consuming than more traditional teaching practice arrangements. Time specifically allocated for discussion and evaluation is required if associates are going to be effectively encouraged to explore a range of strategies and styles, and to reflect sensitively on the investigative pedagogy involved.

In order to probe the opportunities available for mentor/associate collaboration mentors were asked to state the frequency and form of their discussions with associates for discussion, planning and evaluation. This gives no indication of the quality of these encounters, which are not explored in this study but the issue would certainly merit extensive inquiry. Twenty three per cent of the mentors indicated that they frequently had non-contact time to be devoted to helping their associate. A further 40 per cent were sometimes given non-contact time and 26 per cent had never had any non-contact time to work with their associate. Sixty six per cent of the mentors frequently planned weekly sessions with their associate before or after school, and a further 17 per cent sometimes did this. (Fourteen never had a regular weekly encounter.) The most frequently used method for giving feedback and evaluation was on a spontaneous basis. This was unplanned and would occur whenever the opportunity and time presented themselves. Seventy one per cent of mentors relied on this method and the remaining mentors (29 per cent) sometimes operated in this way. This is an important way of communicating, since it can be within a more appropriate context and relate to a very specific incident. Furthermore, it can prompt action to be taken when it is still of use.

The implication of these findings is that considerable time is being spent by the mentors out of school hours, or, in some cases, restricted only to spontaneous encounters. In this latter case, the discussion seems to be prompted by particular events, problems or difficulties which need to be tackled. However, issues concerning classroom practice which are not problematic but still need to be questioned and discussed may be excluded. In the regular weekly sessions, especially if these are done after or before school, the amount of time allocated may well allow only for immediate and pressing considerations to be discussed. Certainly, it seems essential that mentoring, in the sense outlined at the beginning of this chapter, needs to be recognised by all partners as being a process which needs to be planned for. Such planning requires opportunities for mentors and associates to use time wisely, reflecting on their respective roles and practices.

Each partnership school received a sum of money for each associate they had. It was suggested to headteachers that part of this was used to make some supply cover available so that mentors and associates could have non-contact time together on a limited number of occasions. However, at this stage in the partnership no contract had been formally agreed for making this a requirement. Future developments in partnership may need to address this issue more directly.

If time is to be given to mentoring then the role of a teacher has a new component, which has a broader bearing on the nature of the profession. It is this new dimension of teaching, and its implications which is examined more closely in the next section.

A new dimension to the teaching profession

Models of professionalism are changing, in Elliott's terms (1991) from infallible expert to reflective practitioner. However, the status of the profession for equipping and preparing future members remains crucial. Indeed, in teaching this is certainly an area of change. The new Teacher Training Agency is just one recent step in this process, the implications of which are not yet fully known. If the model of professionalism is shifting in the way Elliott suggests, then the role of teachers becomes vital as participants in the process of inducting new entrants into a reflective culture within a school context. However, teachers' views on this matter may not be so clear. The pressures on classroom teachers, amidst so many demanding changes, may leave little time or energy for these additional responsibilities.

In order to probe this further, the mentors were asked to indicate, with a reason, the extent to which they welcomed the increased role which teachers now have in the training of teachers.

Greatly	Moderately	Marginally	Not at all
40%	43% (3%)	11%	3%

The accompanying comments reflect several tensions. Thirty per cent of the mentors claimed that the best way to learn to teach was to try it in a supportive context and this addressed the previous imbalance of theory and practice (6 per cent). These mentors indicated the belief that increased school involvement was welcomed for the benefit of more effective training and experience. However, 29 per cent of the mentors claimed that they felt the increased involvement was an extra work load which was to some extent problematic. Additionally 8 per cent were of the opinion that it was merely a form of training 'on the cheap'. Another dimension to the responses indicated that there were direct influences on their own development resulting from the training experience. Encouraging the teacher to be more reflective, introducing new ideas and techniques, and adding a new challenge to the job each reflected 6 per cent of the responses.

Some concerns were also expressed relating to the support which teachers would receive in the mentoring process. Six per cent highlighted the need for the continued support of HEI and three referred to the need to moderate teaching experiences because of the inevitable variations from school to school. Part of the purpose of retaining HEI involvement is to select and oversee school experience and, as Rudduck states (1991) to offer 'a perspective that shapes consciousness in schools and classrooms and provides students with the variety of frameworks for making sense of what is happening' (p.322)

The continued support of a HEI seemed to be desired from the responses which the mentors gave to a question seeking to elicit the extent to which they would like their training role to be further increased. They were asked to indicate whether or not they would like to be involved in: course design (31 per cent said that they would like to be); marking assignments (11 per cent); teaching 'Professional Development' courses, for example assessment, classroom organisation and equal opportunities (29 per cent); selecting students for the course (23 per cent) and teaching foundation subjects (37 per cent). The percentages indicated show the yes responses. They indicate some interest in taking on additional responsibilities. Eight per cent indicated 'yes' responses to them all (23 per cent to three or more) whilst 40 per cent said 'no' to them all.

The desire for HEI support was also evident in the mentors' responses to the question relating to the mentor training sessions. Not more than 3 per cent indicated that the training had been unhelpful in: conveying the details of the course, providing a support network; offering strategies to support the associates; enhancing professional development; explaining associate assessment procedures and dealing with problems and difficulties. The support which the HEI offers need to offer very different needs in the first year of mentoring than in subsequent years. This further adds to the differing ways in which support needs to be offered throughout the development of mentoring.

Mentors' responses clearly indicated some concerns in the relationship between the principles and practices of mentoring. Although the principle of increased teacher involvement in school-focused ITT is largely welcomed, the reality of the experience creates difficulties when trying to implement it within a context not extensively designed to cater for its needs. The issue, therefore, can be related more directly to the priorities and pressures of the teaching role, and the lack of status which mentoring is currently given within primary schools.

This new dimension to teaching has several implications for the profession. To some extent it extends the responsibilities of the profession. This is an important step for the profession, whether construed in a traditional sense (Hoyle 1969) or more reflective sense (Elliott 1991). There is, however, a great concern looming, the impact of which is difficult to predict. This relates to the potentially restrictive nature of mentor selection. The whole notion of mentoring, within the context of school-focused training, relies firstly on the identification of partnership schools and secondly on the selection of mentors within them. These are to be chosen by headteachers for their particular qualities. Mentoring can thus be an exclusive activity, available to but a few. It is likely to be the case that some teachers would not want to participate, even if given the opportunity. There are, however, some teachers who have previously enjoyed the experience of having a student who might not be considered for a mentoring role. As Furlong (1994) contends, a mentor is more than a successful teacher and requires sophisticated training skills. A certain air of disquiet may arise if only a few teachers repeatedly have students/associates, for longer durations, when others are excluded. Headteachers involved in the partnerships at Keele have already indicated that a problem may occur in the future as the implications of the new arrangements become more evident.

Conclusion

Transition to mentoring seems to have been an experience producing mixed emotions. To some extent it seemed clear to the teachers that they were embarking on something which was markedly different from previous expectations and experiences. The positive benefits which students can gain and the increased time demanded from teachers produced some tensions. Teachers seem to have a remarkable facility for juggling a multitude of demands made on them. In fact, their adeptness is so often taken for granted, not least within the context of current change and reform, that it is perhaps pushed to its limits. If the potential which the task of mentoring may offer in terms of bringing together theory and practice, enhancing professionalism and giving greater opportunity for reflective practice is to be realised, then the role will need to be recognised more fully within primary schools and HEIs. This will need to secure a commitment to training which, under current pressures, may not be a priority.

The relationship of schools and HEIs is to be different within a partnership framework. The accountability of both partners therefore needs to be secured through more formal agreements. Agendas have changed and are continuing to change. Without the sustained support of teachers mentoring will not work. Having a student for a few weeks is a very different experience from the commitment required in mentoring. If primary school teachers seek to take on the mentoring task without appropriate support and allocated time then the initiative, instead of enriching and enhancing the profession, may be hindering it.

6 Further professional encounters: Students and their school tutors

Hilary Constable, Jerry Norton and Gill Hubbard

Introduction

Teacher education reform in the last five years has posed a challenge to both schools and higher education institutions. The response has been highly professional, as is evident in both the programmes which have been put into operation and in the systematic scrutiny which has been devoted to monitoring and improving them (see Booth, Furlong and Wilkin 1990; Furlong, Hirst, Pocklington and Miles 1988; Reid, Constable and Griffiths 1994). As responses have been devised a number of issues have emerged, including the costs of teacher education; the nature and quality of the student learning experience; and the complementary demand on schools, on teachers and on higher education to provide this experience, and as programmes have become implemented it has been possible to revisit some of the issues first raised.

This chapter reports on the professional encounters between students and their school tutors. In earlier work (Constable and Norton 1994) we had been curious to find out about the conversations students had had about their work. In the first instance we needed to know who students actually talked to about their work, and what they talked about. We had ideas from our own experience as students, teachers and teacher educators what might be found but, as researchers, we had no clear or definitive picture constructed from data which had been gathered systematically. The meetings and discussions which students had with other adults about the student's teaching were termed professional encounters. The defining characteristic was that an encounter or meeting should contain some discussion about the student's professional practice. Where and when these encounters took place, who initiated them and who took part might vary, and the encounter may be brief, hardly long enough to merit the title 'meeting'. The encounter, to be so defined, should however contain discussion of the student's professional practice rather than be, say, a purely social conversation. The aim of the first investigation (1994) had been to delineate and analyse this important element of the everyday experience of being a student teacher. Specifically the research was intended to provide insight into the frequency and content of professional encounters taking place in schools.

Both the first and second studies drew on students in initial training at the University of Sunderland. The first investigation took the form of asking students to complete a self-report inventory detailing the number of professional encounters they made over a three day period. School staff and higher education tutors were asked to complement this by also filling in self-report inventories. Subsequently some of the participating group were interviewed about the content of the professional encounters. The results were surprising. Far from the lonely student struggling on unaided with never a tutor in sight, nor a teacher available, the picture was one of frequent, sometimes very frequent, professional encounters. The average was high, ten, and the highest end of the range, 25, startling. Naturally there was also a low end to the range, one, but two thirds of students recorded between five and 15 encounters.

We were interested to know whether this was typical or an accident of timing or some other cause. The first set of figures for encounters had seemed surprisingly high. Possible causes were the effect on the participants of being studied, the newness of some of the partnership models in their first year of operation, and anxiety to demonstrate professionalism under the onslaught of hostile attention to teacher education from the radical right and media. Another source of the particular pattern may have been institutional habit. Any or all of these factors may have continued to play a part. Accordingly the investigation was repeated. In the second round, some three years after the first, students and their school-based tutors - known respectively as generic tutors and subject tutors - were once again asked to complete a self-report inventory detailing the professional encounters they had had (see figure 6.1). A sub-sample of each group was interviewed and the self-report inventory was used to stimulate recall of the content of one of the professional encounters.

The replication aimed to investigate the persistence of the patterns found in the first study, and to analyse these patterns in some further detail. The second study built on the first in that greater attention was paid to the content of the professional encounter conversations. Naturally, as time had moved on, programmes of teacher education had developed and hence the cohort examined for the replication study differed in composition. In the replications study all students were on a new secondary route compared with the first where some had been on established courses and others on new and others on new routes, and in the first study some had been in training for primary education and others for secondary. In the new course a significant feature was the use of a profile of competence for organising student experience as well as for assessment. In the first study, higher education tutors and class teachers or subject teachers were asked to keep records of encounters to complement those of the students, whereas in the replication the students' records were complemented by generic and subject tutors, both groups being teachers in the secondary schools.

Frequency and duration of professional encounters

The figures for professional encounters confirmed the picture for 1991 (see table 6.1) and are worth reporting in some detail. Students were once again talking to their tutors frequently about their work. The range in the number of encounters was extensive, from five to 25, a mean of nearly eleven encounters over three days, the median at 9.5 and a mode of 7 and a standard deviation of 4.5. The similarity with figures for the earlier cohort is marked.

Table 6.1: Frequency of professional encounters recorded over three days.

Mean number of encounters recorded over a three day period.			
	1993 cohort		1991 cohort
Students	10.9	Students	10
Generic tutors	5.1	School staff	5
Subject tutors	5.8	University tutors	5.1

If the total number of encounters was surprising, then their duration was more so. Many individual encounters were short but a great many lasted for a long time and the total time spent in them was startling. The time spent was calculated from the start and finish times recorded on the self-report inventories. Individual encounters ranged from as short as one minute to three hours. Students recorded a mean time spent in an encounter of 29 minutes, mode of five minutes and a median of 15 minutes. The mean length of meeting recorded by generic tutors was 20 minutes. The range behind this was considerable with the longest meeting being two hours and 58 minutes and the shortest one minute. There was a sufficient cluster at five minutes to produce a mode. The median length of meeting was ten minutes and 30 per cent of meetings were 20 minutes or longer. Subject tutors tended to spend longer in their encounters with a mean of 32 minutes and a mode of 15 minutes. Here the median was 20 minutes - that is half of all the meetings were longer than this.

Over the three day recording period the mean of the total time spent in encounters was: for students, five hours 14 minutes; for generic tutors, one hour 33 minutes; and for subject tutors, three hours 9 minutes. Whatever way one looks at this, a great amount of time was spent in encounters, so much so that the time spent raised a number of questions, not least of which concerned the opportunity cost and logistics. Where did this time come from and how was it fitted in? The time spent in encounters was so large that it was hard to see how it could all have been fitted in. The reports showed however that there was no possible opportunity which remained unused. Meetings took place from before school started (6 per cent of events) to after school finished (8.3 per cent) and included registration periods (3.6 per cent), parents' evenings (1 per cent), lunch and break (30 per cent) as well as before (7.7 per cent), during (28 per cent) and after (3 per cent) lessons.

Table 6.2: When encounters took place

	Numbers of encounters and (percentage of encounters for that role in that time)		
	Generic tutors	Students	Subject tutors
Other times	40 (53%)	149 (43%)	52 (41%)
During lessons	7 (9%)	96 (28%)	48 (38%)
Breaks and after school	29 (38%)	101 (29%)	27 (21%)

In planning the course and initially working with school-based tutors, it had been envisaged that non-teaching periods would be heavily used for encounters. Evidently they were used, but formed a relatively low percentage of the meetings: 17.8 per cent for students, 12.5 per cent for generic tutors and 7.7 per cent for subject tutors and 14.8 per cent overall took place in non-teaching periods. For both subject tutors and students a high proportion of encounters took place during lessons as well as in breaks (see table 6.2). For subject tutors 38 per cent of the encounters took place in lesson time, although it should be noted that there was also a major encroachment on teacher break time. One of the advantages of school-based training is the possibility of on-the-spot help; one of the disadvantages is that the time is taken from elsewhere. In terms of the opportunity cost, the grouping used in table 6.2 roughly corresponds to pupils' time (during lessons), teachers' time (breaks) and school time (other). ('Breaks' includes lunch as well as before and after school; 'other' includes non-teaching periods, generic sessions and parents' evenings.)

The interviews provided some further information on what motivated the initiation of encounters. School tutors and students together identified the completion of competence profiles as a reason for initiating encounters. Tutors mentioned making sure there were 'no gaps' in school experience and support in areas where they perceived the student to lack confidence. Students had other motivations as well; they initiated encounters in order to sort out timetable and other organisational issues and to discuss comparisons of the present school with previous school experience.

The interviews also revealed some aspects of continuity of experience for students. The discussions were quite commonly a continuation of a previous conversation, although the encounters were not necessarily pre-arranged; that is meetings were arranged to discuss situations as they arose. Subject tutors had more daily contact with students, and encounters with them tended to be more informal. Several students and subject tutors remarked that there was no need to have formal meetings as they had easy access to subject tutors. Encounters with the generic tutor were more likely to be pre-arranged, indeed pre-arranged meetings with the generic tutor were often on a weekly basis and with other students.

The content and purpose of encounters

A question left largely unresolved from the earlier study had been in what ways these numerous, and sometimes lengthy, conversations added up to support for beginning teachers' professional development. The self-report inventories and interviews were used to investigate the content and purpose of the encounters. In these, the participants had been asked to record the purpose or content of the encounters. The most striking feature of the records was the range and diversity of the topics mentioned. There was widespread direct attention to the development of teaching competence as defined by Circular 9/92 (DFE 1992) and as portrayed in the student competence profiles in use on the programme. Other matters received attention as well, in particular administrative matters were mentioned frequently. Besides the general prominence of competence related discussions and administration (overlapping categories in any case), another striking feature was the way the records gave a glimpse of everyday life in a secondary school. For instance, a chat about how the school review (LEA pre-inspection) was going; demonstration of calculation of numbers at the bottom of the register; an account of appointments procedures for senior posts in Durham schools; and mention of how to acquire room keys were all recorded on the self-report inventories.

A more exploratory investigation of the content of the encounters was made through interview. A selection of participants was interviewed. Each respondent, as they were interviewed, selected one encounter to talk about, aided by reviewing the self-report inventory. Four broad categories in the discussion emerged. Firstly, students and tutors were concerned to discuss lesson planning. They commented on continuity and progression as an aspect of lesson planning and the application of subject knowledge and the identification of learning outcomes were important issues. Secondly, participants discussed assessment and record keeping. This involved discussion of special educational needs, equal opportunities, ethnic minorities and cultural differences, and school marking schemes. Thirdly, there was a major emphasis on practical advice and support. The fourth category concerned the structure and arrangements for the school experience. Tutors and students were keen to ensure that students received wide exposure to different issues and teaching styles, including post-16 education, special educational needs as well as teaching styles in other subjects and departments. Another topic which was revealed through the interviews concerned differences between expectations, work schedules and teaching styles between first and second school placements. The prominence of this may have been due to the survey taking place early in the second block of school experience.

The purposes and content of the encounter conversations were reviewed in terms of the competences expected of newly qualified teachers as outlined in Circular 9/92. The DFE competence areas, assessment and recording of pupils' progress, and subject application, were both identifiable categories as reported in the interviews. However the two DFE competence areas, class management and subject knowledge, tended to arise not as separately identifiable categories but as sub-categories of conversations that focused on purpose and planning in the classroom.

Discussion

The number of encounters and the amount of time spent on them was high, and at least comparable with our previous study. The average figure of over five hours contact during a three day period for students and their school-based tutors indicates a high level of professional commitment. It also indicates a high level of resource commitment. There are of course some additional resources for schools. One of the advantages of school-based training is the possibility of on-the-spot help; one of the disadvantages is that the time beyond this resource is taken from other activities. Each of these times was previously in use for personal or organisational purposes; much of the time for students comes from what was previously pupils' time, teachers' time and school time. Even here the equation is not simple; the student may well be relieving staff of a teaching commitment and allowing, with appropriate supervision, other tasks to be carried out, and there are other gains as well (Haylock 1994). In terms of long term development the diversion of resource into teacher education will need to be monitored as much for its opportunity cost implications as for the maintenance of quality in teacher education.

There was a difference between the type of encounter that took place between these secondary teacher training students and subject tutors, and that between the students and generic tutors. Subject tutors encountered students often but informally; generic tutors less often and perhaps with other students, but this was quite likely to have been formally arranged and with particular aims. This arrangement may well have been acceptable to students and tutors, however student experience is uneven within and between schools, a situation identified in this and other studies (see Booth, Furlong and Wilkin 1990; Reid, Constable and Griffiths 1994) and what this experience of encounters adds up to is still not entirely clear.

The study showed some lack of match between the Circular 9/92 categories and the content of the professional dialogues amongst students and tutors. Concerns sometimes but not always presented themselves in the categories presented by the DFE. In particular the two DFE competence areas, class management and subject knowledge, tended to arise not as those discrete categories but as part of conversations more specifically focused on purpose and planning in the classroom. They may be important in relation to the relative importance of the competences. Are the competences equally important and, if not, how is this signalled to a student (and tutor) who is presented with a list to be completed? In practice this may also be exaggerated by differential student experience in schools.

The University of Sunderland has, like other institutions, moved to the use of a competence based profile for the identification of student teachers' progress and qualification. This is a change from the assessment criteria and procedures which were used at the time of the previous study (Constable and Norton 1994) and proved to be an important new factor in the study of encounters. However that is not to say that the professional concerns of students and tutors were qualitatively different in practice. Nevertheless it might be felt, and the evidence suggests, that issues are likely to be more closely focused by the competence demands. Whether or not this is at the expense of a more holistic approach to teacher development or poses a threat to the long-term improvement of schooling remains unresolved. The students on the course researched have two major assessed teaching placements. Adjustment to different schools was a concern. What are the competencies that a teacher needs to accommodate a change of school, the understanding of, and adjustment to, context? Indeed at this level of professional engagement is the notion of competence identifiable or helpful?

A picture has emerged of a high level of interaction between students and tutors during school experience and furthermore it was possible to identify a pattern in the content of the encounters. A profile of issues has emerged related to personal and institutional demands and needs. The introduction of a competence based approach to teacher education appears to have developed a dynamic between the competence-driven assessment profile and the ongoing concerns and discussions between students and their school based tutors. Whether or not this tension ensures, at least, a minimum level of professional practice, and whether or not it is a diversion from the education of pro-active and emancipated teachers remains a matter for continuing debate.

There is rather more at stake than simply the relocation of teacher education in schools. Nor even is it merely a matter of developing effective partnership practices. It is not even a matter of implementing new practices. Education for teachers who will have most of their working lives in the first quarter or third of the twenty-first century is being <u>created</u> now. What actually happens now is an operational statement of teacher education and training. It is clear that both critical analysis and empirical research continue to be needed to inform decisions about whether what is happening is what is required.

Acknowledgements   Thanks are due to Ian Neale, Carol Glover and Rachael Harker for their help and support for this project.

Figure 6.1: Self-Report Inventory

Professional Encounters

Your Name:
Name of School:
Your Role in School (eg. Head of Dept):
Your Role (Please Tick): Student ☐   *Generic Tutor* ☐   *Subject Tutor* ☐

Day	Who was the Encounter with? (Initials & Role)	Start Time	Finish Time	Where did it take place? (eg. corridor, office etc.)	When did it take place? (eg. break, between lessons, during the lesson etc.)	What was the content/purpose of the Encounter
Tue Jan 25						
Wed Jan 26						
Thur Jan 27						

81

7   Initial teacher training and partnership: A management perspective

Terry Martin

Introduction and context

For the past five years the author has been planning and running Masters' courses in Management in Education. Week by week he has engaged with professionals from diverse backgrounds on issues such as managing change, motivation, theories of organisations, teambuilding and leadership. All these issues have been immediately relevant to his own professional life and the institutional context within which he works, not least the on-going drama of the school-based PGCE course. The perspective on Initial Teacher Training (ITT) offered here will be both personal and derive particularly from reflecting on these experiences in Management Education.

Secondary ITT has been reorganised nationally in response to Circular 9/92 (DFE 1992) which set the ground rules for all new courses from 1994 onwards. Like most Higher Education Institutions (HEIs), Southampton University initiated a partnership scheme for 1993-4, one year in advance of the required deadline. The new PGCE course is not developing in isolation from other changes in HE which impinge upon it. The following factors illustrate the context in which the changes are taking place:

1.   increasing emphasis upon research, driven by the Research Assessment Exercise nationally and a new Vice-Chancellor locally;

2.   quality Assessment audits of teaching undertaken by the Higher Education Funding Council (HEFC); Schools of Education however are being audited or inspected by OFSTED;

3.   increases in student numbers not matched by increases in human or material resources.

The following data give the total number of students successfully completing the Southampton PGCE course in the year concerned.

Year	87/88	88/89	89/90	90/91	91/92	92/93	93/94	94/95
Total	100	109	89	106	141	158	178	(215)

In 1993-94 a new main subject Physical Education was offered for the first time and in 1994-95 Religious Education is being offered as a new main subject for the first time in association with a local college of higher education. These two new subjects account for some of the increase in student numbers indicated above; the dominant factor, however, has been the increases in quota for existing main subject courses.

This combination of contextual factors has greatly increased the difficulties of setting up and operating a Partnership Scheme. Most staff, and certainly those individuals on full-time HEFC funded posts, feel increasing pressures to publish. Quality assurance procedures, whilst laudable in intent, have proliferated paperwork and engendered considerable hostility and scepticism about the reliability and validity of the whole exercise. The increase in student numbers, exceeding the capacity of both human and material resources, has led to the creation of a complex system which is inherently difficult to manage.

The structural and organisational changes

The content of the changes is relatively simple to describe but exceedingly complex in its implications and repercussions:

1. students must spend at least two-thirds of the 36 week course in schools;

2. schools/teachers will have control of ITT courses;

3. assessment will be focussed on performance as formulated in a list of prescribed competences;

4. schools will receive a proportion of the fees which students bring on registration.

84

Students have been spending an increasing amount of time in school on PGCE courses in recent years but this new course brings significant changes in the nature of the work they undertake in school. The reduced amount of time in the university combined with the increase in the number of students has meant a reduced involvement with the students by university staff. The university has responsibility for an enterprise over which it has diminishing control, and this is difficult to reconcile with the demands for Quality Assurance.

A competency-based assessment has brought some advantages in the formative stages of students' development but has proved cumbersome at the summative stage. It is difficult to reconcile with the aim of enabling students to become reflective practitioners. There is no intrinsic reason why being a competent teacher should be incompatible with being a reflective teacher; practical pressures are however shifting the balance towards pragmatic concerns at the expense of theoretical and critical ones. In their anxiety to please schools, students, in fact, are feeling increasing pressures which are leading them to become uncritical practitioners.

Some indicative figures for the 1994-95 course may help to give a feel for the size, complexity and cost of the Partnership Scheme for ITT which has been set up:

215 students in seven subject groups, spending 24 weeks in 40 schools under the supervision of 200 professional and curriculum mentors, and spending 12 weeks in the university and college of higher education with 20 link and curriculum tutors and three administrators;

200 sheets of paper generated and exchanged;

£180,000 being transferred to schools.

ITT is and always has been a highly labour intensive operation; much learning occurs in the intimacy of a one-to-one tutorial. This is reflected in the high staff-student ratio. However, although the students have a full-time commitment to their training, almost everyone else has other roles and responsibilities to perform.

Expectations, roles and responsibilities

In any complex human endeavour or organisation, like running the new PGCE course, it is customary to assign different roles to the individuals involved:

> Role is a psychological concept dealing with behaviour enactment arising from interaction with other human beings. The various offices or positions in an organisation carry with them certain expectations of behaviour held by both onlookers and by the person occupying the role. These expectations generally define role, with some additional expectation that the individual will exhibit some idiosyncratic personality in role behaviour (Owens 1981: 69).

Roles are thus created and sustained by the expectations individuals have of themselves and each other in the context of the situations within which they interact.

Actual behaviour is a subtle interplay of role and individual personality. Too much reliance on role definition and the enterprise becomes rigid and legalistic; too much reliance on personality and the enterprise becomes too dependent upon the idiosyncrasies of individuals.

For an organisation to operate efficiently it is helpful for expectations to be:

Communicated

Clear

Complementary

For a well established organisation roles are pre-determined and have often receded into the background of people's awareness. Individuals have grown accustomed to what they expect of each other, mutually live up to these expectations and take each other for granted. However in setting up a *new* structure for ITT, roles have to be created afresh by and for everyone involved.

In the Partnership Scheme the main roles have been:

| In schools: | Professional Mentor |
| | Curriculum Mentor |

| In the University: | Professional Tutor |
| | Curriculum Tutor |

Achieving common understandings of expectations and roles in a new initiative is a process of checking out, negotiating and agreeing, and re-defining in the light of actual experience. Unless carefully checked out, each participant will independently create definitions of their own and others' roles which may lead to inconsistencies and confusion.

In the mentor handbook and training programme produced before the course, attention was drawn to some likely problems that might arise and therefore could be usefully anticipated and avoided:

failure to check out exactly what each other's expectations are;

over reliance on previous definitions of similar roles;

defining unrealistic and unattainable roles.

Sadly, many of these problems have still arisen and despite attempts to formalise the responsibilities of the different roles in terms of more explicit job descriptions and entitlements, many ambiguities and tensions remain. The school-based roles have been relatively easy to define, although not surprisingly they have created role overload due to insufficient time being allowed to carry out the necessary duties. Some mentors have perceived their role as essentially a tutoring one, with the consequent duplication of some activities in school and university.

The university-based roles have proved problematic. The curriculum tutor role has been implicitly defined in terms of previous experience; the professional tutor role is new and subject to role ambiguity. It has now been redefined and renamed as link tutor to emphasise that the relationship is between the tutor and the school rather than with the students placed within it. The number of roles, however, still exceeds the number of people available and willing to undertake them with consequent problems of role conflict and role overload.

It is important not to forget the role of students; the expectations of them as adult learners will influence the way in which both mentors and tutors relate to them and seek to facilitate their professional development. The students' expectations of the course will probably be different from theirs, and it is important to consider how to resolve some of the conflicts that may arise from this. The concept of student entitlement is proving helpful in resolving some of the role ambiguities mentioned above.

In order to gain some insight into the student perspective and experience an analysis of the course based upon a curriculum audit with some approximate figures may be helpful. Assuming a five hour day for five days a week for 36 weeks the students spend 900 hours on the course in the following manner:

in the university and college of HE (57 days / 285 hours),

15 hours in a group of 200 on professional themes;

15 hours in a small group on professional themes;

80 hours in a curriculum subject group of 20-30 with a curriculum tutor;

75 hours in unsupervised small group subject work;

10 hours in groups on information technology;

15 hours in a group of 20 on a special study;

25 hours in individual private study;

30 hours in leisure activities;

20 hours in administrative activities;

in schools (123 days / 615 hours),

30 hours in professional groups with a professional mentor;

30 hours individually with a curriculum mentor;

125 hours observing and performing school-based tasks;

180 hours preparation, marking, etc.;

220 hours teaching classes;

30 hours on school half-term and bank holidays.

The students certainly have a varied experience; whether it is a coherent experience is another matter. In any learning situation it takes individuals time to familiarise themselves with the environment and context within which learning is taking place. The rapidity with which students move from one group to another and the fleeting contact they have with the many mentors and tutors involved in the course puts the quality of the learning experience significantly at risk. It also takes time to build up relationships both individually and with groups through which effective learning is mediated (a fact well understood by teachers). Nevertheless, in this respect and others, many of the pedagogic principles advocated to the students are actively negated. The nature and quality of the learning experiences for the students should exemplify and model the principles being taught.

The process of change

Fullan (1991) points out that it is not just the content or substance of a particular educational change which is important but the process by which it is brought about.

Some important points about the process of these changes to ITT are:

1. they have been imposed by a government distrustful and contemptuous of HEI;

2. they have been brought about quickly and with a minimum of consultation;

3. apart from Transitional Funding for two years, no additional resources have been allocated.

The combination of imposition, speed and inadequate resourcing, sadly all too familiar in most educational and social change, is proving damaging for a change which, if properly thought through and managed, could bring some real benefits to all the parties involved.

The following general points about the process of change, derived from Fullan (1991), are also relevant to this argument:

1. change cannot necessarily be equated with progress;

2. structural changes are easier to bring about than normative ones;

3. attempts at planned change rarely succeed as intended;

4.   we need to understand the phenomenology of change, how people experience it;

5.   there is a problem of finding meaning in change;

6.   solutions come through the development of shared meanings;

7.   often we find meaning only by trying something.

Fullan convincingly argues that centrally imposed changes are futile. This is a message that has finally registered in the Canadian context in which he writes but it has been strenuously ignored in this country. The starting point has to be the individual experience of those most implicated in the changes, and the considerable effort required by those people to make personal sense of what is happening. This separation of content from process is exemplified in Benton's (1990) account of the Oxford Internship scheme. The content of those changes is similar to those imposed by Circular 9/92. Indeed the Oxford scheme has been a forerunner of school-based training, yet the process whereby that particular change was brought about was vastly different. A substantial period of careful negotiation and the building up of common understandings preceded the actual implementation of the new scheme.

Change is often experienced as a threat and a loss as familiar patterns dissolve and individuals attempt to restabilise themselves and their lives in a new environment. If the attempt fails then they are condemned to a never-ending succession of fruitless and frustrating encounters where fundamental issues remain unresolved and tensions at an individual and institutional level generate increasing levels of anxiety and stress. The cost in human and organisational terms is enormous.

Back to basics

It is a good management principle to bring solutions not just problems; workable solutions must be based upon shared principles and understandings. Only then can a more productive and sustainable partnership develop. The following suggestions are offered tentatively as important considerations in guiding the process of restructuring a partnership scheme.

1.   There is a need to create, through an ongoing process of dialogue and negotiation, a shared understanding of the purpose of the partnership, and the values and principles upon which it is based.

2.   There is a need to agree models of students, teachers and children from which understandings of learning derive. The understandings of students as adult learners is fundamental to the pedagogic principles of the scheme.

3.   The funding of the course, including the maintenance of the partnership and administration, needs to be derived from real costings of the tasks actually performed. In the absence of any increase in overall funding levels this will entail some hard decisions about the commitment of time by mentors and tutors. However, given the understanding of students as adult learners mentioned above, much of their learning can arise through productive engagement with clearly defined but unsupervised tasks.

4.   The contributions made by the university staff and school staff need to be coherently related to the points above and to the complementary strengths which individuals and institutions can bring.

5.   It may be helpful explicitly to distinguish the difference in roles of mentors and tutors, from the difference in institutional context, school and university, within which the partnership operates. There are already excellent examples of mentor involvement with university-based sessions. The sessions are based in the university for reasons of economy and scale, and for the practical necessity of working with an entire curriculum group that would, for an entirely school-based scheme, be dispersed throughout a large number of schools.

Large and complex systems, both physical and social, are particularly vulnerable to instabilities (Senge 1990) which arise locally through some unanticipated combination of circumstances and events and propagate quickly throughout the entire system, often with disastrous consequences.

It seems that the present arrangements for ITT are arbitrary and ad hoc and cannot be sustained in either the short or long term; they create constant instability in a system which is perilously close to collapse. A structure which will be robust and stable against such instability will arise from the trust and understandings built up through the processes outlined above. When individuals share common understandings and exhibit trust then there is less need for cumbersome and unmanageable structures and procedures which rise through needs for control and power.

Conclusion

Marris (1986) explores the deep parallels between the experience of change and that of bereavement. The psychological impact of changes on those who will be most affected by them are often massively underestimated by those initiating them. People need time to absorb the impact of change and to reorientate themselves. This has enormous implications for those who aspire, often with great presumption, to be agents of change.

> When those who have power to manipulate changes act as if they have only to explain, and when their explanations are not at once accepted, shrug off opposition as ignorance or prejudice, they express a profound contempt for the meaning of lives other than their own (Marris 1986 : 155).

During the last few years many of those professionally involved with teacher education feel that they have been treated with profound contempt by those for whom they now reciprocate similar feelings. This cannot be healthy; an underlying value in education must be the worth and value of all people whose relationships are based upon mutual trust and respect. A revaluing of the enterprise of teacher education is a change worth striving for.

8 Long memories: Lessons for the induction and support of student teachers in schools

David Kerr

Introduction

This chapter is not a theorised account of the changes in teacher education; instead it seeks to describe the experiences of student teachers in the move toward more school-based teacher education in one particular context, that of the Partnership Scheme, the secondary Postgraduate Certificate of Education (PGCE) course at Leicester University. It is based on the findings of a survey of the induction and staff support experiences of student teachers in partnership schools. It is research in progress and the conclusions are tentative. However, the emergent issues at Leicester and their implications may hold lessons for others involved in school-based teacher education.

The Leicester Partnership Scheme

The School of Education at Leicester has a tradition of a close working relationship with local schools. In the 1960s, Professor Brian Simon pioneered a co-tutor system which was extended in the 1980s by Dr Pat Ashton through the IT-INSET model of teacher education (Ashton et al 1989; Everton and Impey 1989). The existing Partnership Scheme has grown from these earlier developments (Everton and White 1992). The decision to increase the proportion of school-based work in PGCE secondary courses (DFE 1992) has had little overall effect on the Leicester PGCE programme because student teachers were already spending approximately 60 per cent of their time in schools. However, it has meant the advent of more formalised arrangements which clearly define the complementary and distinctive contributions of schools and the University to the initial training partnership (Kerr 1994).

How does the Partnership Scheme work?

In the autumn and spring terms, student teachers spend two days a week in a particular cluster of partnership schools. They spend six days in the cluster early in the autumn term, followed by a six week block teaching practice in one of the schools in the cluster. They spend 18 days in schools during the spring term, and, following a second teaching practice (of eight weeks) in different schools, they return to their partnership clusters for a further 12 day block period at the end of the summer term. Whenever possible each student teacher works as one of a pair of student teachers attached to a subject department in a partnership school. They work closely with a teacher in the department (the co-tutor), planning teaching and discussing their work as a team. Subject tutors at the School of Education liaise closely with the subject co-tutors.

In 1993-1994, 261 student teachers were registered on the secondary PGCE course and 51 Leicestershire and Northamptonshire schools were involved in the Partnership Scheme grouped into 17 clusters. Roughly 16 student teachers were attached to each cluster (the number in each school ranging from four to ten). Each school has a professional tutor who co-ordinates the student teachers' programme in their school. Attached to each cluster is a School of Education link tutor responsible, in consultation with the schools' professional tutors, for co-ordinating the work of the student teachers in the cluster.

Study background

The survey arose from collaboration with the course's external consultant (EC). The EC is an important component of the quality assurance procedures at Leicester and reinforces the partnership between the University and local schools. The current external consultant is Peter Macdonald Pearce, Principal of Uppingham Community College, an 11 to 16 co-educational institution in the partnership. Peter and I agreed to focus on the quality of the school-based component of the partnership for student teachers. This decision was taken for a number of reasons.

First, it was taken to underline the importance of the student teachers' perspective in initial teacher education (ITE). They experience the course and are the fundamental link between its various components - school and university - yet they are often the 'missing voice' in the debates about teacher education. Their opinions are either presumed or subsumed. The literature on

94

school-based teacher education contains much on what student teachers require and receive but lacks systematic evidence of their thoughts and experiences on the current changes (beyond Furlong et al 1988; Furlong 1990; Booth 1993). In many ways their views should be the basis on which decisions are made, particularly as it is their training requirements which are at the heart of the debates. The survey was an attempt to redress this in the context of the Leicester Partnership Scheme.

Second, the current changes in teacher education accelerate the move toward school-based teacher education which has been pioneered on a number of initial teacher training (ITT) courses, including Leicester. They have major implications for schools and for the roles and responsibilities of staff who work closely with student teachers. The fundamental challenge is to assist school staff in maximising the potential for school-based teacher education in their particular institution. To be able to do this it is vital to first find out what is happening at present in order to inform future practice. It is imperative that school staff do not perceive the current reforms as merely 'taking on the role of University tutors' (Pendry 1992).

Third, a recent HMI report on the Partnership Scheme raised questions about: variation in the nature and quality of the training provided by schools to student teachers; the integration of the school and university-based elements; the quality assurance mechanisms for monitoring the school-based element and the planned training for school staff in preparation for their new roles and responsibilities (HMI 1994). The survey was an opportunity to substantiate the nature and extent of these issues.

Fourth, we were keen to identify elements of 'satisfactory or better' and 'unsatisfactory' practice across the partnership which could be fed into the training programme for school staff in 1994 and 1995.

Study method

A questionnaire was issued to 241 PGCE students with follow up subject group discussions of the main issues in January 1994. The purpose was to gauge student teachers' conceptions of the school-based course component experienced in the autumn term. In particular, we wanted to evaluate their experiences concerning: first, induction to the Partnership Scheme in schools - how well had they been received and what had been the effect on their perceptions and behaviour? - and second, the roles and responsibilities of school staff who had worked closely with them - how had they been supported by school staff and what had been the impact on relationships at professional and subject level?

Study findings

Induction

Seventy-six per cent of student teachers judged the induction process satisfactory or better while 24 per cent found it unsatisfactory. Two features made the induction process satisfactory or better. First, positive responses from staff and pupils to their presence in school and second, the existence of well-planned, flexible training programmes at both professional and subject level. Many student teachers commented that they were 'made to feel welcome' in a school and this led to 'a sense of belonging' and of 'feeling valued'. A number of student teachers also stressed the reassurance of a friendly staff room. Student teachers found it particularly helpful to be given suitable school documents. A high priority for all student teachers was a well-planned and well-structured partnership programme where 'we were told in advance what we were doing'.

The key features which made the induction process unsatisfactory were the converse of the satisfactory elements, namely poor or non-existent staff responses and lack of a planned training programme. Student teachers referred to the need for schools to spell out 'what was expected from us'. Many schools did not appear to have a clear grasp of their training role and responsibilities vis-à-vis student teachers and student teachers commented on being 'left to sink or swim'. It is not surprising therefore to find a great deal of frustration among student teachers as encapsulated in this comment:

> The school didn't seem to realise that there was training and learning taking place. Perhaps they thought it happened somewhere else or that simply by being in the school I would take it in by osmosis.

This is particularly significant given that the last time many student teachers were in school was as pupils themselves.

Roles and responsibilities of school staff

The majority of student teachers (69 per cent) confirmed that the professional tutor had overall responsibility for their training.

Professional issues

Overall, 51 per cent judged the arrangements for developing their skills in wider professional areas in school satisfactory or better and 49 per cent regarded them as unsatisfactory. The principal reasons for unsatisfactory arrangements concerned lack of time and commitment from professional tutors and the lack of status of wider professional issues in schools. In many schools the professional tutor role was combined with other responsibilities. Many commented on 'compromises over time' because the professional tutor was too busy with other things or with student teachers from other universities. Professional tutors were thus often unable to provide the breadth and depth of insight into professional issues student teachers required. In some instances they were reduced to a fleeting figure who snatched brief words in passing. This contributed to the perception of student teachers that wider professional issues were not a high priority in the school.

Subject issues

Sixty seven per cent stated that skills development in their subject area was satisfactory or better while 33 per cent felt it was unsatisfactory. Three key features stand out in making the subject experience satisfactory or better: first, positive responses from staff in the subject department; second, the influence of balanced advice and feedback and third, regular opportunities to meet with a co-tutor who has clear expectations of the subject partnership and of the development needs of student teachers.

Student teachers underlined the importance of feeling welcome and valued in the department. They worked best in a climate of encouragement tempered with constructive criticism and advice as evidenced by this comment:

> Staff in the department are very supportive offering advice but not crowding me. Every day someone asks me how it is going and really is interested in discussing it. I feel trusted by staff in the department to get on with things and it is an amazing confidence boost.

They also placed high value on timetabled opportunities to discuss their personal concerns with co-tutors. This was most productive where they had worked alongside the co-tutor in the classroom.

The commonest key feature for unsatisfactory skills development was the lack of time. Fifty five per cent of student teachers felt that their co-tutor had insufficient time to work with them on teaching skills. Many stated that the co-tutor was busy with other commitments and this brought an overwhelming sense of guilt if they had to take up precious personal time at break or lunch. The following comment is typical:

> The co-tutor is run into the ground with other commitments. She never has a minute. If you can grab her for five minutes she does her best but it's always rushed and you feel like a huge burden as if you should apologise for being there.

Even when specific time had been set aside it was often interrupted. Student teachers found the constant need to request opportunities to meet with co-tutors demotivating.

Two other unsatisfactory features were frequently mentioned. First, staff insensitivity to student teacher concerns allied to conflicting advice, and second, co-tutor ignorance of training responsibilities and of course requirements. Student teachers complained that some staff revelled in picking on their classroom failings rather than successes. Some co-tutors neither worked with the student teachers in the classroom nor observed them teaching.

Emergent issues

The survey findings throw up many issues for discussion. On the positive side, there is much that student teachers find satisfactory or better in their current school experiences. This is testimony to the considerable efforts of the partners in building a strong and effective partnership. On the negative side, there are unsatisfactory aspects which correspond with the variability issues raised by HMI. Clearly, the partnership must look to consolidate and nurture the positive elements while ironing out the negative aspects. However, the situation is not that simple. The issues must be viewed within the context of a Partnership Scheme in flux as it responds more precisely to the requirements of Circular 9/92. The response is centred in particular on the partners managing the significant shift required in the roles and responsibilities of school staff who work closely with student teachers. In order to assist this task, I want to concentrate on the lessons of the survey for partnership schools and their staff. This is where the survey findings can be applied to maximum benefit for the partnership.

Induction

This is clearly an important process for student teachers. The quality of the induction frames not only their impressions of a school and its staff, but also informs their subsequent actions while in the school. The more knowledge and understanding of the institution - staff, pupils, working practices, status of student teachers - the school is able to provide through induction the more quickly the student teacher is likely to settle, interact positively with staff and pupils and begin to discuss their particular training requirements. Above all, student teachers need to feel welcome and valued and that their needs, however trivial they may appear to experienced staff, are respected. Earley and Kinder (1993) have shown that effective induction for new teachers is best negotiated rather than imposed and founded on flexibility, responsiveness and responsibility. The same holds true for the effective induction of student teachers.

Roles and responsibilities of school staff

The professional tutor Schools are experiencing obvious difficulties in meeting the requirements of this role. Clearly, at present, staff designated professional tutor neither have the time nor the commitment to develop the role fully and link it with subject work. This may be a reflection of the lack of status of wider professional issues among staff in schools combined with the notion that because of the link tutor role such issues are more the domain of the university than schools. This is happening despite the presence of documentation designed specifically to assist school staff. The professional topics file (a ten topic 'protofile' of supported self-study material produced to support the professional course by the School of Education) is badly under-utilised by school staff in working with student teachers.

The co-tutor This role is much more familiar and established for school staff than that of professional tutor. The survey findings reinforce much of the research findings about the relationship between co-tutors and student teachers both from the perspective of the co-tutor (Booth et al 1990; McIntyre et al 1993; Dart and Drake 1993; Williams 1993) and from the student teacher (Furlong et al 1988; Williams et al 1992; Booth 1993). At present, staff in this role neither have sufficient time to devote to it nor fully understand what it involves, particularly in relation to the development needs of student teachers as beginning teachers. The result is a variety of practice not only across schools but also across subject areas. It raises questions as to who should be a co-tutor and what they should be doing.

The co-tutor role is a highly responsible one and can be very time-consuming particularly when student teachers are first in school. Co-tutors need to understand the role in the light of 9/92 before agreeing to proceed. Clearly, they understand some of the requirements based on the collected wisdom of past experience. For example, they realise the need to create a supportive environment within which the professional relationship between co-tutor and student teachers can develop, often referred to as an 'ethic of caring'. However, many currently fall short in terms of how best to help student teachers in the classroom.

It is clear from the survey that the majority of co-tutors see their role as supervision rather than training of student teachers (Maynard and Furlong 1993). they are more staff managers and counsellors than educators. They are not making the most of their contextual knowledge, understanding and skills - the strengths of school-based teacher education. This is in part because of the time pressures but also because they have limited access to the growing research base on teacher education and development with respect to student teachers. In particular, they have little understanding of the complex process of learning to teach for student teachers. Maynard and Furlong (1993) suggest five stages of student teacher classroom development, namely early idealism, survival, recognising differences, hitting the plateau, and moving on. The survey suggests that many student teachers progress through the first three stages, i.e. to a point where they are deemed competent in the classroom and can be left safely with classes while the normal teacher attends to other matters. Progression relates more to co-tutor 'arbitrariness and idiosyncrasy' (McIntyre and Hagger 1993) than uniform systematic training. Movement from the plateau is currently only possible when the student teacher initiates it.

There are also signs of tension in some schools between the needs of student teachers and co-tutor requirements. The personal development needs of the student teacher are not always compatible with the institutional priorities of the co-tutor and the school. Some student teachers feel pressurised to adopt a similar teaching style to their co-tutor or to opt for safe teaching and learning approaches.

Whole-school experiences

Few schools view initial teacher education within a whole-school context nor make the rationale for the training programme for student teachers explicit. Schools need to look at their provision for initial teacher education in totality, particularly where they work with a number of universities. The school-based training of student teachers can no longer be left to the whim of individuals or be broken up into disparate segments. Schools need to agree their approach to initial teacher education, to spell out the training programme more clearly and to better co-ordinate and monitor student teacher experiences in the school. It is vital there is clear communication between the professional tutor and the co-tutors and that subject work dovetails with wider professional concerns. Central to staff roles and responsibilities is the importance of interpersonal skills and the need to create a supportive environment in which student teachers are encouraged to learn through reflection and structured support. At present, student teachers are acutely aware of the different cultures that exist in a school and are left to weave their way amongst them. Some are more successful at this than others. It raises the question of how far, as part of their training, student teachers should be versed in the political and micro-political skills they need to work in schools (Calderhead 1994).

Training for school staff

The student teacher responses point to the need for considerable training for school staff to improve current practices and meet the requirements of Circular 9/92. Their comments suggest the training should encompass several strands. First, the context of teacher education including Circular 9/92. Many staff are unclear about their roles and responsibilities in working with student teachers. Second, understanding of the rationale of the Partnership Scheme covering all its components - school, university, subject and professional aspects. Third, the skills required to meet the specific roles and responsibilities of the professional tutor and co-tutor. This requires school staff access to the growing research base on ITE and consideration of the implications for their particular institution and practice. Finally, coverage of the partnership assessment requirements and supporting documentation is essential.

Final thoughts

How successful partnership schools will be in responding to the survey findings as they strive to meet the revised criteria for school-based teacher education remains to be seen. The partners are working hard in this direction and a number of survey issues may well be eased by the new formalised arrangements for partnership in 1994-1995. These include a signed partnership agreement between individual schools and the university which sets out the financial basis of the partnership and establishes a minimum time requirement for school staff to work with student teachers across the year; documentation to support the work of professional tutors (now renamed ITT co-ordinators) with student teachers given the abolition of the link tutor role, and quality assurance mechanisms to monitor the school-based component.

Despite these developments there remain tensions in the Leicester Partnership. These stem from a series of considerations for the partners, notably for:

1.   schools and their staff:

  - how seriously will they take their increased ITE responsibilities given all their other commitments?

  - how far do they possess the 'reflective, professional development culture' which underpins the partnership and links wider professional concerns to subject work?

  - can they resolve the conflict between the financial versus the social and practical imperatives of ITE involvement?

  - how will they resolve the tension between institutional priorities and the development needs of the student teacher?

2.   the university and its staff:

  - what is the university's future role in school-based teacher education?

  - how will staff reconcile the pressure to scale down the support to student teachers in school at a time when it could be argued those needs are greater than ever before?

3.   training for school staff:

  - how much training do school staff require for particular roles?

  - how much can be usefully achieved in the limited training time available beyond coverage of administrative procedures?

- how applicable is the growing research base on ITE practice and student teacher development? Certainly the experience of schemes at Oxford, Sussex, Cambridge and Leicester can assist staff training (Benton 1990; Hake 1993; Dart and Drake 1993; Kerr 1994). However, the present context is much changed from the one in which those schemes were set up with significant shifts in the relationship between schools and universities, in the number of partner schools involved, in the short time scale in which the changes to courses are to be made and, crucially, in the size of available resources. Past conceptions and experiences of ITE may have only limited use and, as I have argued elsewhere, may actually prove a hindrance (Kerr 1994).

Above all, the student teacher responses strongly suggest that if these questions are to be successfully resolved then the university and its partner schools need to ensure two things. First, that they are extremely careful how they frame the training partnership in relation to Circular 9/92 and second, that they remain ever vigilant in the monitoring of the actual training practice. There is always the danger of a gap developing between the rhetoric of partnership and the reality of its practice in a school. The findings suggest such a gap already exists in the practice of some partnership schools.

The danger for the future partnership under 9/92 is that the current context of initial teacher education may increase the negative variable aspects of school-based practice at the cost of the positive ones. The recent reforms of initial teacher education are predicated on a 'social market' view of teacher training with an internal market which encourages competition between training conceptions and providers. The competing conceptions include, on the one side, the apprenticeship or 'sitting with Nellie' model - based on the concept of the student teacher working alongside and imitating the experienced teacher - and, on the other, the reflective practitioner model - based on the student teacher learning to teach through reflective practice. The former has driven much of the political rhetoric behind Circular 9/92 (O'Hear 1988; Hillgate Group 1989; Lawlor 1990) while the latter has informed the development of many ITE courses (Barrett et al 1992), including the Leicester Partnership, over the past 15 years. The competing providers range from existing HEIs to new entrants, notably the Open University and various school-centred consortia.

The threat for the Leicester Partnership Scheme is that despite the best intentions of the partners Circular 9/92 may widen the gap between the rhetoric and the reality of partnership in many more partnership schools. The rhetoric of partnership, as outlined in this chapter, may be for reflective practice but the reality may be far removed from this. Instead, there may be a potential mismatch between what is desired and what is achievable given the increased pressures of ITE involvement on school staff on top of their other commitments. The reality may be nearer the apprenticeship model in many partnership schools, at least in the short term. Fullan (1992) talks about the 'implementation dip' when introducing new initiatives. This may be what we are about to experience in ITE. A growing number of teacher educators are worried about the combined effects of the implementation of the Education Reform Act (1988) and school-based teacher training on the teaching profession (Dart and Drake 1993; John and Lucas 1994). The question is whether we will come out of this dip and to what extent? The answer has serious implications for the professional development of teachers and for the future of initial teacher training. Some recent research suggests that those who become co-tutors often fall back on the experiences of their own training in working with student teachers (Elliott and Calderhead 1993). The training experiences of current student teachers may well have repercussions when those student teachers themselves become co-tutors and professional tutors.

It is therefore vital that schools and universities should think about the sort of ITE training partnership they want and how partners can best achieve it given the reality of education today. Much will depend on the attitude of schools and their staffs to the requirements of Circular 9/92 and on the ability of university staff to help them begin to fulfil the expectations of their revised roles and responsibilities in working with student teachers. Surveying the school experiences of student teachers and learning from the findings is a vital part of this assistance. This is what we are attempting in the Leicester Partnership though we must await the verdict of future student teachers to see if our efforts have been rewarded. Our actions are based on the belief that the partnership is involved not only in training student teachers to be teachers but may also be influencing their practices as teacher trainers of the future. It is not only elephants which have long memories.

9 Primary school-based teacher education in France

Penny Cotton

Introduction

Whilst the United Kingdom is beginning to develop a more school-based approach to teacher education, other European countries have been working in this way for many years. France, for example, is very experienced in training its maîtres formateurs - specially selected teachers who take on the role of student supervision in primary schools. These maîtres formateurs/ master teachers, after undertaking a substantial university-based training course/exam, work alongside tutors from university institutions. In addition to guiding/supervising students during school experience, the maîtres formateurs often organise workshops in the university which prepare students for teaching and support research. This chapter reviews these arrangements and considers possible implications for the United Kingdom.

Primary school-based teacher education in France

In a book of this nature which focuses on the development of school-based teacher education in the United Kingdom insights may be gained by looking further afield at other education systems which have been working in a similar way for some time. The French education system is an obvious example from which lessons may be learned, as its formation of instituteurs (primary teachers) has been very much based in schools with maîtres formateurs (master teachers) playing an important role.

In fact, until quite recently France has had a very centralised, school-based approach to teacher education which has been highly structured and well resourced. In line with other European countries, France had its roots in the evolution of publicly financed schooling which was the response to the

105

emergence of a modern industrialised society with its commercial, technological and social needs (Miller and Taylor 1993).

Since the mid-nineteenth century, the education systems in France and England have undergone many changes, but in relation to the education of primary teachers they appear to have been working in completely opposite directions. Table 9.1 enables one to see that after 1870, when Jules Ferry declared that he would devote all his time to 'the education of the people' (Némo 1991), it was the Écoles Normales that were set up to train teachers. These 'normal schools' were initially where motivated students would finish secondary schooling and continue their studies and apprenticeship working alongside primary teachers in schools.

Although there have been changes in entry qualifications and time spent on training primary teachers in France since the end of the last century, the Écoles Normales have remained. It was not until 1989 that the Bancel report proposed to put all teacher education into the University sector by 1992, for three main reasons: to recruit more staff; to give equal status to both primary and secondary teachers; and to standardise teacher training (Greaves and Shaw 1992). This is in striking contrast to teacher education in England where recommendations were made at the end of the last century to establish University departments of education. Amazingly, it was also in 1992 that a proposal was made by the English secretary of state to place the bulk of teacher training in schools.

A complete move in opposite directions leads one to question not only why these changes have evolved but also, in terms of school-based teacher training, what is it about the French system that has been successful over so many years.

Currently, France is moving from a very centralised to a more de-centralised education system which has implications for both pedagogic structure and curriculum content. To be able to understand French teacher training more fully, however, it may be helpful to look at its development and progression - especially in relation to qualifications, training, links with schools, and the maîtres formateurs/master teachers who have for many years facilitated the link between theory and practice for numerous prospective French primary teachers.

106

Table 9.1: Comparative development of teacher education in France and England

France	England
19th Century	
Duality in training of teachers	
Split between elementary/higher secondary schools	
Most gifted pupils stayed on at school as monitors; then combination of secondary school and professional training. **Governed by State** 1870 Jules Ferry declared that he would devote his time to 'the education of the people'. 1879 Traditional form of Écoles Normales set up by Ferry in all départements. 1880 Education Act supporting this 1897 Jules Ferry became 'Ministre de l'Instruction Publique', and his concept of teacher training changed very little until after World War II. 1945 Gradual change in Écoles Normales began. 1952 Lycée teachers needed new qualification: CAPES 1959-63 School reforms: primary not elementary. Secondary education for all. Influenced teacher training. 1960 Instituteurs could improve their qualifications. 1968 Faure's Law proposed to offer university education for all teachers. 1969 Training changed from ONE to TWO years. 1971 Closing of preparatory classes for BAC in Écoles Normales. 1979 A new reform - decisive step towards a university training for all. 1986 Colloque d'Amiens THREE year courses 1989 Four Year courses, leading to: CAPES/DEUG+2 Jospin: Loi d'Orientation Bancel report: idea of IUFM and more theory-based teacher education. 1990 Three pilot IUFMs 1992 Instituts UNIVERSITAIRES de Formation des Maîtres responsible for education of ALL teachers.	Set in denominational training colleges. **Absence of State control** 1839 Denominational opposition to idea of a 'State Normal' school. 1888 Cross Commission recommended UNIVERSITY departments of Education. Two-year courses at day training colleges were established in universities. 1891 ONE year course set up for graduates.(ie 4 years to acquire teacher status) 1903 Introduction of Local Authority colleges. 1927 Some co-ordination of these three providers of education through the joint boards. 1944 McNair report recommended the creation of University Schools of Education to be responsible for training in their areas. 1948 Area training organisations set up. 1952 Last of 4 year university students admitted. 1963 Robbins Report: New B.Ed degree. 1970s reduced numbers into teaching; closure of some colleges/integration with universities/polys. Some became colleges of H.E. 1970 All graduates entering primary education now had to complete a PGCE training year 1974 The same for secondary (not Maths & Science) 1984 C.A.T.E. established course recognition/approval by Secretary of State. 1990s Many polytechnics/H.E. colleges became universities. 1992 Proposal by Secretary of State that the bulk of teacher training should be placed in SCHOOLS in England.

Evolution of training establishments

The pattern of teacher training in France has changed considerably during the later part of this century. It has moved from a very much school-based approach, where students began their 'apprenticeship' by choosing to prepare for their BAC (similar to 'A' levels) at 15 in an École Normale (teacher training college), to a 'post university' course at an IUFM (Institut Universitaire de Formation des Maîtres). These university institutes were established in 1991, with the aim of raising the status of instituteurs (primary teachers) to professeurs d'écoles, and training them alongside secondary teachers. ThisFollowed the Loi d'Orientation introduced by Lionel Jospin, the French Education Minister, in 1989. In the past, not only were the two levels of teachers 'formed' in different ways, they also received different salaries. Now, however, there will be no divide.

When stagières (students) finish their two year course at the IUFM they now go into schools with their elevated salaries and status, and work alongside 'instituteurs' who have a great deal of practical experience, though possibly not the same academic qualifications. As September 1993 was the first year that the 'professeurs d'écoles' were qualified, it is uncertain how this dual level of qualifications will work in the future. Most instituteurs do not foresee too much of a problem, as many can either take additional INSET courses or already have the relevant number of points to augment their salary. Some students, on the other hand, feel that they may be resented by instituteurs, and hope that the new qualifications will not cause a divide between primary teachers.

Three main phases of development in French teacher training

The development of teacher training courses has progressed through three major phases since Jules Ferry's nineteenth century model of bright children from poor families becoming teachers.

Initially, students decided at the age of 15 if they wished to teach. In many cases it was the brightest children in the class who really wanted to become teachers. 'Historically, the École Normale had offered the bright pupil a way out of his/her modest family circumstances' (Neather 1993). The status of the profession was very high then, as one directeur of an école d'application confirmed when interviewed. After preparing for and completing the BAC, students would study for one further year at the École Normale, before commencing their teaching. Three months of this period was spent working in schools.

After the school reforms of 1959 and 1963, prospective teachers could take their BAC in secondary schools, subsequently moving to the Écoles Normales. Here they followed a two year course which would prepare them for teaching (Eurydice 1991).

The beginning of the third phase in 1991 saw the setting up of the IUFM, which are mainly based in the old Écoles Normales, and tend to be grouped into regions with about five IUFMs linking to a Central IUFM - there are now 29 in France. Students are recruited to these university institutes after they have studied for three years at university. The directeur of the école d'application suggested that sometimes the students who take this option do so because they don't know what else to do, and may only just have scraped through their university course (Follain 1994).

Current courses

The first year prepares students for the concours, an exam to see whether they will be able to continue into the second. Most of this year is theoretically based, with only a small amount of time in schools. The concours relates very much to theoretical issues, and some students elect to take this preparation year at their own university.

Successful students, once they have passed the competitive concours, become fonctionaires (civil servants) and receive a salary. They spend about 50 per cent of their time in school and the remainder discussing theoretical issues. Philosophy of education is high on the agenda. The aims and objectives of the course are to make links between theory and practice, forming a bridge between the two. The courses are so designed that stagières work alongside tutors in college; alongside maîtres formateurs whilst they are on their stage accompagnée; and alongside conseiller pedagogiques/ inspecteurs/ tutors when they are alone in the classroom on their stage de responsibilité. All students have the opportunity to work in both écoles primaires and écoles maternelles.

Links between theory and practice

There is very close liaison between the IUFM and the schools in which the students are based. The links are made through stages sur le terrain (school experience); ateliers pedagogiques (school-based workshops); some supervision of memoires (dissertations); and occasional research projects. In many of the IUFM, the écoles d'applications are either next door or attached to the university institute and facilitate the important link between college tutors and maîtres formateurs in schools. These specially qualified teachers provide a vital bridge between theory and practice in the early stages of the students' understanding of the learning process.

Structure of the French education system

Children begin compulsory education at six years of age, spending five years in primary school rather than six, as in the United Kingdom. Most of them, however, attend an école maternelle for three or four years beforehand . The ministry of education decides on the number of hours that children will spend on each subject within the primary school , and the classes have the following United Kingdom equivalence:

Cours Preparatoire	=	Year 2
Cours Elémentaire 1	=	Year 3
Cours Elémentaire 2	=	Year 4
Cours Moyen 1	=	Year 5
Cours Moyen 2	=	Year 6

Function of the écoles d'application

In general, most écoles normales would have either one or two écoles d'application (annexes) on the same campus. These would be the schools having the most liaison with the training establishment and a very high proportion of the teaching staff would be maîtres formateurs. In addition, a large proportion of schools within the catchment area of the écoles normales would be designated écoles d'application with a significant number of maîtres formateurs on the staff.

The function of the écoles d'application is, therefore, to receive students on school experience and to guide and develop their learning, gradually allowing them to be responsible for a primary class. In addition, time is allocated to maîtres formateurs in order for them to discuss pedagogy and teaching programmes as well as run ateliers pedagogiques in the écoles normales and supervise student dissertations (IUFM-Douai 1991).

Since 1992, when students are initially received in school it is always to work alongside a maître formateur known to be capable of helping them to progress. Placing stagières in specifically designated écoles d'applications helps the IUFM tutors, as they know which placements are available and that

110

the teachers are suitably qualified to develop students' thinking and teaching, and children's learning within the classroom context.

The écoles d'applications, which have been chosen for the training of teachers, receive students during their stage accompagnée- short periods in school during the initial stages of the course. The final school experience, frequently two four-week periods, can be in any school - students are now considered to be qualified and should be able to teach by themselves.

Currently, some areas of France are changing the ways in which they work with the écoles d'application and, under the new system, fewer maîtres formateurs are often available. This has caused many students to express concern about the new arrangement, as the quality of some teachers does not present a good model for emulation.

Role of the maîtres formateurs

One of the biggest differences between teacher education in France and that here relates to the training and role of the maîtres formateurs, who are responsible for the supervision and development of students within schools sur le terrain. The terminology of 'master teacher' itself suggests a different task. Supervisors of school experience in the United Kingdom tend to have time to do just that; maîtres formateurs are allocated hours within their timetables so that they can become involved in the actual 'formation' of students.

Tutors, or professeurs, in the IUFM are often recruited for their academic ability and many have taught in secondary schools, but very few have primary experience. As a consequence, they are not expected to make frequent visits to see students in school. Maîtres formateurs, on the other hand, are teachers with at least five years' teaching experience, often more, who have usually but not always been singled out by the inspecteur as being excellent practitioners. It is then suggested that they follow a course to prepare them for the role. Teachers can qualify without attending a course, but it is up to individuals to decide. The courses are usually run by the inspecteur of the IUFM, who also sits on the selection 'jury' for the rigorous three part exam. This jury usually comprises: the directeur of the IUFM; two tutors from the IUFM; one directeur of an école d'application; one maître formateur; and the Inspecteur.

Qualifications

To qualify, teachers must pass each part of the exam which lasts over a period of one year, and consists of three parts.

1. The first part is taken between September and December, when a teacher is seen teaching his/her own class in front of a jury and must achieve 15/20 in order to progress to part two.

2. The second part is taken between January and April, where the teacher gives a presentation of his/her written thesis to the same jury. The theme for this is usually decided upon in collaboration with a maître formateur.

3. The third part is taken between April and June, when the teacher is seen by the jury whilst analysing a student's teaching/giving feedback.

Once the teachers have passed the exam, they have to wait until a post as maître formateur becomes available in an école d'application of their choice; sometimes this may be two or three years, but often it is immediate. Now they are able to receive students into their classrooms, and only teach for 18 hours a week; six are left to work with students and three for administration and personal research.

Liaison

As well as receiving students into their classrooms, most maîtres formateurs teach for a number of hours at the IUFM usually on courses of a practical nature related to atelier pédagogiques. Some also supervise dissertations and run specific INSET courses. In addition to this, many work with IUFM tutors in their own classrooms, trying out new teaching methods and projects, which often go towards publications for the benefit of other teachers. All see part of their role as helping colleagues and improving pedagogy.

Theoretical aspects

One important issue which appears to mark a difference in attitude towards the training of teachers in France and the United Kingdom is the relevance of theory. Whilst in England the government is looking towards a more school-based approach, in France the theoretical side of training takes up about 50 per cent of the course, and is considered an extremely important element, especially by the University and the Ministère de l'Education Nationale. Some students and teachers, however, are not so sure of its relevance, even though they know it is important to have a theoretical background.

Practical aspects

The stages in school progress in a very structured way in France. During the first one-and-a-half years, for example, the students work in pairs, alongside the maîtres formateurs, observing and analysing with a fellow student. The analysis of these sessions serves to develop and inform future sessions and therefore helps in the planning and progression of work done in school. Each maître formateur is given six hours every week to be with students either in class or in the IUFM, plus three hours for administration. In the final 'stage de responsibilité' the students are completely alone in the class and can be placed in any classroom, often not with a maître formateur. (Under the old system most students spent all their time with a maître formateur but currently students are often placed with less experienced teachers.)

Status

In general the status of a maître formateur within the French primary education system is high. S/he is respected for having been successful in the concours (the exam where only a certain number will pass), which shows an excellence in teaching; the ability to think analytically and theoretically about educational issues; and an aptitude for relating well to students and facilitating their learning. These qualities are seen as essential for both working with colleagues, and enhancing students' ability to relate theory learned in college to practical aspects in school. In addition, tutors and students welcome their expertise and advice on practical pedagogical matters.

Supervision of students

The bulk of supervision is usually in the domain of the maître formateur in an école d'application, especially in the early part of the course. In year one, students are always placed in an école d'application with a maître formateur. They work in pairs, and often spend a great deal of time observing the teacher.

Once they begin teaching, they plan their work together with the help of the maître formateur. Often s/he will take the first lesson of a sequence and all three will analyse it in detail. After this, both students will plan the second lesson and one will teach whilst the other evaluates, often aided by the teacher. Sometimes the maître formateur will interrupt the teaching, but students welcome this and feel that are being helped rather than criticised. In most cases, there are desks at the back of the classroom for students or tutors, and the children become accustomed to the constant stream of visitors to their school. (Usually the écoles d'application are quite prestigious and very popular with parents, due to the high quality of teaching.)

The college tutor will only visit once, or twice if students request it, but this can be for as long as three to four hours if necessary. It is felt that one long visit where a complete lesson can be seen and then analysed in depth is of most benefit to both student and tutor (IUFM-Douai 1991).

Later in the course, when students are alone in the class for longer periods of time, the tutor will still only visit once, unless there are exceptional circumstances; practice is often for the inspecteur or conseiller pedagogiques (assistant inspector) to also see students once. In this way, s/he will be aware of prospective primary teachers in the area, as students are usually employed in the region where they qualify.

Placement of students

There appear to be a number of advantages for French institutions in terms of general status and control over students in school:

1. the IUFM prepares and is involved in the selection of maîtres formateurs, and therefore can decide which teachers are capable of receiving students;

2. the IUFM knows how many students may be placed in each school, and plans for the whole region;

3. the IUFM has overall responsibility for the assessment of students;

4. the IUFM runs many INSET courses for teachers.

Practical implications for the United Kingdom

Now that the French system is becoming less centralised, and the IUFM are not dependent on the government to the same extent, each region of France is developing its own way of educating teachers. Nord/Pas de Calais, for example, is currently retaining its écoles d'applications, whereas Brittany is slowly phasing them out. One of the reasons may well be expense.

France has not been without its problems concerning development and change within teacher education but, from insights gained so far, there may well be lessons to be learned. It would appear that, to develop an efficient school-based system of teacher education, a considerable amount of planning and expense is required. If supervision of school experience is to be successful and maîtres formateurs/mentors are to gain confidence and expertise when working with students, the following points need to be given some consideration.

1. Those responsible for supervision of students should be adequately qualified in terms of:

   - performance in the classroom;
   - proven supervision of students;
   - academic ability/theoretical knowledge.

2. Activities such as ateliers pedagogiques (workshops) in both college and school should be encouraged, in order to make the crucial link between theory and practice.

3. Mentors should be involved in dissertation supervision in order to give them academic status and keep up-to-date with educational debate and discussion.

4. If university tutors were involved in the selection of mentors, and knew how many there were in each school, the placement of students would be far more efficient. In addition, it might also be possible to assess strengths and weaknesses in order to match students with teachers.

So why are we moving in opposite directions?

In France, like many other European countries, the move is to upgrade the academic input of courses and to leave much of the supervision of teaching practice to those working in schools. In many cases this has evolved because of the division between academic and professional work in the training institutions. It is only in the United Kingdom that teacher educators need to have taught in school and are regularly required to update their classroom experience.

Whilst the implications for mentor training outlined in this paper may appear rather demanding, the maîtres formateurs in French primary schools have been a reality and a much respected part of French education for some time. When, however, post 1950, a similar but less structured system was developed in the secondary sector, the 80 per cent school-based system failed. The following reasons for this were given in a report published by the Institut National de Recherche Pédagogique in 1987.

1. Lack of coherence. When training was carried out by a number of schools, it was difficult to ensure that the complete syllabus was delivered.

2. Lack of ownership. Educators were marginalised due to the small amount of time under their control, whilst schools regarded teaching children, rather than training teachers, as their main priority.

3. Personal weakness. Most teacher mentors failed to see themselves as trainers and were unable to 'exteriorise' the principles behind their own sound classroom practice.

4. Danger of establishing a model. Students complained that teaching in these model schools in no way prepared them for the real schools in which they would undertake their first jobs.

5. Producing clones. A very highly school-based training tended to encourage students to emulate the teachers with whom they were working, rather than find their own teaching styles.

This system was therefore rejected and, in the early 1990s, led to the incorporation of both primary and secondary teacher education within the university sector. The newly formed IUFMs would now provide the academic input.

Conclusion

The French school-based experience undoubtedly has implications for the development of any school-basing policy and practice in the United Kingdom. Insights can be gained from work in the primary sector which show that for school-based teacher training to be successful, a very carefully woven network of expertise is essential. Caution, however, is necessary when undertaking such a scheme, as the French secondary experience indicates that increasing the school-based element of teacher training beyond 50 per cent distances educators from the goal of a balanced professional training.

10 Value conflicts in school-based initial teacher education

David Blake, Vincent Hanley, Mike Jennings and Michele Lloyd

Introduction

This chapter explores some of the dilemmas presented when more initial teacher education is located in schools. In 1993-4 we studied the operation of Department for Education (DFE) Circular 9/92 as it applied to the Chichester Institute's Post Graduate Certificate in Education (PGCE) course for intending secondary teachers. In 1994-5 we focus on the operation of the Institute's course for PGCE primary teachers, operating under DFE Circular 14/93. The circulars represent government policy on initial teacher education in England and Wales, in relation to control of the content of training and insistence on a higher proportion of training taking place in workplace settings.

We identify and review aspects of values and conflicts in professional training illuminated by our empirical research. Data were gathered from semi-structured in depth interviews with 12 students, 12 teachers in partner schools and six college tutors. Of particular interest are the terminology of school-based training, the impact of a new form of training on the personnel engaged in it, the criteria by which quality training is judged and commitment to equal opportunities.

Terminology

Our findings suggest that students are trying to make sense of their training according to their own definitions of key terms and the meanings they attribute to them. An occupational lexicon is being substituted for the language of professionalism. It is this substitution and the values associated with it that help to mould students' perceptions and give meaning to their experience. In what follows, the process through which certain key terms were deployed to construct a particular configuration of meaning (John and Lucas 1994b) will be examined.

'School-based', as understood by many students, appeared to signal reproval for the HEI and approval for the school; the consequence was that 'on the job learning' had been increased and, in time, the school became the more important centre of influence. Further analysis then revealed how - and why - the student's relationship with the subject mentor in school was highly prioritised. Not surprisingly - and as happens so often in initial teacher education - practice exerted a strong purchase on students' judgement of their progress. What they may have been less conscious of was the configuration of meaning within which they made their judgements.

'School-based' had already acquired meanings and imparted values as a label for the new course; it was also a marker to distinguish the new course from the old. Furthermore, we do not believe that the term emerged as a casual outcome of disinterestedness. Instead, it is a product of intentionality that positions the school at the centre of things and, by implication, removes the HEI to the periphery. In the new relationship between the partners, students believed that the school was in the ascendant. Arguably, the term might be justified by the increased amount of time and course activity transferred to the school. It is an important justification but its effects may be even more important; since 'school-based' affords priority and status to the school and classroom environments and locates the student in particularised practice, there is a danger that it may diminish expectations of a wider professionalism. In other words, the term may lend credence to students' narrow preoccupation with teaching as work at the expense of broader initial teacher education. In this sense, therefore, 'school-based' is neither arbitrary nor neutral.

We cannot be certain that the surge of interest in competency based education and training in the 1980s forced 'competences' onto the teacher education agenda as a necessary outcome of training. Now, it is much in vogue and, like 'school-based', is effectively located in the configuration of meaning. But how is it defined? And how does it relate to, and interact with, 'school-based' and other terms? Circular 9/92 throws no direct light on the subject; DFE assumptions are buried under prescriptive statements. Circular 14/93 is broadly based on the same format, although it does mention 'practical teaching competences'. Examination of the statements in both documents shows that 'competences' are derived from an analysis of teachers' occupational tasks, responsibilities and duties. The lists are extensive and indicate minimum levels of outcome related to normative, newly-qualified teacher (NQT) performance. It is clear to us that this approach to formulating

120

'competences', identified by Burke et al (1975) and Tuxworth (1989) has a strong functional bias, implicit in the language of demands 'to demonstrate', 'be able to', 'produce', 'use' and so on - all with their relative values and knowledge.

One of the dangers in using this kind of minimalist vocabulary is that it tends to emphasise a standardised performance and, because profiling is a high priority, there is a steady socialising and orienting of students into the acceptance of boundaries, control and limited horizons of the profile. 'Competences' may not drive an obvious wedge between theory and practice but, with so much emphasis on teaching, they may be discouraging students from engaging more widely with education and with a fuller professionality.

In the configuration of meaning, 'school-based' and 'competences', as currently defined and used, may be reinforcing acceptance of a narrow view of teaching and of a circumscribed teacher's role in keeping with the government's interest and agenda. As terms, they are not value free and whatever the level of staff training and development to achieve consistency, the terms can never be wholly independent of context. The situation is fraught with difficulties; for example, if 'competences' become reified, the value base of newly trained teachers may narrow as teachers concentrate on performance and not, as Pring (1994) advocates, serve the pupil to the best of their interest rather than someone to be exploited to the best of one's own. A truly competent teacher is not - and can never be - an accumulated sum of compartmentalised elements.

Role conflict among training personnel

Findings from our research into the secondary PGCE illuminate various sources of role conflict for both teachers in partner schools and college-based tutors. In this section we draw on interview data to consider how school-based forms of ITE inevitably impact upon the professional roles of training personnel.

A number of teachers in the sample made reference to intra-institutional tensions with colleagues who repudiated the ideological agenda behind government moves towards school-based training and who consequently felt it pertinent that their school withdraw from the scheme. This raises the question of the extent to which ITE is recognised as a whole-school responsibility. In a small minority of schools in the sample whole-school responsibility had not been accepted; professional tutors and subject mentors sometimes had to cope with varying degrees of disinterest or lack of commitment to ITE. In these situations, some students felt marginalised when teachers (in the same departments) ignored them or only casually briefed them when handing over classes.

Opposed to the idea of school-based ITE, a minority of teachers were reported to be rather resentful of the amount of time that professional tutors and mentors were spending with students. Some of the mentors in this sample endeavoured to address inter-personal tensions of this kind by being more sensitive to the balance between the needs of students and colleagues in school. Aware of the demands and potential role conflict within mentoring, a number of respondents were also keen to emphasise that a teacher's prime responsibility is to the children and their parents; mentoring is a secondary role (see also Stark 1994).

A further difficulty identified by mentors was the lack of formal dialogue with HE tutor precipitated by the new training arrangements. However, these communication constraints were not willingly accepted by mentors. With college tutors making fewer school visits, some mentors determined that it was now all the more important to maintain inter-institutional discourse on an informal basis.

Tensions within the role of tutors based at the Chichester Institute were also unveiled in the research. Their views on the PGCE provide substantial indications of theory-practice or ideal-actual conflicts and, possibly most strongly of all, vulnerability to external influences. In the case of the current situation in teacher education, vulnerability to political influence threatens the continued existence of the HE tutor role. The interview transcripts give considerable evidence of tutors' own view of their marginalisation. The form in which this concern was expressed was to question the extent to which allocation of time for the role and contact with students in school were sufficient. Given the centrality of teaching to the purpose of the course, it is hard not to sympathise with the view of PGCE course tutors that not to see students at work in the classroom somehow negates or compromises this role.

Value orientation is another dimension of role conflict problematic for HE tutors in this case study. There is evidence of incongruity between tutors' values and the values and concerns of their role in its enactment (Wilson 1962). In the interviews tutors expressed concerns about values which may be changing on the PGCE. There is the question of what constitutes an effective programme of professional development, how much theory students should have, what kind of theory, what kind of introduction to issues concerned with aspects of equal opportunities. Put another way, how can college tutors help to construct an agenda which looks beyond the immediate, and beyond students' overwhelming concern with classroom relevance, to shape an experience which is in students' and schools' longer term interests?

So how are teachers and tutors responding to the conflicting elements of their training roles? In his seminal study of the teacher's role Grace (1972) reviewed three possible responses to role conflict in teaching. In summary these are redefinition of the situation, adaptation to incompatible expectations and retreatism. Elements of all these responses may be discerned in the present case study.

Redefining the situation is the most self-confident, positive and potentially rewarding response. It embodies a kind of militant reformism which may imply integrity to core professional values. It may be argued that events have moved beyond the control of teacher educators, that they are simply compliantly reacting to externally driven change and have lost all professional autonomy. Alternatively, it could be argued that the construction of a new PGCE course with a locally defined value base is itself a significant redefinition of the situation, which has enabled new, valuable roles to be constructed.

Adaptation to conflicting expectations appears to be the closest response to teachers' and HE tutors' reports of what is going on. Grace describes various kinds of adaptive behaviour, for example conforming to the expectations of those perceived as significant, rejecting expectations of the role at the margins because of their professional illegitimacy or balance legitimate expectations against considerations of self interest (Grace 1972: 8-9). The latter 'average person' response approaches what mentors and tutors say they are doing. In other words they are living with the situation, trying to change it at the margins, trying to improve the conditions in which they operate, trying to form strong formal and informal inter-institutional links which embody a practical and ideal version of partnership, trying to make a complex scheme work and trying to maintain a robust value base. Yet it is also possible to perceive a retreatist attitude, that is a loss of interest in the activities of the role and a kind of shoulder-shrugging acceptance of a disliked state of affairs which is impossible to change.

There is a perennial argument between those who see role conflict as dysfunctional and those who believe it is an essential, almost stimulating, part of work and life. Those who see it as dysfunctional maintain that it is a broadly negative influence on harmony and social adjustment. Those who argue for role conflict as a stimulant see it promoting analysis of problems and eventual reform. In the context of teacher education in the 1990s, and specifically in relation to the role of the college tutor, it is hard not to take the view that role conflict is broadly dysfunctional. The interviews with teachers and college tutors do give grounds for an optimistic interpretation of future development, but there is also evidence of job dissatisfaction, reduced confidence, strain and role conflict.

The framework for the inspection of secondary initial teacher training

In October 1993 the Office for Standards in Education (OFSTED) issued a collection of working papers on the inspection process for secondary initial teacher training (OFSTED 1993a). The purpose was 'to make explicit the criteria and procedures used by HMI in the inspection of teacher training' (p.2). It was considered to be especially important to make this information public when schools are becoming involved in the training. This is a document of 45 pages, full of detail about the process of inspection, with a further 50 pages of material contained in the annexes. The working papers enable us to explore the values which underpin the process of inspection so that we can respond to the question, what is OFSTED's view of good quality teacher training?

The papers provide a view of inspection which is about control and central direction. There is little overt reference to improvement or development through inspection. Rather, there is repeated reference in the working papers to the need 'to provide evidence about compliance with the Secretary of State's requirements for the approval of ITT courses' (p.2). In order to do this, the first focus is on 'the standards of students' work and the range of competences they achieve as student teachers' (p.2). Inspection itself is set in a market framework. It is claimed that the process will provide 'information to prospective students and the wider community about course quality on ITT' (p.2).

Certain assumptions about good practice in teacher education recur in these papers. There is uncritical acceptance of the notion that partnership, of schools and HEIs, is the key to effective training and therefore much concentration on the management of that partnership according to certain criteria. It is assumed that good teaching, and therefore good teacher training, is best expressed through a set of competences which find expression in a profile which will be useful for prospective employers. It is assumed that we are concerned with a training rather than an education process. It is assumed that the main, if not the sole, emphasis in training will be the national curriculum and its assessment. Within that emphasis, it is assumed that most of what good teaching is about can be summed up in the terms subject knowledge and subject application. This is a bleak litany of conformist, limited expectations, confining teacher education to a straitjacket of the imag-

124

ination and intellect.

The experience, care and professionalism of HMI in their approach to inspection is well-known and merits widespread respect. Nevertheless, in these papers, as in the *Handbook for the Inspection of Schools* (OFSTED 1993b), we see a bureaucratic, mechanistic and formulaic system at work. It takes four pages to detail the responsibilities of the reporting inspector. There are eight different forms, or schedules, associated with an inspection visit. There are 22 pages of criteria for the completion of the eight schedules, indicating what constitutes satisfactory or very good performance. Every inspection report is constructed in the same way, following the template provided in the working papers. And in the end quality judgements are collapsed into five categories (very good, good, satisfactory, unsatisfactory and poor) with bald and slightly odd summary descriptions. These look like the procedures and values of a conservative and compliant government agency. Is there even a flicker of the flame of the former independent values of HMI?

The working papers are infused with the vocabulary of a slightly *passé* managerialism. Teaching itself is inspected but there is an overlay of more macho ideas like course delivery, quality control, forward-planning, funding allocations and accountability, performance indicators (PIs), value-added, wastage, match to training needs and various kinds of implementation. Staff development is given expected emphasis, although the criterion of staff awareness of the requirements of relevant government circulars throws up an alarming image of collusive conformity. The management values in these working papers are dominated by systems, procedures and controls. Some areas of supposed management competence (criteria for the selection of schools and departments, effectiveness of resource allocation, criteria for student selection) are question-begging and unrealistic.

Equal opportunities

How will equal opportunity issues be addressed as a more school-based teacher training system evolves? The development of more equal opportunity in respect of 'race', gender, class and special educational needs is a fundamental democratic commitment embedded in notions of justice and freedom. Since negative attitudes which impair achievement are to some extend constructed and sustained by schooling (Figueroa 1991), it follows that the education system and schooling have a key role to play in combating racism and inequality. How will tomorrow's teachers develop this professional commitment in the new training programmes?

The prospects are not encouraging. When government training circulars are compared, there is a marked reduction in requirements in respect of equal opportunities. In 1989 (DES 1989b) there was reference to the need for students 'to appreciate their tasks as teachers within the broad framework of the purposes of education ...., the values and the economic and other foundations of the free and civilised society in which their pupils are growing up ....' (para. 6.1: 10). This entailed awareness of cross curricular dimensions such as equal opportunities, multicultural education and personal and social education (para. 6.2: 10). It required awareness of 'the diversity of ability, behaviour, social background and ethnic and cultural origin they are likely to encounter among pupils in ordinary schools' (para. 6.3: 10). Students were to 'guard against preconceptions based on race, gender, religion or other attributes of pupils and understand the need to promote equal opportunities' (para. 6.3: 10). It was expected that courses would help students to see the school in a wider social context 'including issues of culture, gender and race' (para. 6.7: 11). By 1993 the emphasis had almost completely changed. The new primary criteria (DFE 1993d), replacing those of Circular 24/89, ignore the above agenda. There is no explicit reference to equal opportunities. Instead there is a slighter, less explicit terminology of individual differences, diversity of talent, provision for pupils with special needs and reference to pupils' spiritual, moral, social and cultural development.

The commitment of government to consideration of equal opportunity issues within training programmes, then, is reducing. It is instructive to note the more rounded view of nurse education and training adopted in Project 2000 (UKCC 1986) with the idea of the practitioner as both a 'doer' and a 'knowledgeable doer'. It is argued in nursing that the knowledgeable doer cannot be divorced from his/her political, social and economic context, and indeed needs a grounding in the policy issues surrounding practice. The nurse is said to require an awareness of the social and political factors which relate to health care. Only four years ago the government's National Curriculum Council (1991) in its much criticised document on initial teacher training encouragingly argued that newly trained teachers would require a coherent view of the whole curriculum. Part of the reason for this was to expand the horizons of all pupils 'so that they can understand and respect, learn from and contribute to the multicultural society around them' (NCC 1991: 7).

The attacks by the new right on the place of equal opportunities within the teacher education curriculum have been virulent and sustained, amounting to a campaign for its removal. Anthony O'Hear (1988), for example, characterised teacher training courses as obsessed with questions of race and

126

inequality while Dennis O'Keeffe (1990) wrote about the hydra-headed cults of equal opportunities. Teacher trainers are said by O'Keeffe to have conducted a gigantic experiment in social engineering and to have promoted an intolerant proto-totalitarian ideology. O'Keeffe claimed that the colleges have taught an egalitarian philosophy which ignores pupils' real needs.

The actual evidence is less alarming. The survey by HMI of the performance of new teachers in school (OFSTED 1993c) included reports on aspects of the students' training. There is no evidence that the amount of time given to educational studies, or to equal opportunities issues within them, is excessive or distorted. On the contrary, HMI reported greater student satisfaction with educational studies in 1993 than in their previous 1987 report and found students who generally felt they had a good understanding of equal opportunities practice (OFSTED 1993c: 46).

What is worrying, however, is the reduced emphasis on equal opportunities in OFSTED's recent publications. The tone may have been set by a dismissive reference in the Alexander, Rose and Woodhead report on primary school organisation and practice (DES 1992c) which saw research on social factors in educational achievement as somewhat unhelpful, 'absolving teacher and school of any responsibility' (p.14). There are no references at all to equal opportunities in the two follow-up OFSTED papers to the Alexander report (OFSTED 1993d, 1994). It is also noticeable that the working papers on the inspection of secondary initial teacher training (OFSTED 1993a) make no explicit reference to 'race', gender or equal opportunities. There is little doubt that OFSTED's stance is a negative one, both with regard to theoretical issues in general and equal opportunities in particular, as is evident from an astonishing 'finding' on the training of primary school teachers in 1993:

> The balance in educational studies has shifted appropriately from a focus on theoretical issues such as how pupils learn and develop to practical matters such as classroom management and organisation. (OFSTED 1993e: 2-3).

The values inherent in a commitment to equal opportunities in the teacher education curriculum are under attack. These values should be defended and reaffirmed.

Conclusion

We have shown how a new teacher education is being constructed and how that construction is positioned by a particular terminology. We have reported perceptions of personnel engaged in school-based training of the value conflicts inherent in their new roles and responsibilities. We have taken OFSTED's quality control procedures to illustrate the value assumptions which underlie the inspection of teacher education. Finally we have focused on the area of equal opportunities to show how rapid is the shift in government agencies' views of what should be included in the curriculum of initial teacher education. The limited conception of the teacher as a competent technician diminishes the potential role of the teacher in our society. We believe there is a need for a new and more enlightened vision which reasserts the need for theory in teacher education, identifies the need for beginning teachers to be competent in the area of equal opportunities and conceptualises teaching as both a practical and intellectual activity.

Part 3
CASE STUDIES

11 Planning for partnership in the primary sector: A Welsh perspective

David Ellis

Introduction

'In many ways, partnership between schools and teacher education institutions is an obvious, necessary and indeed desirable relationship' (Crozier, Menter and Pollard 1990: 44). In fact, partnerships in teacher training have always existed in some form (Furlong 1994), as have school-based approaches. 'To be fair, the policy of making initial teacher training more school-based has been with us a long time. Years before the government purloined the idea, the intention among educationists had been to make courses directly relevant to, and based upon, real children in real schools' (Cullingford 1994: 22). What is currently high on the agenda of the initial teacher training (ITT) debate, however, is the nature and balance of this partnership and the ownership of the school-based elements. The arguments are underpinned by differing views of teaching and how to prepare an effective teacher. For example, the professional development model, as articulated by such authors as Pollard and Tann (1993) and Calderhead and Gates (1993) and supported by the majority of the profession, is based on the conviction that teachers need to understand the education process by theorising and reflecting on their practice. On the other hand, the apprenticeship model claims that fundamentally teachers only need to develop certain practical skills and competences in order to perform their role proficiently. This is a view that is reflected particularly in the publications of the political right wing by such writers as Lawlor (1990). Consequently, whilst higher education institutions and schools are attempting to establish cooperative arrangements which exploit the expertise of all parties involved in the partnerships, the government is deliberately introducing changes to shift the control of teacher education away from its traditional higher education domain. As Crozier, Menter and Pollard (1990:44) continue, 'The notion of partnership thus illustrates an uneasy relationship, with the rhetoric and ideologies of both the government and professional groups intermingling in a way which, whilst often using a similar vocabulary, has been underpinned by very different values and has been intended to achieve different goals'.

Ideological considerations are thus an unavoidable and fundamental aspect of the planning for partnership process, yet as Wilkin (1994) points out, opposing views should not prevent progress being made or the profession exploiting the government guidelines to its own advantage. In fact, HEIs are likely to encounter greater difficulties in relation to the practical implications of the DFE criteria. For example, the vast majority of schools are reluctant to take on more responsibilities and to take the lead in partnership developments (Holden 1994, Pyke 1994b). Similarly, teacher educators are having to balance what they consider to be in the best interests of their students with the parameters imposed by individual schools. These difficulties are compounded in the primary sector by the number of students involved, a dearth of research evidence and the lack of HEIs' and schools' previous experience of partnership arrangements except for one or two HEIs such as Bedford and Chichester (formerly West Sussex). There is, though, a growing body of recent literature, for example from the Teacher Education and Mentorship (TEAM) project (Yeomans and Sampson 1994) and the Primary Initial Teacher Education (PITE) project (McCulloch and Lock 1994). However, Circulars 14/93 (DFE) and 62/93 (Welsh Office) insist that in a very short time schools must take on a greater role in the planning and management of teacher education courses and in the selection, training and assessment of students, even though the government notes that the situation in the primary context is somewhat more complex. There must be an effective partnership between HEIs and schools with the latter playing a much larger and influential role in course design and in the delivery and development of the application of practical skills. Moreover, the increased contribution of schools must be reflected in the transfer of resources from the HEIs to their partner schools, which will be negotiated locally and made public. To achieve this in the space of two to three years presents a great challenge to those institutions providing primary teacher education, a challenge in fact which one or two institutions have already decided not to accept.

The Welsh context

In Wales the teacher training institutions are fortunate to be small in number and to have a good working relationship with the Welsh Office through which government policy is directed. Additionally, all the HEIs in Wales which provide ITT courses are part of, or affiliated to, the University of Wales. The deans of education from the constituent and affiliated colleges meet regularly as part of the University Subject Panel for Education which serves as a forum for reaching multilateral policy decisions, as well as acting as the vehicle for the validation and approval of courses. Similarly, the all-Wales Teacher Education Group, formed from the former Welsh Advisory Body's committee on ITT, and now representing both the public and university sectors, meets periodically to discuss major ITT issues and has direct representative access to the Welsh Office. There are, therefore, effective channels for communication and cooperation which enable a good measure of uniformity and consistency to be achieved between the various ITT institutions in the Principality. For example, in 1992, following the publication of Welsh Office (WO) Circular 35/92, a South-East Wales consortium was established, involving the three HEIs in the region training teachers, namely Cardiff Institute, Gwent College and the Faculty of Consumer Affairs and Hospitality Management at University College, Cardiff. This consortium agreed on a number of cooperative measures in relation to the new secondary partnership arrangements, including the memoranda of agreement with schools, the level of funding to be paid to schools and mentor training programmes. More recently, following a meeting in 1994 with representatives from the Welsh Office and the Higher Education Funding Council for Wales (HEFCW), the deans of education from all the institutions in Wales met to agree that three year primary B.Ed. courses should be developed in the Principality. With the new Teacher Training Agency not applying to Wales, at least at the time of writing, there thus appears to be a good chance that the HEIs in Wales will be able to continue to meet the new criteria through a process of cooperation and shared understandings.

At Cardiff Institute of Higher Education the basic principles and ground rules underpinning the development of primary school partnerships have been the subject of much discussion since the publication of Circular 62/93 (WO). The Institute has a long history of close cooperation with local schools and has always worked in partnership with them through such ventures as IT-Inset, the Artist-in-Residence scheme and more recently the National Primary Centre (Wales). Additionally all the Institute's secondary courses have recently been converted to meet the new requirements of Circular 35/92 (WO). However, although this level of traditional cooperation has assisted the Institute in coping with the dramatic changes in ITT over the last decade, the new criteria present several challenges which individual HEIs must resolve for themselves. For example, in the South-East Wales region no primary schools have come forward voluntarily to offer themselves as partners under the new arrangements since the publication of Circular 62/93. Additionally, the scale of the exercise is immense. Each year the Institute has to place approximately 850 BA (Education) and PGCE (Primary) students in schools, involving almost all the primaries in South Glamorgan and the majority of those in Mid Glamorgan. Moreover, there is no control over which teachers are allocated students, as this depends on the decision of the headteachers. This, of course, has serious implications when the teachers are required to take responsibility for assessing the students.

Principles

Within this context, staff at Cardiff Institute are basing the revision of their current primary courses on a number of significant premises. First, a system of mentoring involving teachers in school will be essential. While not specifically mentioning mentoring, the new criteria quite clearly imply that this will be necessary if the regulations are to be properly implemented. As Furlong (1994: 7) notes, 'In this new vision of ITT, the role of the mentor is central'. However, it will be impossible and probably undesirable to base a mentoring system on the current teaching practice process, since this would involve having to train every teacher in every school as a mentor. Similarly, the current arrangements for mentoring in secondary schools would seem to be inappropriate and unworkable in the primary sector, due to the scale of the operation and the different organisational nature of primary education. This is a point emphasised by Yeomans and Sampson (1994: 1) who stress that, '.... assumptions about mentoring derived from secondary school experiences may not apply to the primary context'. Consequently a radical new approach to mentoring needs to be developed and this will inevitably involve controlling in some way the choice and range of schools and teachers, if quality and consistency are to be ensured.

Secondly, schools should be involved in discussions on the design and development of the courses from the outset, although it is almost certain that the initial proposals will of necessity have to come from the Institute. As in most other areas of England and Wales (Holden 1994), the indications from primary schools in the South-East Wales region are that they wish to be involved in the partnership arrangements, but only if this does not increase their workloads. Moreover, from preliminary discussions with schools in the area, there appears to be a general consensus that the HEIs should retain the overall responsibility for planning and developing ITT courses since they possess the necessary expertise and understanding of teacher education and current directives. Consequently, as mentioned above, the schools are almost all unwilling to take the initiative, preferring the Institute to present proposals to which they can agree or dissent.

Thirdly, training for both mentors and participating faculty staff will be essential:

> .... mentors in schools do not know how to do the job because it is not only a demanding one but also quite different from anything they have done before, while people based in universities [and colleges] do not know how to do the job because it is quite different from anything they have done or studied. There are no experts on how to do the job of mentoring in initial teacher education (McIntyre et al. 1993: 19).

Finally, a research project will be undertaken by a seconded member of staff to identify the best practice and to ascertain the most appropriate way forward. It is intended to experiment with three or four different approaches resulting in a composite model by Easter 1995, so that mentor and staff training can occur in the summer term for full implementation of the new partnership arrangements in the academic year 1995-1996.

A possible model

One way forward, arising out of the Institute's initial deliberations with a number of interested parties and schools, would be to base the partnership arrangements on a limited number of teaching or training schools. Those willing to be involved would have to commit themselves to taking regularly four or five students per term. To reduce the over-use of the same classes, schools would normally have to be of a certain size and the first practice on both the BA (Education) and PGCE courses could be paired. There would have to be a balance of different kinds of schools and different locations (for example, urban and rural) and perhaps special arrangements could be made for smaller schools to participate, maybe as associate partners. Based on an approximate calculation of six teaching practices per year (three BA Education and three PGCE - maximum 150 students per practice) with four students per school for each practice, somewhere in the region of 40 schools would be required. All participating schools would be asked to sign a memorandum of agreement and receive staff development in the new arrangements as a whole school in addition to the mentor training undertaken by individual teachers. No students would be placed in any school that was not part of the partnership/mentoring programme and which was not properly prepared. In line with Circular 62/93 (WO) all schools would be invited to participate, but they would have to guarantee that they could meet the requirements outlined above which the scheme would demand. However, in order not to deny any school the opportunity to be in partnership, as the Circular decrees, a rolling programme of partner schools could operate or alternative models could be available. As indicated above, though, the current evidence suggests that the Institute will not be overwhelmed with applications for partner primary schools, despite the long-standing and valued tradition of mutual cooperation. Furthermore, it must be recognised that not all the schools that apply would necessarily be suitable, and so clearly negotiations with these would have to be handled sensitively and with care. As Yeomans and Sampson (1994: 212) conclude from their research evidence, '.... we have tried to show that the commitment of time and energy required to be an effective mentor demands mentor qualities and conditions which will not be achievable in all primary schools'.

Within each teaching school, a mentor, known perhaps as a teacher-tutor, could be specifically trained to supervise the students across all the classes. Similar to the Swedish model, this person would have a teaching commitment within the school, but possibly not a class responsibility (for example, the deputy head). This would help to alleviate the problem of class teachers having to spend time away from their own classes, which Yeomans and Sampson (1994: 201) note can cause difficulties: 'The role conflict for mentors who need time away from their own class to fulfil the role of mentor effectively, yet perceive that they need time with their children if they are to be effective teachers, is a limitation on the expansion of mentorship schemes in primary schools'. Alternatively, the teacher-tutor could be a college tutor who wished to transfer to this kind of role or alternatively the position could rotate between members of staff from year to year thus promoting a whole school approach, although this would have implications for the mentor training programme. The time taken by the teacher-tutor for supervisory and other duties would be funded by the resources transferred from the college. If an hour per week were allocated per student for supervising, writing reports and other responsibilities, and there were four students regularly in the school, then it could be estimated that teacher-tutors would need to be released for approximately a quarter of their duties. The teacher-tutor could also make contributions, possibly to the college based course, and receive credits towards in-service awards on an accredited prior experiential learning (APEL) basis. In fact, whatever scheme is adopted, it is likely that mentors will have privileged access to in-service courses, and this is already being offered to mentors as part of the Institute's secondary partnership package.

One definite outcome of the research programme, whichever model is adopted, will be the publication of a manual of open learning materials for teacher-tutors to use with students. Combined with a mentor training programme, the school experience handbook and other documentation, such as the lesson feedback forms, mentors should thus have a comprehensive yet easy to follow set of guidelines and instructions. This should lead to reasonable consistency between schools and enable the programme to be quality assured effectively. Additionally, a few specifically trained college tutors could be linked to a cluster of schools, for example, five tutors with eight schools each, who would visit the schools periodically to monitor the programme and to assist and moderate the teacher-tutors rather than supervising the students. However, they could mediate if disputes arose and observe students in the classroom if a second opinion was required. This clearly would lead to many college tutors, who currently supervise students in school in the traditional manner, losing this aspect of their teacher education role. However, this does appear inevitable to a certain degree in light of the new criteria, whatever model or approach is adopted, especially as a level of funding will be transferred to the schools.

Finally, there would be a comprehensive profile of the students' practical classroom competences as part of their records of achievement and final confidential reports. Currently this is compiled by the Institute for both the college-based and school-based parts of the course, but under the new arrangements the assessment and recording of classroom competences would be a responsibility of the teacher-tutor. Since the teacher-tutors would also have the ultimate authority to pass or fail students on their practical classroom abilities, the Institute would have to consider returning to a simple pass/fail basis for school experience rather than the five point scale currently used on the final practice. The main reason for this would be the difficulties involved in ensuring compatibility and consistency between schools when the moderator's role is reduced only to that of an adviser, although it could be argued that, if there were only a small number of teacher-tutors (for example, one for each teaching school), then moderation meetings involving mentors and college tutors could be feasible, perhaps in cluster groups. It could also be argued that consistency between college tutors has never been achieved using traditional supervision methods, and there is much evidence to support this view (Ellis 1988). For similar reasons the Institute would also have to review its intention to link classroom performance to degree classifications.

Three years ago, the University of Wales accepted a proposal that the five point scale for the assessment of practical teaching could contribute to the overall degree classification on the BA (Honours) Primary Education course on a compensation basis. However, the Institute has never implemented this procedure in light of the development of the new primary ITT criteria. To guarantee such a level of consistency which would be fair to students would now appear to be impracticable, whatever quality assurance procedures might be introduced.

Conclusion

In summary, the planning process at Cardiff Institute, in relation to meeting the requirements of Circular 62/93 (WO), has involved the consideration of both ideological and practical issues. These are being resolved through collegial discussions with other ITT institutions in Wales, in liaison with the Welsh Office and the HEFCW, and through the goodwill and advice of local schools. However, all the evidence indicates that ultimately it will be the Institute's role to devise a strategy which will be acceptable to the local primary schools while at the same time meeting the government's criteria. Careful planning is therefore essential if these objectives are to be achieved. A research project has thus been established to test out a number of approaches and to indicate the most appropriate way forward. Preliminary investigations suggest that there appears to be a general consensus in South-East Wales that partnership schemes in the primary sector can form the basis for the effective preparation of teachers, but clearly these must be well considered and must be seen to benefit all parties involved.

12 New partnerships in schools: Comparing teaching practice supervision in Accredited Assessment Schools (AAS) and Professional Development Schools (PDS)

Jane Maloney and Andrew Powell

Introduction

New PGCE courses had to be developed to meet the requirements of Circular 9/92. A specific requirement to be met was the transfer of some resources from HEIs to schools. Clearly this had serious financial implications for the HEIs. In the light of these economic implications, five HEIs in South-West London formed a consortium with schools to make the construction of such a course viable. It was also beneficial to the schools as they could now take their students from just one source yet cover a much wider range of National Curriculum subjects. The five HEIs in the consortium are Brunel University, St. Mary's College, Kingston University, West London Institute and Roehampton Institute. The course set up had different implications for each of the HEIs.

For Kingston, the time students spent in school on block school experience (affectionately known as BSE by the students) involved very little change. However, one of the new developments for the University was the increase in time for serial practice; now students spend two days a week in their teaching practice (TP) school from the beginning of the college term to ensure a continuous strand of school experience throughout their course.

Another key innovation was the development of new partnerships with schools. Schools traditionally played a key role in the supervision of students on TP but this was largely unremunerated and relied on the goodwill of the school staff. The consortium has developed a new partnership scheme known as the Professional Development School (PDS) in which the school undertakes a wide range of initial teacher training support. Programmes to facilitate the students' development of subject application skills and the study of educational issues were set up in the PD schools. Other schools providing the more traditional support are known as Accredited Assessment Schools.

139

The academic year 1993-1994 was the pilot year for these new arrangements. The focus of this project was to evaluate the contribution that the PD schools made to the experience of Kingston University students on TP. It is hoped that the research will continue into 1994-1995 to evaluate the PD schools within the whole consortium rather than just those used by Kingston University.

The aims of the project

The original aims were to:-

> evaluate those areas of the course delivered by the schools;

> compare and contrast the delivery of the school-based teacher training in the PDS and the AAS;

> evaluate the partnership of members of the consortium.

> The aims completed for this report were focused on the first two as the partnership is being evaluated by other colleagues.

The focus of the research

The questions to be addressed were:-

1. Are there any significant differences between the students' experiences at a PDS and those at an AAS?

2. Where differences are identified, are these positive points for PD schools?

3. What makes these positive areas more successful?

4. Should we therefore encourage AA schools to become PDS?

5. If AA schools wish to become PDS, what systems should be set in place to facilitate these changes?

6.   How have the professional tutors in the PD schools evaluated the pilot year?

7.   What improvements can be made to the existing schemes for next year?

Methodology

There were 64 students on the PGCE Secondary Course at the beginning of the autumn term 1993. Over 40 schools had offered to take students for the serial and block practice A. Of these schools, six were PD schools used in both teaching practices and there was another PD school only used on the second TP. Thus there was a total of seven PDSs where Kingston University students completed their teaching practices. Overall 22 students attend a PDS on one or other of their TPs. Their other TP was at an AA school.

All of these students were sent a questionnaire to complete after the Easter break whilst they were on their second TP. Despite follow up procedures on return to college, only 18 returned a completed questionnaire (82 per cent). Of these, eight were at a PDS on the first TP and ten on the second TP. The results were analysed separately in case there was a significant difference between the two groups.

All seven professional tutors at the PD schools were interviewed towards the end of the second TP (May 1994).

Results

Although the data were analysed for those students who went to a PDS on their first TP and those who went there on the second TP separately, the results for the separate groups are not shown as there was no significant difference between their responses. 'All students' refers to the 18 students who completed the questionnaire.

The students were asked if there was a planned professional development programme at their PDS. Three students seemed to be unaware that there was such a programme. These students were in PDS where another student at the same school had been aware of the programme. However it is important that this possible lack of communication is addressed by the University and schools next year.

The students were asked to rate the amount of support given to them on serial practice by the AAS and the PDS. The responses for the AASs were much more varied, ranging from 'very good' to 'poor' with 11 of the 18 at 'good' or above (61 per cent). Although one PDS was assessed as 'poor' there was a significantly higher proportion of 'good' or above responses - 15 of the 18 (83 per cent). At the PD schools, students had the opportunity to work with students from other HEIs on a formal basis and they also met with other members of staff on the professional development programme. In some schools they were able to request topics to be discussed and this opportunity for their own input was appreciated. Professional tutors believed that the schools were able to build up stronger relationships with the students in the PDS system. More time was given by the staff to the students in the schools particularly by heads of departments (HODs) and although this time allocation is an issue for next year's course, there is a significantly higher appreciation of the support given to students at PD schools.

One criticism made concerned the use of the serial practice booklet. This booklet suggested tasks that the students could carry out whilst on practice but did not appear compatible with the programmes devised by the PD schools. This issue is already being addressed by the university for next year as this became apparent early on in the pilot project.

A significant point that becomes clear when each written response is studied is the experience of the individual student. This can be illustrated by the example of the student, who described the overall support given as 'first rate in both schools'. As this was unlikely to be the case for all students, all the questionnaires were studied to see if other students had received such good support or whether some students had experienced poor support in both schools. On closer inspection it was noted that ten students (56 per cent) had rated their experiences as 'very good' or 'good' on both TPs . Of those who had an 'average' or 'poor' experience in one school, six had a 'very good' or 'good' experience in the other school. However, two students had support that they considered to be 'average' in both their TP schools. This has implications for the placing of students on TP and this will be discussed again later on in this chapter.

The students were asked to rate the overall written feedback given by the AAS and the PDS. Again the AAS elicited a varied response with only seven (39 per cent) of the students judging the written feedback to be 'very good' or 'good'. At the PD schools 15 (83 per cent) judged the written feedback to be 'very good' or 'good'. Both the quantity and quality of the written feedback was commented upon. At the PD school feedback was more regular and given soon after the lesson. However one student found the teachers from the PDS who were on a mentoring course a little over enthusiastic and in some cases the student considered that some staff were unsure of what they were saying. Four of the PD schools had staff who had already received mentor training and the other three expressed interest for the future as they could appreciate the value of such training for their staff. It was noted that some staff were involved with newly qualified teacher (NQT) mentoring but the school felt, on reflection, that this did involve different skills. The university is already addressing this issue and will be implementing new procedures so that there is more uniformity for written feedback in all schools.

Students were asked to rate verbal feedback given at the AAS and PDS. Interestingly, there was no significant difference between the verbal feedback given at the AA schools and the PD schools. Students greatly appreciated the time given by all teachers in discussion of their progress. Students commented upon the speed at which spoken feedback was given; rapid feedback was considered most helpful. Key issues to be addressed in some schools (PDS and AAS alike) is the consistency of advice given as one student reported being given conflicting advice by the department. The amount of feedback from individual teachers also varied considerably. The guidance given should be linked with the competency forms as it is on these competences that the student is assessed.

It would seem that teachers are more confident in giving verbal feedback as this has been part of the traditional role of schools with students in their department. Staff are happy to give time to discuss and share their expertise on this more informal basis and students obviously gain a tremendous amount from this help. This reinforces the need for training teachers in the skills of giving written feedback and the need for the university to set up systems which facilitate consistency of feedback for the students.

Students were asked how often they were observed in the classroom by different staff, for example HOD, class teacher, professional tutor. There were no significant differences between the number of people and the number of times the students were observed in AA or PD schools. One interesting point is the variation within the PD schools and the role of the professional tutor. In some PDSs the professional tutor did not observe the students at all. Other students were observed occasionally and in one school the student was seen once a week. The schools have developed the role of the professional tutor in different ways and one PDS reported that the tutor would observe the student at the student's request but the main observation role is given to the HOD. It is significant to note that in schools where the professional tutor did not observe the student teach, the overall support was still considered to be 'very good' or 'good' in all but two cases. This indicates that although schools have developed a different role for the professional tutor this has not affected the overall quality of support in any way.

Students were asked how they felt the schools had contributed to their training in the five competency areas of subject knowledge, subject application, classroom management, assessment and recording, and professional development. These are the five areas on which the students are assessed at the end of the teaching practices. They are given the competency statements (which differ for the two practices) before they start their TP. Therefore they, and the schools, are aware of what should be covered in each of the areas. Students found no important differences between the AA and the PD schools, except in the competences of classroom management and professional development where the PD schools had contributed more successfully than AA schools. This was not always the case and many AA schools were given high praise. When asked which areas of the training the PD schools should be contributing to, the professional tutors felt that classroom management was most significant along with coursework and lesson planning, personal and social education (PSE) and the role of the form tutor.

An important point highlighted by this research is the training of students in the skills of assessment and recording. Some students gave positive responses when they were given helpful advice on the marking and recording of pupils' work or where there was a '....well prepared system for marking and recording'. This section elicited the most varied responses with some students reporting that they '....were left to their own systems in both schools'. Some AA and PD schools provided good guidance and support to students and some schools had very clear procedures. However, this is an area in which there needs to be more parity for the students' experiences between all schools whether AAS or PDS.

The students were asked if they would like their training to be more school-based. Ten (56 per cent) were very happy with the balance as it is at present or wanted less time in school. They emphasised the need to have time to discuss matters with other students back at college and that a university input ensured consistency of standards. Six (33 per cent) students gave qualified answers as they believed it could be a good idea if certain factors were in place. They emphasised the need for more training for the school staff, more links to be made with the university or more time to be given by the school if the university input was to be reduced. Two students (11 per cent) were in favour of spending more time in school, with one of them commenting that '....the professional attitude would develop quicker'. The other believed that more time in school might result in less emphasis on written assignments which the student had not found helpful to the classroom.

The professional tutors at the PD schools were also asked this question and two schools felt that they could take on more of the role in the training of teachers if sufficient resources were given. They envisaged buying in of the university services to extend their present programme. The other PD professional tutors opposed the move away from the partnership with some expressing strong feelings that such a move would devalue the qualification and signify training 'on the cheap'. They considered that the students would receive too narrow a view of schools and the overall education system. They believe that the partnership draws on the strengths of both schools and HEIs, a point echoed by some students' responses. From the schools' point of view, the tutors also felt that they should consider their role very carefully as their main purpose was to teach children and more school-based training could mean that children are taught by too many students and more time is spent out of the classroom by the best teachers. The view of parents was also raised as an issue.

Summary

Some PD schools are providing excellent training experiences for the students and so are AA schools. There are many areas in which the schools provide good quality support for the training of teachers with the limited time and financial resources available to them. The PD schools are clearly much more aware of what is required in the written feedback given to students and the professional development programmes have been appreciated by the students. However, there are key issues that need to be considered by the HEIs and schools if this initiative is to develop further and to encourage AA schools to become PDS.

The key points drawn out from comments made by teachers and students are:-

1.   students and HEI staff need to be fully aware of the difference between AA and PD schools;

2.   the HEIs need to ensure parity of course provision between all PD schools;

3.   schools require more guidance on the content of their professional dev-elopment programme and more information on the HEI's programme and assignments for students (this is already being addressed);

4.   PDS staff would like to meet to share expertise and discuss problems;

5.   schools accept that more funding is a difficult issue but the HEIs could contribute to schools' in service training (INSET) programme (now being done with some schools);

6.   a formal evaluation procedure needs to be set up so schools can receive feedback from the students and the partner HEIs.

From the university's viewpoint, the above are either in place for next year or being considered as part of development following the pilot year.

The university also has to address the issue of students' experiences on TP. It needs to ensure that the students receive good quality support in whatever TP school they attend. Should there be any difficulties in the first TP, then the university must select the second school to make certain the student's next experience compensates for the first TP experience. The university also needs to identify schools in which poor support is given to students in order that steps can be taken to improve the quality of the students' experiences.

The university also needs to consider how students are trained in the competences of assessment and recording in all schools and in the university programme. If AA schools are to be encouraged to become PDS then they need to meet with the PDS staff to discuss the advantages of being a PDS. The university will need to facilitate this meeting and then work with the AAS to assess the school's training needs and set up a support structure to bring about the move to PDS.

Discussion

Although the sample in this survey was small (involving just 18 students), responses to the questionnaire have highlighted important points when considering the process of school-based teacher training. However, there is a need to extend the research to study PDSs used by students at other HEIs to gain wider perspectives from students in other departments as this research only involved music and science students. Furthermore, analysis of the data needs to be carried out to ascertain whether students at the same school but in different departments have different perceptions of the support given. On initial inspection the data show that there can be considerable variation even within the same department. In one case where two students were in the same

146

department at a PDS at the same time. one of them rated the support given by the school as 'very good' and the other as 'average'. Students were asked to compare their experiences at their two TP schools and therefore their responses will depend on the quality of support they received at the AA school. One of the students reported that it was difficult to compare her two schools as the schools she attended were so different - one a mixed 11-16 boarding school and the other a single sex 11-18 secondary school. Students also identified that the verbal and written feedback can vary among the school staff with one student indicating that feedback was '....poor to very good, depending on the teacher' but she rated the overall written feedback as 'poor' on the questionnaire.

The variation in support given to students by individual teachers is not new and not a great discovery. However, if teacher training is to become more school-based then these variations will become crucial. If a school were to take on total responsibility for training, as indeed some have, there may be no .consistency in quality of training from school to school. It should be considered good practice that HEIs should only work with schools in which the quality of support is known to be good. This may seem obvious but it may become increasingly difficult with many schools announcing their intention of withdrawing from having students for teaching practice. HEIs could be struggling to place their students in a school at all. Another danger of using only 'good' schools is that the student may experience teaching in a school that bears little relationship to the school in which the trainee will eventually teach (Whitty 1991).

If a student is in a school in which there are few discipline problems how will they practice class management strategies and reflect on and learn from the success or failure of these different methods? One student at such a school, when asked how well prepared she felt she had been in the skills of class management, responded, 'Well prepared in AAS due to higher discipline problems therefore necessity driven'. Similar cases were described but the discipline problems were in the PDSs thus emphasising the variation in experience students receive.

According to an HMI report on school-based initial teacher training (DES 1991: 7) students are expected to acquire a range of knowledge and skills before they take up their teaching post and they suggest that 'no single person or institution can offer all the expertise they require'. If students need to attend several institutions to gain the necessary knowledge and expertise then how can a totally school-based programme deliver this requirement? Of course schools could form consortia and devise their own course and provide a range of experience for their trainees. But this seems to still be a contenti-

147

ous issue between the two Houses of Parliament (Pyke 1994a), thereby fuelling the debate on whether or not initial teacher education should become totally school-based.

The argument against teacher training being the total responsibility of schools is not just based on the quality of the training the students would receive but also on the fact that there are financial implications. Cullingford (1994) claims that school-centred courses are twice as expensive as the cost-effective partnership between schools and higher education. Interestingly some professional tutors interviewed as part of this research considered that training students totally in school was training 'on the cheap'. One of the tutors who felt that the school could provide a good training programme if adequately resourced suggested that schools would need libraries, places for students to work, and access to halls of residence. These points led to the suggestion that it would be more sensible to have a central place for students (such as an HEI?) and for them to work in schools which have a partnership with the central institution.

Another more fundamental issue is the approach taken to the training of the teachers. Busher and Simmons (1992) believe that the CATE criteria are atheoretical and they suggest that they offer a political agenda for promoting a particular type of teacher through a limited model of teacher training. Whilst many agree that the changes in teacher training since Circular 3/84 (DES 1984) may be part of a political agenda (Hill 1989, Whitty 1991), it does not necessarily mean that using such criteria will prevent teachers from becoming the self reflective practitioners that leads to high quality teaching.

Cullingford (1994) recognises a dilemma in teacher training in that the trainees need to know a great deal before they enter the classroom but that this only makes sense when they have been in the classroom. He suggested that 'Experience and reflection go together. Just coping in the classroom is not enough' (1994: 22). This research project would indicate that 'coping in the classroom' is the area that most schools concentrate on and it is the HEIs that facilitate the reflection on these experiences. It is true that some schools are able to provide some forum for this with the students but many comment on the need to share their problems and successes with a number of students. They also benefit from the sharing of experiences of students in a very wide range of teaching establishments. Students involved in this project went to schools that were mixed, single sex, grammar, independent, 11-16, 11-18, sixth form colleges, boarding, GMS and LEA based. Such a mixed experience would be almost impossible if the trainee teachers were on school-centred courses without an HEI link.

148

It must be remembered that this was a pilot year for the consortium of the HEIs and for the development of new partnerships. The other evaluations being carried out will no doubt highlight areas in which improvements can be made in the future. One of the purposes of this research was to assess whether there are key differences between the experiences of students at PDSs and AASs and to suggest whether AA schools should be encouraged to become PD schools. The value of a PD school seems to fit into two categories: one the traditional support role of the student, and the other the professional development programme run by the school for all the students in the school.

Many of the AA schools provide excellent support as shown in the students' responses. Where an improvement could be made is in the production of quality written feedback and this would come through good mentor training. However to devise and implement a professional development programme takes considerable time as the most successful PD schools in this survey were building on programmes already in place, not initiating them. It may be possible to arrange that AA schools could work alongside PD schools at first, but this would rely on geographical factors and may cause financial problems.

There are over 40 schools used by Kingston University alone and only seven of these are PDS at the moment. It would not be realistic to suppose that the AA schools could be developed into PDS very quickly even if the schools were willing. There are also financial implications for the HEIs as more money is paid per student to the PD schools.

There are complications in running two systems at once. One difficulty is the duplication of work at the HEI and PDS. Schools are welcoming guidance about what should be included in their programmes and they are receiving information about the university's programme the term before the students arrive. This should overcome this problem for the next cohort of students. The other factor is ensuring parity of school experience for students since less than 50 per cent attended a PDS in this cohort of students. However there are many AA schools offering very good support and as long as the professional development programme is complemented at the HEI then this problem may be avoided as far as it is possible to bring about some consistency of experience. Quality assurance and consistency of provision from school to school is, as Cullingford (1994) describes, something of a challenge.

Finally, the research illustrates some of the inherent problems of making the training of teachers totally school-based. If there is variation in the support trainees are given, as indicated by these findings, how much more would there be without some central institution providing at least some consistency of experience? This point can be summarised by a student's response to the following question:

> What would be your opinion if more of the teacher-training you experienced were to be moved to schools?
> It would be a serious detriment to the profession as even the PDS staff's inexperience is obvious when compared to the training ability of university's staff. I feel that students would either leave or be moulded in a specific and too narrow field just to fit that particular school. University input ensures consistency of standards.

Schools may have inexperienced training staff at present but obviously this can be overcome. The narrowness of experience and inconsistency of standards can be addressed by rooting the training of teachers in an institute of higher education forming strong partnerships with the other place of training, the schools.

13 The development of professional competences

Tim Cain and Catherine Kickham

Introduction

Early in 1992, La Sainte Union (LSU) College of Higher Education began to develop a four year BA/BSc honours degree with qualified teacher status (QTS). This coincided with an increasing emphasis on competence-based approaches to teacher education and a vigorous debate about the respective roles of colleges and schools in the educative process.

The introduction of the course gave those of us involved - teachers, students and college tutors - the opportunity to re-think our respective roles in the process of preparing primary school teachers for their first posts. It enabled us to identify those elements of the process which could most effectively be undertaken in school and those more suited to the college environment and to consider which types of assessment are most appropriate for each. More importantly, it prompted us to spend some time considering our notion of professionalism and to develop a professional model which could reflect our shared understandings and effectively meet the needs of primary schools in the 1990s. During the development stage we were aware of the need to meet the Secretary of State's requirements in the initial training of teachers (Circular 24/89 and later 14/93) and endeavoured to do so within a consistent philosophical framework.

Philosophy and guiding principles

Before starting work on the project, those involved met to agree a philosophy which would underpin the work and establish a clear set of guiding principles. The college has traditionally promoted a reflective practitioner model of teacher education and it was agreed that this approach, which had provided a successful foundation for previous course design, should continue to inform our thinking. We believe our model acknowledges the clear value base which informs professional practice (Schon 1983).

In addition, there was a commitment to empower students to identify their own learning goals and development needs and take ownership of and responsibility for their progress, enabling supervisors to take supporting, guiding or directing roles as appropriate. We were aware of the government-led drive to provide clearly documented evidence of achievements which could be used to inform a variety of audiences and acknowledged that competency-based approaches lend themselves to clear and precise reporting of achievement.

Finally, there was agreement that any effective system of assessing student teachers must acknowledge the complexity of the profession and so avoid atomistic and over simplistic notions of competence. We recognised that competent teachers not only demonstrate a range of professional skills, underpinned by a large body of knowledge and understanding, but possess professional qualities which permeate and inform their actions.

Tensions

As we worked, we were made aware of a number of tensions which we had to resolve. The debate concerning competency approaches to the assessment of professional capability was gaining momentum. There was a tension between the notion of competence and a more norm-related approach. In a competence-driven model, the student is judged to be competent (or not yet competent) in a particular situation. In the norm-referenced approach, a student can be judged on a scale which can run from poor to excellent, with any number of stages in between. Whitty (1991) points out that many teacher educators reject the idea of competency-based teacher education on the grounds that it encourages an over emphasis on skills and techniques. Initially, many of the professionals we consulted - teachers, governors, tutors and headteachers - were concerned that a competence approach would lead to a behaviouristic model of teacher education with teaching reduced to a series of meaningless behaviours. There was a clear view that the norm-related approach provided a more appropriate way of assessing student teachers, despite the emphasis on the acquisition of competences in the circulars coming from the DFE.

Others pointed out that more than one approach to the notion of competence can be discerned in the literature. (Whitty and Wilmott (1991) had identified two quite different approaches. On the one hand there was:

> competence characterised by an ability to perform a task satisfactorily, the task being clearly defined and the criteria of success being set out alongside this

and on the other hand:

> competence characterised as wider than this, encompassing intellectual, cognitive and attitudinal dimensions, as well as performance.

The Department of Education, Northern Ireland also outlined two distinct approaches to the notice of competences (DENI 1993):

> One school of thought defines them in terms of series of behaviours or performances of which the execution at an acceptable level can readily be identified by observation. In this model individual competences are identified by analysis of tasks and roles, and the analysis proceeds by breaking down competent performance into a number of discrete parts.

> Another approach is to assign much greater importance to the part played by knowledge, understanding and attitudes as central to the whole process of developing professional competence, and to view them as permeating and affecting practice in an integrative way.

The authors point out that little is gained by possession of a competence if one cannot judge how to use it and that this perspective can accommodate the strong dimension of values present in teaching. It was this second approach which we believed more accurately reflected our perceptions of the professional role of the teacher and which we decided to adopt.

Other tensions arose, for instance between the desire to avoid any form of assessment which might lead to hundreds of tick-boxes and the need to cover as much as possible, or certainly as much as necessary. Another concerned the need to keep the paperwork to the minimum, whilst making it sufficient to enable a large range of supervisors, including teacher mentors, college tutors, associate tutors and external examiners, to have roughly the same criteria for judging students' competences. These and other tensions were resolved through a process of talking and listening to hundreds of students, tutors and teachers.

Development

Initial preparatory work was undertaken in the latter part of 1992 when the development team worked with over 50 experienced headteachers, teachers, LSU tutors and students to identify those Newly Qualified Teacher competences which they believed reflected the needs of schools.

From the beginning, the team took the view that a competence approach would be used to assess students only in a school setting, while subject knowledge would be assessed through a variety of means. This was partly driven by practical considerations: subject knowledge is taught partly in a modular system within the college and many modules are available to students not on an ITE course. Introducing a competence approach in these modules would not have been appropriate.

At an early stage, the development team was influenced by the approaches used by the School Management South Project (Earley 1992). This project was initiated to facilitate the professional development of experienced teachers and emphasises management development within the teaching role. Drawing on this work, the first set of LSU competences was organised into the following categories:

- the management of procedures, which included planning and record keeping.

- the management of people, which included teaching and relating to children and others in school.

- the management of resources.

Each statement of competence was precisely described in terms of its range, statement descriptions and performance indicators. In addition to these classroom competences, tutors and teachers described subject specific competences which could be developed through curriculum courses in school and college. As a result of this process a large number of generic competences was compiled together with a volume of detailed and precise, supporting documentation.

At this point, those involved in the project expressed misgivings about two issues. One concerned the large amount of paperwork which was being generated. Formative assessment needs to be comprehended quickly on a day-to-day basis, and this cannot be done if there is too much to read. Secondly, the language which had been derived from the School Management

South project was thought to be too far removed from the student experience of the primary classroom. When practitioners considered this first set of categories, they believed that some adjustment would be necessary. The management of resources was thought to be not important enough to require its own category. Planning, however, was thought to be sufficiently different from record keeping to warrant a separate statement of competence. Hence the competences were reformulated in language which better reflected teachers' perceptions of their jobs. The original competences were reduced in number and organised into categories relating to planning, teaching, managing children's behaviour, assessing children's progress and, underpinning each of these, evaluating the student's own practice.

At about the same time, the development group became interested in the approach to the assessment of professional competence used in the ASSET (Accrediting Social Services and Teaching) project (Essex County Council and Anglia University). We found this relevant because of the way in which it addresses the question commonly asked by members of our project, 'How many times do students have to demonstrate competence before they can be deemed to be competent?' ASSET's answer is that there is a range of core competences which are being addressed at various different times, in a range of contexts. In this way, the core competences are being continually reinforced.

The group felt that this two dimensional model of assessment could be applied in an educational setting. One dimension would be the generic competences which underpin successful teaching in any curriculum area (this later became formulated as figure 13.1). The other dimension would be the competences allied to specific subjects. A view was expressed to the effect that there were no particular approaches which are characteristic of specific areas of the curriculum, but that the feature which distinguishes one area from another is subject knowledge. However, subject specialists from diverse areas including drama, music and science showed that these subjects require not only specific knowledge but also have characteristic teaching styles and methods of working.

The pilot project

In February 1993, the course was validated with the proviso that development of the competences should continue over the following 18 months. The following month, a small group of LSU tutors, teachers and students began to prepare a lesson observation schedule which built on successful elements of

155

the previous schedule and incorporated the generic competences.

In April and May 1993 during the four week Year One teaching practice (TP), the competences and schedule were trialled in school with approximately 10 BEd students. Half way through the trial period participants (including students) met and suggested modifications and the schedule was reworked. It was agreed that although the categories should remain, the statements of competence needed some clarification. Students and teachers involved in the trials felt strongly that in order for the schedule to be purposeful and formative, students should have an opportunity to note their own evaluations together with an agreed action plan (see figure 13.2).

Further development

In June 1993 a group of approximately 30 experienced headteachers, teachers, LSU tutors and final year students met for a day in order to review the competences identified so far. Initially, the practitioners worked in small groups to list those things a newly qualified teacher needs to be able to do in his or her first post, both in and out of the classroom. This was done without reference to the competences drawn up previously. Practitioners then compared their identified competences with those trialled in April-May. Missing competences were identified and suggestions for improving the lesson observation schedule were noted.

During this period, it became obvious that students could not simply be judged competent or not competent, but that a more appropriate tool had to be designed to reflect stages in the development of competence. Accordingly, a three-point scale was devised (figures 13.4, 13.5 and 13.6). This scale was devised by TP supervisors and descriptions of each level were drawn from accounts of classroom observations of students.

The BA/BSc (QTS) is a four year course with blocks of school experience in each year. Some practitioners argued in favour of a four level scale. However, after attempting to discern levels of development supervisors agreed that a maximum of three levels of student development could be distinguished with ease and clarity. Further discrimination would require time-consuming and detailed scrutiny of minor differences.

Analysis

In July 1993 a group of headteachers, teachers, LSU tutors and final year BEd students analysed the documentation produced by each group on the June development day. At this point, they decided to distinguish competences (which could be observed with a degree of objectivity on specific occasions) from professional qualities (personal characteristics which teachers would be expected to have, and which would permeate all aspects of professional life although not necessarily evident on specific occasions). This accords with the formulation expressed by the DES (1983) that those awarded QTS should possess personal qualities, academic standards and professional knowledge and skills (quoted in Tickle 1992).

This is a departure from our original view of competence as embracing aspects of professional qualities. However, it clearly reflects the view of the teachers on the team that competences can be observed on a day-to-day basis, but that professional qualities are better identified in a conference involving the student, the supervisor and the class teacher, using evidence from a variety of sources and occasions, at the conclusion of a teaching practice.

The generic competences were reduced to four categories: planning, teaching, assessing and evaluating, since it was evident from the June reports that practitioners believed that the fifth category (managing children's behaviour) was too closely bound up with teaching to be assessed independently.

The materials

In October 1993 the development group, in consultation with 12 LSU teacher mentors, drew on the work compiled so far to devise a set of materials which were trialled and modified on five teaching practices between November 1993 and May 1994. As a result of these trials, discussions and modifications the following materials have been produced.

Generic classroom competences developed from practitioners' constructs and modified as a result of extensive classroom trails in primary schools (figure 13.1). These are recorded on the lesson observation schedule (figure 13. 2). The assessment of generic classroom competences is supported by descriptions of evidence of generic competences at three levels: beginning student, intermediate student and final student (figure 13.4, 13.5 and 13.6). We are currently using evidence from teaching practices to develop these further.

Subject specific competences identified by experienced specialists, including subject co-ordinators from primary schools. Evidence of these can be obtained when students undertake specific directed tasks. The assessment of subject specific tasks is supported by descriptions of evidence which include unique non-generic features specifically related to the subject. In addition to subject specific competences, we are encouraging practitioners to devise further competences not specific to subjects, which would relate to activities such as planning a school visit or taking a class assembly.

Teaching practice schedule devised by experienced teachers, tutors and students. The lesson observation schedule (figure 13.2) is used to observe students in the classroom. Before a period of observation the student and tutor decide which competences will be observed and commented on. The end of practice schedule is used at the end of TP (figure 13.3) to record progress and identify targets for future periods of school experience.

Professional qualities (figure 13.7) for instance the ability to form effective relationships with children and staff, flexibility and commitment to continuous professional development. These have been documented and will need to be evident as a student progresses through each period of school experience.

The procedures

Before each period of school experience, students will have all relevant documentation, including reports of any previous periods of school experience, and a clear indication of what will be expected of them in the practice. Students and supervisors will review the documentation and identify an action plan for development throughout the school experience.

During each period of school experience, students will collect evidence of competence. This may be found in lesson observations, written plans, evaluations and documentation and must be verified by supervisors. Students will maintain records of achievements in their files and use these to reflect on their practice and identify future targets. The supervisor will support, direct or guide students in this and students will retain copies of TP documentation. Duplicates will be stored centrally. At the end of each TP students, supervisors and class teachers will review evidence of competence and complete the end of school experience schedules.

As the four year programme progresses, students will build up a record of achievement which will be used to inform their development and ultimately to compile references.

Conclusions

Teaching is not an exact science, so the method of assessment we have developed is not and cannot be accurate or exact. Essentially, what we believe we have done is to describe a complex range of behaviours clearly and efficiently. These may not add up to a complete list of every competence needed by an NQT, but a large number of teachers, headteachers, students and college tutors are satisfied that it is sufficiently comprehensive. They are also satisfied that the formulation of competences and personal qualities reflects accurately the role of a beginning teacher.

The first cohort onto the BA/BSc (QTS) started in September 1994, so we will not know the advantages of this approach until 1996 or 1997. However, it would be foolish to enter into this development work without some advantages in mind and we believe that there are three.

Advantages to the students

From the beginning of their course, students will be aware of the competences they have to demonstrate. We expect that, during their 20 days of serial teaching experience and later, in their six-and eight-week block practices, they will quickly get to know what is expected of them and become adept at demonstrating their capability. Those areas which need further development will quickly emerge and we expect that students will focus clearly on strategies for obtaining the knowledge and skills necessary to achieve them. We believe that they will gain recognition for demonstrating a range of competences including those required to teach the National Curriculum and so be motivated to attempt to teach subjects which, under the present system, they can sometimes avoid.

Advantages to teachers and assessors

With a norm-referenced system of assessment, assessors can be tempted to give a poor pass grade to students they believe are not quite competent. We hope that this will no longer be possible in a competency approach. There is also potential for considerable staff development, both for college staff and teacher mentors. Teachers, students and college tutors have commented that they have benefited from developing and using subject-specific competences. As these are used in the classroom, it is to be hoped that a greater shared understanding of the nature of each subject is achieved, not only by the students, but the teacher mentors and college tutors.

Advantages to future courses

Courses come and go very fast, often at an alarming rate. The BA/BSc (QTS) has considerable advantages as a four-year course, half of which is spent on teaching studies and half on a combined-studies BA or BSc. However, it is expensive and although we prefer to be optimistic, we cannot assume that it will have a long life expectancy.

Descriptions of competence, if they are clear and manageable, might prove more durable and we expect ours to inform courses in the future. Because of their focus on output rather than input, they could be useful not only for college-based courses, but also for school-based ITE. They could be used on the PGCE course and perhaps it is possible that with some adaptation, they could be used to inform the shape of teachers' further professional development.

Above all, we believe that our competences go quite a long way to describe the challenging and complex job of teaching. One American approach is said to have identified 121 separate statements of competence (see Gitlin and Smyth 1989). We have heard it derided for its obvious lack of practicality. Yet we have some sympathy, for it is not easy to describe teaching in only 121 statements. We believe that we have been able to develop an approach which allows for many separate assessments without being impossibly complicated.

Figure 13.1

GENERIC CRITERION No. 1: Plan

This includes the ability to:

a) identify learning outcomes *e.g. skills, concepts, knowledge and attitudes and National Curriculum requirements;*

b) prepare relevant activities *e.g. building on previous work, meeting individual needs;*

c) choose appropriate resources *e.g. appropriate stationery, information technology;*

d) plan teaching techniques *e.g. explaining, questioning, giving instructions, demonstrating, asking a child to demonstrate;*

e) select appropriate organisational strategies *e.g. individuals, pairs, groups, whole class;*

f) identify assessment opportunities *e.g. activities which could be used to assess specific Statements of Attainment.*

GENERIC CRITERION No.2: Teach

This includes the ability to:

a) organise the learning environment effectively *e.g. use appropriate groupings, displays;*

b) gain and maintain attention *e.g. motivating children by effective voice control, body language*

c) form positive, professional relationships *e.g. listen to children, show an interest in them;*

d) set clear standards of behaviour *e.g. give clear instructions and consistently apply appropriate rewards and sanctions;*

e) vary teaching methods appropriately *e.g. promoting discussion, individual research;*

f) communicate effectively *e.g. through choice of language, audio-visual aids;*

g) respond appropriately to individual needs *e.g. explaining ideas, providing opportunities for supplementary work;*

h) keep children on task *e.g. use time targets or incentives to complete work;*

i) pace a lesson or activity effectively *e.g. introduce, sustain and conclude a lesson or activity within a given time-span.*

GENERIC CRITERION No.3: Assess

This includes the ability to:

a) set aside time to monitor children;

b) use appropriate methods to assess *e.g. observation, discussion, looking at their work and encouraging self-evaluation;*

c) provide focused feedback *e.g. written and oral, celebrating achievement and offering encouragement as appropriate;*

d) use and update records;

e) produce informative reports *e.g. progress of an individual child for a Special Needs teacher;*

f) use assessment to inform planning *e.g. plan to re-visit a skill or concept which children have not fully grasped.*

GENERIC CRITERION No.4: Evaluate

This includes the ability to:

a) alter planning, teaching and assessing according to the immediate context *e.g. alter teaching techniques when children have not fully understood something;*

b) evaluate and record personal performance *e.g. note positive aspects and areas for further development in plans, teaching and assessing;*

c) draw up achievable action plans *e.g. for the next week;*

d) seek help when appropriate *e.g. ask class teacher or supervisor for advice, read up on aspects of the curriculum.*

Figure 13.2

Lesson observation: Account of evidence
© LSU 1994

Name:	Type of activity :

1 = competent beginner   2 = competent at a higher level   3 = competent NQT

Plan ☐
- learning outcomes
- rekevant activities
- appropriate resources
- teaching techniques
- organisational strategies
- assessment opportunities

Teach ☐
- organise environment
- gain attention
- form relationships
- set standards of behaviour
- vary teaching methods
- communicate effectively
- respond to individual needs
- keep children on task
- pace the lesson

Assess ☐
- monitor children
- assess appropriately
- provide feedback
- use records
- produce reports
- use assessment to inform planning

Evaluate ☐
- evaluate the immediate context
- record personal performance
- draw up action plans
- seek help as appropriate

Competences demonstrated / required

General comments	Future action

Signed (assessor):   Date:
Signed (student):

Figure 13.3

End of practice record
© LSU 1994

Name:

School details:

Class details:

Dates:

Account of competence achieved (include comments about personal qualities):

Action plan for next practice:

Signed: Date:

163

Figure 13.4

The beginning student

Plan

All the competences noted in the Schedule have been addressed.
Short term planning enables children to use their time profitably and engage in activities which are relevant. National Curriculum is referred to.

Teach

All the competences noted in the Schedule have been addressed.
Can begin to form professional relationships with children, capture their interest and teach using an organisational strategy and one or more teaching techniques.   Can pace a lesson.   The children understand activities and undertake them.

Assess

All the competences noted in the Schedule have been addressed.
Obtains feed back from children and records the achievements of a small group in Mathematics and English.

Evaluate

All the competences noted in the Schedule have been addressed.
Can describe positive aspects and areas which need improvement and can draw up a simple action plan.

Figure 13.5

The intermediate student

Plan

All competences noted in the Schedule have been addressed.
Short term planning is differentiated, related to children's needs, builds on previous work and is located within an overall Scheme.

Teach

All competences noted in the Schedule have been addressed.
Can form appropriate professional relationships in the classroom and can capture and maintain children's interest.
Uses a variety of organisation strategies and teaching techniques.
Paces lessons effectively. The children understand what is expected of them and show positive attitudes towards learning.

Assess

All competences noted in the Schedule have been addressed.
Uses a variety of methods to obtain feedback from children and records children's achievements in the core subjects.

Evaluate

All competences noted in the Schedule have been addressed.
Begins to analyse why some aspects of teaching are positive and others need improvement. Draws up relevant action plans.

Figure 13.6

The final student

Plan

All the competences noted in the Schedule have been addressed.
Thorough short and long term planning takes account of different levels of ability. Planning builds on previous work and supports and challenges children at their own levels. National Curriculum requirements indicated, are met as appropriate.

Teach

All the competences noted in the Schedule have been addressed.
Is able to form positive and appropriate professional relationships with children and motivate them. Can organise the learning environments effectively using appropriate groupings and use a range of teaching techniques. Can pace lessons effectively and manage time. Children know what is expected of them in terms of work and behaviour and respond positively.
Interacts effectively with other adults.

Assess

All the competences noted in the Schedule have been addressed.
Uses a variety of methods to assess children.
Records children's achievements in core subjects and uses records effectively.

Evaluate

All the competences noted in the Schedule have been addressed.
Can evaluate, analyse and record personal performance noting positive aspects and areas for further development. Can draw up an achievable action plan and identify sources of additional support.

Figure 13.7

Professional qualities

It is intended that on completion of the programme, all students will possess the following professional qualities.

The ability to:

1. form positive professional relationships with children and adults, including the ability to present an appropriately professional manner;

2. communicate effectively, including the ability to listen to others;

3. organise effectively self and children, including the ability to pace oneself effectively in terms of time;

4. demonstrate a commitment to continuous professional development, including the ability to learn from others, to be flexible and open to alternatives, to evaluate one's own work and be willing to seek advice;

5. analyse, synthesise and apply learning within a practical context.

These qualities should be evident as students progress through periods of school experience and noted in the end of school experience schedule.
Evidence of these qualities may be obtained from a variety of sources including observation.

14 Change in teacher education: Interpreting and experiencing new professional roles

David Blake, Vincent Hanley, Mike Jennings and Michele Lloyd

Introduction

The concept of partnership between schools and HEIs is central to the government's plan for initial teacher education (ITE), and much depends on how it is interpreted and embraced by partners. Establishing more teacher training in schools has forced - and continues to force - redefinitions of existing partnerships and, in so doing, has demanded new roles for teachers and college tutors in the training of students.

The aim of our research was to investigate how the new secondary school-based PGCE operating under DFE Circular 9/92 was being experienced by those engaged in the training programme at the Chichester Institute of Higher Education *(ChIHE). We elicited a multi-perspective view of the course by focusing our research on the three main participants centrally involved in the scheme: the students, teachers and college tutors. We were particularly interested in the new professional roles that were being devised to support student teachers' learning. As well as investigating students' new training experiences, we were concerned with the ways in which teachers and college tutors defined, experienced and reported their new roles.

The project entailed empirical research in the form of questionnaire surveys and semi-structured, in depth interviews with purposive samples (Cohen and Manion 1994: 89). This chapter draws on our findings from the three groups of respondents.

* At the time the research was conducted, the Institute's name was the West Sussex Institute of Higher Education, hence interviewees' quotations refer to 'WSIHE' and 'West Sussex'.

The view from the students

Although the main foci of our project were the definition and conceptualisation of new professional roles, neither can be researched in isolation from the students' experience. Our work with students, therefore, was intended to provide insights into this experience and, through them, to discover ways in which professional roles - i.e. those of subject mentors and professional tutors in schools, link tutors and subject tutors in college - were being interpreted in practice.

The findings presented here focus on just one area of student experience, namely serial experience and teaching practice in schools, referred to in course documents as school A and school B. Data were collected in two questionnaire surveys (one at the conclusion of each school placement) and interviews with a purposive sample of 12 students. This section of the chapter is arranged under the following sub-headings: background, terminology, relationships with school personnel, and guidance and support.

Background

Sixty-one students registered for the programme in September 1993 in the subject specialisms of English, history and mathematics. There had been no evidence to suggest that school-based, as a label for the government's new training, had had any effect on normal recruitment; the group was typical of previous intakes in background and categories of degree classifications.

Students were placed in 24 partner schools across West Sussex, Hampshire and Surrey, all of which had previous strong links with ChIHE, although not necessarily for PGCE placements. The majority of the schools were classified as urban and had between 440 and 1,500 pupils on roll. Most of the schools were comprehensive; there was one single sex school and one (selective) minor public school.

The number of placements in each school ranged from one to six. Some schools also had partnerships with other HEIs and so had to cope with different patterns of course requirements. In the ChIHE programme equal amounts of time were spent in schools A and B in which periods of serial experience preceded and followed block practice. Most students' overall school placement was managed by professional tutors, while at subject teaching level they were supported by subject mentors. The immediate contacts with college were link tutors and subject tutors.

170

Terminology

One of the important induction tasks in any ITE programme is defining key terms. Definitions, it could be argued, help to provide understanding of the aims and coherence of the intended training and are crucial, explanatory statements. As statements, they are often embedded in descriptions of courses and activities at the operational level and, as the mode of training changes, new definitions are required. In the larger context of reform of teacher education, John and Lucas (1994: 158) note how 'an occupational lexicon' has ousted 'the language of professionalism'.

In our case study, 'school-focused' had been replaced by 'school-based' as a key term in the new PGCE. As researchers, we were interested in students' definitions of the new key term and the extent to which they raised expectations or guided perceptions of teachers' and college tutors' roles. Students were reminded that practice and theory were interrelated and that the programme's definition of 'school-based' did not imply a narrow preoccupation with the technicalities of teaching. The 12 interviewees, therefore, were aware of the programme's broad view of the term and had completed more than half the course when interviewed.

Despite the programme's broad view, there was much evidence to suggest that students' definitions had crystallised narrowly and concisely. All were aware that 'school-based' courses demanded more time in school as a government requirement - a requirement they all approved of. However, there was less certainty about how much more time was required but, whatever the addition, it was made at the expense of hourage for college-based taught courses - or what some perceived simply as theory. As students saw things, therefore, the PGCE programme had been forced to allocate two-thirds of its total time to serial experience and block practice in order to redress a perceived imbalance in training in favour of schools. The new balance, it was tentatively hinted, was a corrective in which experience and practice had been elevated above taught courses. The school, therefore, assumed more importance than college as a centre of course influence. Within this centre, students believed they could experience the real world of the classroom and learn how to teach. For them, training in this sphere was characterised as the 'hands on approach', 'on the job learning', or, more straightforwardly:

> ... work experience at school, whether it's observation or actual teaching practice. And you're based at the school rather than college but you have links with the college.

The responses here underline the value placed on experience and the belief that students learn best 'through doing'. The strong belief in the pervasive power of experience and learning of teaching as a craft, is strongly reminiscent of an apprenticeship model even though, as noted in a later section of this chapter, some students preferred to develop their own teaching styles, not those of their subject mentors.

We cannot, of course, be certain of the meanings students give to definitions of terms or of the extent that terms help to determine students' perceptions of professional roles. However, as the report on 'school-based' shows, the term, derived from an 'occupational' lexicon may have been resonant with occupational meaning for students who were trying to make sense of training in schools.

Relationships with school personnel

Analysis of data strongly suggests that most students had realised the importance of the working relationships with professional tutors and subject mentors at an early stage. Much depended on establishing and sustaining the relationships and, as the programme progressed, tutor and mentor - especially the mentor - loomed large in their thinking. When students were asked to list perceived difficulties and successes in both schools their responses showed just how important the relationships were. In both surveys, only 'classroom management and discipline' was a greater perceived difficulty than relationships with the tutor and mentor. As a perceived success, getting on well with the tutor and mentor ranked second only to 'relationships with pupils' in school A and was top of the list in school B. In some instances, students observed, well-intentioned subject mentors found it hard to allow them their independence, a difficulty cited by mentors in Dart and Drake (1993). One student reported that the mentor:

> ... was being slightly 'over-protective' of me when I felt that I really needed to learn things (such as discipline) on my own and by experience - not by having him do it for me.

Establishing autonomy in the classroom proved problematical for others, too:

> I felt that there was undue pressure to adopt a particular method of teaching rather than 'drawing out' our own skills and utilising them.

The crucial matter here is students' expectation of how the mentor should operate. It raises questions about the model of the mentor and all that implies - and, of course, the levels of inter-personal skills, confidence and assertiveness that school-based training may demand of students.

The extent to which the professional tutor and subject mentor were able to fulfil their increased training responsibilities was another key issue. Although students were generally positive about the way in which schools timetabled and ring-fenced periods for tutorials and seminars, many thought the periods did not greatly compensate for the additional pressures (a problem discussed at length by Dart and Drake 1993). School roles in the PGCE programme had usually been assigned to senior members of staff, each having administrative or departmental and teaching responsibilities. A breakdown of statuses show that 60 per cent of subject mentors were heads of departments and 45 per cent of professional tutors were deputy headteachers. A deployment of such senior staff to the programme may have brought an essential breadth of experience to school-based training but, as students pointed out, the demands on their time were heavy. Conscious of these heavy demands, some students felt reluctant to approach them about sudden, unexpected difficulties. Others felt that exchanges under hurried circumstances were sometimes superficial or inadequate.

Guidance and support

To gain some insight into the level of guidance given by professional tutors and subject mentors students were asked to indicate the overall quality of support they had received on a five point scale of excellent / good / fair / poor / none. Interpretation of their responses from school B gives a favourable picture of tutors' and mentors' overall support. Sixty-three per cent of students believed that the support from mentors was 'excellent' while 70 per cent thought that support from tutors was 'good' to 'excellent'. To investigate further, students who were interviewed were asked how school and college personnel could best support them in school. Analysis of responses revealed concerns in the following three areas: attitudes, approaches and time.

Students felt that the attitude of school personnel was crucial, emphasising that teachers should 'want to do the job'. The implication was that, in some schools, tutors and mentors may have been reluctant participants and commitment to teacher training may have been lukewarm. It was desirable, too, that professional tutors and subject mentors should be more proactive in monitoring student progress and in helping to identify and resolve problems. The proactive approach, responses suggested, demanded a sensitivity to students' needs as *adult* learners; they could be encouraged to build on their own experience, skills and knowledge and to develop their own teaching styles - not have one imposed on them. In their work as teacher-trainers, school personnel could best help students by using their time in two ways; first, there should be ring-fenced time for tutorials and seminars; second, schools should recognise that, for a variety of reasons, students need informal access to tutors and mentors and that time for informal access should be taken into account in overall planning.

Reflecting on how college-based tutors could best support students in school, nearly all the student interviewees agreed that the link tutor should see them teach (not a requirement at present) and make more visits to see students, especially during the block practices. Support of this kind, it was claimed, would help to keep students in touch with college and would provide opportunities for them to discuss their progress more frequently.

Implications

We suggested initially that students' perceptions of professional roles may have been influenced by the new vocabulary of teacher training, a suggestion partly borne out by students' early identification of key personnel. The need to demonstrate competence in the classroom, and, as one student put it, 'to survive', helps to explain the emergence of the subject mentor as *the* significant figure in what we interpreted as an apprenticeship model - a model in which the 'student-apprentice' saw herself or himself working with a 'master-teacher'. This practice in the classroom, of course, was the core element of school-based training, orchestrated, in this context, by the professional tutor as manager - a concept in keeping with the occupational lexicon mentioned previously.

Perhaps we should not be too surprised by the apparent marginalisation of college personnel, link tutor and subject tutor, in the school context. Formal descriptions of their roles show limitations on direct observations of students in classrooms - a task for which the subject mentor is responsible. However, these limitations are not willingly accepted by many students who wish to see more linkage with them as individuals, not just with schools.

Overall, the dominant concern was lack of time; it is a recurring theme in the way students contrast the *realities* with the *ideals* of their training, especially in relation to how it affects the professional roles of school and college personnel.

174

The view from the schools

We selected 12 teachers as a purposive sample from the 44 teachers involved in professional tutor and subject mentor roles in the Secondary PGCE programme. The sample reflected the subjects of English, history and mathematics and the proportion of women and men involved in the scheme. Their schools were of varying sizes, geographically spread across Hampshire and West Sussex LEAs. During the interviews we explored four broad areas: the advantages and disadvantages of the school-based PGCE; preparation and training; roles and responsibilities; and overview of the course. The overall responses to these questions are described below and the implications draw out what appear to be some significant issues.

Advantages and disadvantages of the school-based PGCE

In response to the move to make ITE courses more school-based the majority in the sample cautiously welcomed such initiatives. They were all were positive about what their school was gaining from partnership involvement in ITE, such as having fresh visitors and ideas coming into schools and opening up the climate for educational debate. Being involved in the scheme also gave schools opportunities to look beyond the school itself; question approaches; improve the quality of pupils' learning and the learning environment; and acquire some limited funding.

A similarly positive endorsement was given by all respondents to the advantages for both individual teachers and the students coming into school. For some teachers, being involved with students provided them with a break from their routine and many experienced mentoring as a form of revitalisation. They also had opportunities to undertake mentor training and to reflect on their own subject and practice as both a teacher and as a department:

> Students come in with fresh ideas. They're almost, I believe, like an in-service in themselves to the staff. Certainly as a mentor they made me re-evaluate my own classroom practices.

Various advantages for the students were cited. The school-based programme afforded students more time to acclimatise themselves to the ethos of schools and enabled them to work more closely with colleagues. They had the opportunity to see how the institutions they would be joining *really* work, thereby gaining insight into the wider aspects of a teacher's role.

The advantages for the HE tutor were much less obvious to most respondents. Although minor advantages were seen in tutors' closer links with schools (and with students who had more experience in schools), there was a strong feeling that HE tutors had come off worst under the new partnership arrangements:

I sometimes wonder whether they are getting the poorer end of the deal. I can't actually see what advantages they're getting out of this.

For all their positive endorsement of an increase in the school-based element and their involvement in it, the teachers also noted some significant limitations. They had reservations about the workload involved for the school, and the political agenda behind the moves. They all regarded theoretical understanding of education, schooling and training as essential for students and equally felt that the HE role in developing this understanding was essential. Some of them expressed misgivings about the reduced theoretical content of the school-based programme which they felt had adversely affected the extent of students' conceptual understanding of educational issues, particularly in comparison with past student cohorts. As an experienced history mentor noted:

Some of the debates that we took as read, people coming out of college with, no longer seem to be known. For example, one of this year's students said 'Who is this Marwick man?', whereas lots of people would have known about Arthur Marwick's work beforehand.

Concerned about the devaluation of the role of HE in ITE, some mentors warned against a form of school-based training which viewed students as 'nuts and bolts' practitioners who have to cope simply with x or y competence.

For the teachers involved there were further drawbacks to the school-based scheme. Some parents and teachers had voiced concern that children were being taught by lots of students rather than trained, experienced teachers. Weak and failing students involved extra workloads for the school, particularly for the mentor and the department, in supporting and assessing them. Balancing two or more roles as teacher and, say, deputy head and mentor, proved problematical at times for a number of the respondents. Some suggested that teachers and schools should be getting more money for their role as they were now doing the job that the college previously did.

Respondents perceived minor disadvantages for the students in their school too. An initial feeling of being out of place and lacking in confidence may be encountered by some students at the start of the school year. Spending a large proportion of time in school could result in the fragmentation and devaluation of the college-based element of the course.

On the subject of disadvantages for college tutors the teachers amplified their concern that tutors were not able to see students as much, or develop essential social and pedagogic relationships with them. As a consequence tutors were placed under pressure in trying to fit everything into a very limited time with students.

Preparation and training

All the teachers felt strongly that schools had been offered very little concrete support by the government and DFE, particularly in terms of funding for preparation and implementation of the course, or prior consultation. By contrast, they valued the literature they had received from ChIHE which they believed had been far more informative and yet not too prescriptive. The link tutor from college had been particularly helpful in developing their understanding and supporting the implementation of the programme. The school's role in training, however, was not mentioned as significant by any respondents.

The interviewees were unanimous in the view that training for mentors is essential to enable teachers to do the job effectively. For many the key aspect of training was the opportunity to meet other mentors and discuss issues and approaches with them. Their own mentor training days at the institute had been very good and very practical. Training for all mentors was viewed as necessary in helping to ensure common approaches and experiences for students, particularly as most of the course was based in school:

> They [students] experience different schools and I think it's important for them that the mentors are asking the same things of them, that mentors across schools are consistent in their requirements from students.

Roles and responsibilities

When characterising the training responsibilities of the school and the institute the teachers regarded the school's role as introducing the student to the culture of that one school, whereas HE's role was to introduce the student to the culture of education, schools and schooling in broad terms. Respondents also underlined the interdependence of school and the institute:

> If you wanted to be cynical you could say that the school could do without WSIHE, but WSIHE couldn't do without the school. But I'm not being cynical because I think at WSIHE there's a lot of expertise and there's a lot of knowledge and skill there which I haven't got.

As a result, teachers felt that HE can look at wider issues much better than schools can.

While teaching and mentoring were demanding roles, teachers commented that the task of combining these responsibilities had been facilitated by the quality of support and information they had received from the link tutor attached to the school. Working together with college tutors and teacher representatives from other partner schools on the PGCE Management Group had been particularly helpful.

Overview of the course

> When considering the main difficulties that had arisen during their experience as a school-based mentor, the constant and most significant response from the teachers was the lack of time to carry out their role: 'It's a job that can become one's whole job with not too much difficulty'.

Other points mentioned related to the constant pressure of having someone with you all the time, and having a lazy student in a very committed and energetic department. The number of students any school can realistically take on was brought to light by one subject mentor whose school had ITE partnerships with three HEIs and, at one stage, had had 19 students in the staffroom.

On the subject of professional development opportunities, the benefits of being a mentor substantially outweighed any difficulties encountered by the teachers during the year. One respondent particularly valued her mentoring involvement since, she explained, there are gradually fewer opportunities for teachers to do their in-service training away from school, meeting other teachers and hearing their ideas. Mentoring had generally been a very positive experience for both the respondents and their schools. As a professional tutor concluded:

> ... where, as a school, we have frustrations, they're frustrations with 9/92 rather than frustrations in the partnership that we now have with West Sussex.

Of the 12 interviewees, one did not wish to act as mentor with the next cohort of students, having had two weak students that year. However, the other respondents were keen to continue their partnership involvement. One school, which had already volunteered for the following year, planned to use part of the money for cover to provide extra time for the mentors. The majority of the teachers were looking forward to acting as mentor again: 'Oh yes, yes. It keeps me in touch with college, it keeps us in touch with the wider world'. 'There's a massive amount of willingness to be involved'.

Implications

The responses from the majority of the teachers in the sample to the questions in the interviewing schedule suggest the following conclusions. The professional development advantages for both individual teachers and the school as a whole significantly outweigh any difficulties or disadvantages experienced so far. This was strongly felt, as is revealed by many of the teachers' immediate positive responses, though hearsay reports from other institutions do not confirm universal enthusiasm.

Mentor training is essential and should recognise individual teacher and school needs and experience when developing the training programme. This has implications for a second phase of mentor training much more driven by mentors' expressed needs than HE views of mentors' needs. The main difficulties for teachers in implementing their role are: creating and maintaining time for the work when they already have other major administrative and teaching responsibilities; and assessing weak or fail students which is a more complex, lengthy, intellectual and emotional process than previously realised. Despite these difficulties, almost all the mentors would be very happy to undertake the role again in a continuous involvement with ITE.

The view from the college tutors

Interviews with six Secondary PGCE tutors from one institution

We interviewed six tutors who were the key members of the team responsible for delivering the PGCE course at ChIHE. As stated earlier, two possible roles were available to HE tutors, that of link tutor and subject tutor. Of the six tutors interviewed two were link tutors, two were subject tutors and two acted as both link and subject tutors. The interview schedule explored tutors' general perceptions of the new PGCE as well as more detailed aspects of their role and the ways in which it interacted with others.

A fundamental thread running through the interviews with all six tutors is that of change conceived of in terms of status, control, location and responsibilities within teacher education. These interviews with tutors are peppered with reflections on the way they are personally responding to change in teacher education. The interviews are reported under four headings: the strengths and weaknesses of the school-based PGCE to date; how the responsibilities of school and college personnel are working out in practice; the role of the college subject tutor; and the role of the link tutor.

Strengths and weaknesses of the school-based PGCE

There was a generally shared view that the fact of the course being substantially based in school was itself a major strength. More than that, there was a general view that the quality of the links with schools was excellent, leading to mutual confidence between schools and the institute. All tutors made very positive reference to the good team-work, which they believed was essential to the successful operation of a school-based course. This well-developed team-work led to open and effective communication, from staff to staff, students to staff and vice versa, and from school to college. In general, the tutors expressed high levels of satisfaction with the way the new school-based course was working in practice.

Weaknesses were identified. It was considered by two of the subject tutors that arrangements for subject work on the PGCE were unsatisfactory. Tutor A felt that the subject link with the school was probably insufficient and would need to be reviewed. Similarly, tutor B considered that the subjects are on the margins:

For example we have no detailed working knowledge on what happens

180

in school. We don't see the students on teaching practice, we don't know what is going on at levels which are really useful.

Various aspects of the students' experience were identified as weak to some extent. They were felt to be under considerable pressure on the school-based programme, as opposed to previous courses, leading tutor F to consider that course selection procedures would require review. Some tutors discerned that the increased demands of the new course made it hard for students to accept the usefulness of anything beyond the immediately relevant:

Sometimes that [reflective] perspective goes because you're too busy trying to survive, with all the alligators around you, to take any long-term viewpoint.

The fragmented notion of the school-based course was commented on, leading tutor D to argue that 'it's more difficult for us to establish really meaningful relationships with students. There was some inconsistency in the level of schools' commitment to their new role. This was felt to be a very small minority of schools, but it was nonetheless a significant concern in a school-based scheme when commitment, support or competence were in any way at risk. Finally, some tutors felt there had been too much inconsistency in the level of training and preparation of school-based colleagues within the scheme.

The responsibilities of school and college personnel

Although the respective responsibilities are set out in the course handbook, tutors acknowledged that there is variation in people's understanding and knowledge of them. The main problem in reviewing school and college responsibilities is that of control. At one level the notion of control implies ownership and responsibility for the course. At another level, the idea of control refers to responsibility for the quality of the course. Tutor E identified quality control as the main problem in assessing responsibilities, pointing out that professional tutors see it as their responsibility to quality control subject mentors but there is an overall lack of precision about this aspect. Tutor D expressed similar uncertainty about what the lines of accountability mean in practice:

The role of the visiting tutors, be they link or subject tutors, is to ensure a sort of quality on the programme, the effectiveness of the programme. I mean, what do you do if it's not working? You can't sort of work it out yourself. All we can do is make a note of it, suggest to the mentor that these things need looking at, or to the professional tutor, and think about whether we use the school next year.

The subject tutor

Subject tutors' support for students was distinguished from the support provided by subject mentors in school in terms of being more general and less focused on the individual child or class. However, there was a feeling amongst tutors that the subject tutor's role had diminished when compared with previous arrangements and was now a restricted one. Tutor F described how subject tutors formerly had 'an awareness of the needs of the students and how those might be best addressed' but now this was in the hands of the mentor in school. All the subject tutors felt there was a need to look again at the subject tutor's role, especially in respect of involvement with the students in school and making judgements about their teaching.

There was general agreement that subject tutors' knowledge of subject and schools needs to be up-to-date. Restricting their access to schools and teaching could be detrimental to their credibility. As tutor A pointed out:

> One of the reasons they [subject tutors] want to keep in touch with schools and make more visits to schools is because it's about keeping in touch with what's happening in their subject area in schools.

The link tutor

From the viewpoint of HE, the link tutor's role is considered essential. It is seen as a strength that the link tutor brings an objective perspective to the school engaged in training. Tutor D regarded it as important that link tutors are not subject-based, but rather that they are able to look at ITE in the context of whole-school work:

> .... you're really the advocate, if you like, of the importance of the ....professional development courses that we're offering in college, that we think are so important.

182

Over time there are felt to be great opportunities in the role of link tutor even though, in the short term, the main expectation of the role from some schools is to reinforce their viewpoint. There is insufficient time to do the job properly, according to tutor C, and in any case the job should be expanded from making a link with the professional tutor or subject mentor to making a link with the student as well.

Link tutors have contacts with a large number of students, professional tutors and subject mentors, as well as college link and subject tutors. Link tutors had contact with a range of four to 18 students and, routinely, five to seven professional tutors and subject mentors. There was a lot of linking to do and not very much time in which to do it. This number of contacts was contrasted by tutor E with the more generously resourced Articled Teacher Scheme where he had one student in each school and could regularly go into school to work with the student for half a day at a time.

Despite all the careful documentation, training and meetings, tutor D considered that there were continuing problems in getting students and schools to understand the link tutor's role:

> They're used to a different sort of role where tutors came from college into school and observed them teach and it's a different role. And some of the students have been saying things like 'Oh, you haven't come into see us' or 'We haven't had a visit' and that isn't the purpose of the link tutor or the subject tutor's visit. So I think there's a problem there, trying to get that message across, which is interesting because post-grads really have got no prior expectations.

Implications

It is incontrovertible that changes in government policy constitute a direct challenge to the way in which HE tutors have hitherto exercised their professional skills. Tutors were alert to the shifting external environment, as reflected in the interviews. Subject tutors tended to compare the old PGCE with the new, particularly with respect to their greater knowledge of students in the past; the way tutors had structured the former course process so that HE set the students' agenda; and their previous involvement as supervisors of students in school. The challenge posed by the new arrangements was profound, since there was no sense in which subject tutors were critical of professional tutors' and subject mentors' competence and commitment in working with students. Link tutors, too, identified the problematic nature of

183

their role in the midst of a radical political agenda, as graphically summed up by one tutor:

> There's an element that we're stuffing ourselves for Christmas. We've trained the schools and mentors. They've had free training from us. We're paying schools for everything and we're free.

It is difficult for HE teacher educators to feel anything other than anxiety about their status and future prospects. On the whole tutors were positive about the new opportunities for professional development which some aspects of partnership arrangements offered them. But potential incompatibilities and problems may be identified in comments about lack of control and lack of knowledge in respect of the PGCE course model.

Conclusion

Data from this case study suggest that while respondents generally endorse the move towards more school-based forms of Secondary ITE, many of them articulate well-founded reservations about teacher education becoming overly school-based at the expense of valuable HE involvement.

As far as students' observations were concerned, we should remember that the roles to be experienced and interpreted (including their own) were new; they brought no clear preconceptions to the situation. Their understanding of the experience and interpretation were partly rooted in the new terminology that set parameters of meaning and generated student views and concerns, all of which need to be explored further. The exploration, for example, could focus usefully on the 'master-teacher-apprentice model' and the perceived centrality of the subject mentor's and professional tutor's roles. Although the moves to make ITE more school-based were welcomed by the teachers in this sample, they expressed qualifications centring on two main areas. Firstly, they highlighted the need to ensure a complementary balance of school-based and college-based training in which HE continues to have an essential stake; teachers, in this study at least, do not appear to want to have sole responsibility for training. The second concern is that any move to school-based training must not be done 'on the cheap'. Funding must be sufficient for schools to undertake this extra and different commitment and to implement it effectively.

HE tutors articulated clear benefits resulting from more school-based ITE, particularly the enhanced quality of partnership arrangements and students' increased understanding of the world of the school. There was a view that immense energy had been invested by school and HE personnel to produce a genuine and constructive working partnership. But, at the same time, concerns were expressed about the dangers of an increased fragmentation of the student experience and a reduction in that critical, analytical edge about teaching which results from systematic, HE-based professional work. There was also a shared concern amongst students, teachers and tutors alike about the lack of direct involvement of HE tutors in students' teaching in school.

Our findings indicate that Secondary PGCE students do benefit from a more school-based course in one fundamental way - experiencing how an individual school, department and its teachers really work. The severe limitation of this initiative is, however, that students are no longer developing the essential theoretical and analytical frameworks previously provided by a partnership which was HE-centred.

15   The theory practice gap explored: The views of art and physical education students at Cardiff Institute of Higher Education

David Egan

Introduction

This chapter seeks to explore three areas which, it may be claimed, have as of yet received little attention in research on partnership and mentoring in secondary ITT. In the first place, research has largely drawn upon the core National Curriculum subject areas and the foundation subjects of history, geography and modern languages (Benton 1990) - specialist areas such as art design, music and physical education have not thus far received consideration. Secondly it may be said that research into student perceptions and experiences of partnership and mentoring are relatively uncharted territory despite some interesting initial forays into this area (Furlong 1990, Booth 1993). Finally it is apparent that much of the focus in historical partnership experiences such as those at the University of Sussex (Lacey and Lamont 1976) and at Oxford University (Benton 1990) and in more recent developments (Everton and White 1992, Sands and Bishop 1993) has been to establish discrete - but complementary - domains in which teachers and teacher educators can contribute to the development of students' knowledge and learning. Influenced by the findings of a Cambridge-based research project (Furlong, Hirst, Pocklington and Miles 1988) there has been a concern to overcome what that research described as the 'theory practice gap' which is identified as the besetting weakness of traditional, college-based BEd and PGCE courses. One of the participants in the Oxford University Internship Scheme which has pioneered attempts to use partnership and mentoring procedures to bridge this 'gap' has put the argument about separate domains starkly in saying that 'the simple fact is that teacher educators are not teachers' (Haggarty in Benton 1990).

On the basis of research into aspects of the first year (1993-1994) of partnership and mentoring experiences associated with the PGCE Secondary course at Cardiff Institute of Higher Education, this chapter seeks to contribute to scholarly and professional debate in the three areas set out above. It does so through focusing on the art and design and physical education curriculum areas of the course. It draws particularly on evidence gathered from students through an end-of-course evaluation and questionnaire. Finally it concentrates attention on particular and well established aspects of the course in these curriculum areas, which involve a different view of the role of teacher educators in the quest to overcome the theory practice gap.

The PGCE secondary course at Cardiff Institute

The PGCE Secondary course at Cardiff Institute of Higher Education contains two large curriculum studies areas for specialist teachers of art and design and physical education. These are two of the largest courses of their kind in the country and it can be claimed they have a national and international reputation for the quality of experience and training that they offer to students. The art and design course recruits 50-60 students annually from across a wide variety of undergraduate courses in the United Kingdom. The students come from diverse undergraduate areas such as fine art, painting, sculpture, performance, textiles, creative arts and expressive arts. A significant number of the students are mature students who have previously worked in commerce and industry. The physical education course recruits a similar number of students each year (50-60) with the vast majority of these being recruited from undergraduate sports and human movement studies courses within the Faculty of Education and Sport at Cardiff Institute. All PE students must have followed an undergraduate course in which elements of physical education and/or sports studies make up at least 50 per cent of the course. The PE postgraduate course has been the only one of its kind in Wales and is one of the leading specialist courses in the country. The Cardiff PGCE Secondary courses, with these two significant specialist subject components, has long had close partnership-type relationships with local secondary schools which have always been anxious to receive these specialist students and the skills they bring to subject departments. These close relationships pre-date university developed partnerships such as those at Sussex and Oxford, and can be seen to be representative of what Margaret Wilkin has identified as 'an increased commitment to partnership between schools and colleges...particularly apparent in the non-university sector' (Wilkin 1992a:80). In 1992-1993 it was decided to move the course into formal partnership under the terms of the Secondary ITT Criteria set out in WO 35/

92 (DFE 9/92). Partnerships were formed with over 60 Welsh and English medium secondary schools in the counties of Mid-Glamorgan, South Glamorgan and Gwent and the first year of these new partnership and mentoring arrangements has been undertaken in 1993-1994.

The AIR project

In the developing informal partnerships which preceded the onset of the new Secondary ITT arrangements, the art and design and physical education courses had developed particular aspects of school-based work which had become highly valued by all participants - students, schools and tutors - and which had brought wide attention and recognition to the courses.

At the outset of the PGCE year, art and design students become involved in the Artist-in-Residence-Project (AIR). For three days a week, for six weeks, students are hosted as artists in residence, in teams of three, across 20 primary schools in the county of South Glamorgan. Students create studio environments and, pooling together the experience and specialisms they bring from their own practice and undergraduate education, they stimulate, guide and teach children a variety of art and design practices. The contribution this makes to the development of children at Key Stage 2 - where their work is focused - is highly valued by the participating schools (there is a waiting list to become involved), particularly since the development of the art National Curriculum. The AIR Project culminates in a major exhibition of student work at Cardiff Institute, to which all participants are invited. The quality of this exhibition and the experiences embodied in it have led to the course receiving sponsorship from outside bodies and firms such as the Cardiff Bay Hamlyn Foundation. In March 1993 this established quality was recognised by the Higher Education Funding Council for Wales when it awarded the 'recognition of excellence' to the course. The AIR exhibition has proceeded from its launch in Cardiff to a variety of UK institutions and locations and abroad to Holland, Germany and Canada.

The intentions of the AIR project are to provide intending secondary students with an initial opportunity to study and work with pupils at Key Stage 2 so as to be able to:

• experiment with a variety of teaching approaches which will contribute to creative and expressive learning experience;

- develop students' confidence through collaboration with mentors and tutors which will lead to early achievement and recognition;

- provide a theoretical basis in areas such as perception, skills, aesthetics, teaching and learning strategies, which are developed by tutors in the Institute, who together with students will simultaneously address these to practice in the AIR schools.

What is involved here, then, is what the course team call a 'teaching contract' which allows for both students and tutors to work together at the outset of the course, both in college and in school, to develop and demonstrate processes and teaching strategies and then to share and interpret the evidence accumulated through work with children.

In the process of developing partnership and mentoring arrangements in 1992-1993 it was apparent that there was a strong desire from both tutors and schools to sustain the AIR Project within the new arrangements. The enthusiasm of the primary schools for the project has already been pointed out and in the design team which was set up to prepare the partnership mentoring arrangements, secondary schools' representatives were equally committed to maintaining the primary-based AIR work. Commitment was maintained despite the fact that this would mean less transfer of HEI resources to them due to the time spent in primary schools. They made clear their support for the quality of AIR and their awareness of the useful preparation that this teaching contract between schools, tutors and students provided for students who would then proceed to Key Stage 3 and Key Stage 4 in secondary schools. Tutors were also extremely concerned to continue what for them had become a bridge across the 'theory practice gap' to rich pastures of productive partnership. In straitened and threatening times for HEI involvement in ITT, it was necessary to question the amount of tutor time spent in schools which were now being paid to receive students. However, it was decided that the quality of the AIR experience should lead to this type of tutor involvement in classrooms continuing - albeit at a reduced level.

Instructional teaching practice

In physical education within the Cardiff PGCE course there had also long existed a further example of tutor, student and teacher involvement and interaction for training purposes - this is the Instructional Teaching Practice (ITP). ITP involves a group of seven students working with an HEI tutor in

190

seven to eight secondary school PE departments for one day a week for a period of six weeks. Like the AIR Project this is followed in the first term of the PGCE course and serves as an introduction to secondary teaching for PE students before they engage in later collaborative and block practices singly or in pairs. The intention is to introduce students to various teaching situations and strategies in a progressive manner. On the ITP days, students, tutor and mentor prepare to teach the normal PE timetables across age and ability ranges through a variety of strategies including observation of tutor and mentor, micro teaching of small groups and other forms of single and group participation by students. Time is allowed for group discussion and evaluation, where tutor, mentor and students identify and reflect upon basic principles of teaching methodology in the specialist subject area. The involvement of the HEI tutor ensures a continuum of experience and instruction across the college and school course which again seeks to bridge the 'theory practice gap'. Students are perceived to benefit from this gradual, co-operative introduction to teaching situations, drawing upon: the everyday craft knowledge of the mentor; the teacher education experience and specialist expertise of the college tutor (many of whom have taught them in their undergraduate studies); and the pooling of the specialist physical education skills they bring as physical education practitioners themselves.

Again, in moving into formal partnership, there was a strong desire from PE tutors and mentors to sustain ITP as part of formal partnership and mentoring arrangements. Tutors were highly committed to this successful method of achieving the time-long expressed desire of PGCE students to see their HEI lecturers showing them 'how to do it'. Schools were anxious to be involved and the acceptance of such a large group of students was made possible and beneficial by the simultaneous involvement of the college tutor. Although the changing circumstances of the HEI's role in secondary ITT required careful consideration of the resources needed for both tutors and mentors to work in schools with students, it was decided to carry forward the practice of ITP into partnership arrangements with some reduction of tutor involvement.

Student evaluation

Many of the worries of HEI tutors about the effect that partnership and mentoring arrangements would have on their specialist curriculum areas can be seen to have been assuaged by the experience of the first year of partnership. High quality work has been apparent again in both AIR and ITP projects and the commitment of schools and teachers educators to these projects is as high as ever. What of the views of the students who participated in AIR and ITP during the first year of the PGCE partnership? In July 1994 as part of their end-of-course evaluation, students were asked to complete an extensive questionnaire on their experiences, including evaluation of their views of the AIR and ITP projects. Students were asked to rate these experiences on a five point scale (very good, good, satisfactory, unsatisfactory and poor) and to offer additional comments on the quality of AIR and ITP.

Forty-seven of the 55 Physical Education students thought that ITP was satisfactory or better, with 21 believing it to be very good, 14 good and 12 satisfactory. Only one student saw ITP as a poor experience and seven as unsatisfactory, with comments from these students indicating problems with the organisation of ITP. The overwhelming response to ITP, however, was positive, with students often reflecting upon 'security in numbers', 'going into schools in a group gives you confidence' and valuing the opportunity 'to see a variety of teaching styles and try them out'.

Thirty-seven Art and Design students completed the questionnaire and their response to AIR was overwhelmingly enthusiastic. All 37 believed it was a satisfactory or better experience, with 30 seeing it as very good, six as good and one as satisfactory. It was noted that AIR 'gives students the confidence to approach preliminary teaching strategies and to develop ideas', leading to 'a very productive time, which provides an opportunity for self expression and confidence building'. For many it was the best part of the PGCE course and 'possibly the only time ideas could be pushed to their full potential with no constraints put on the project by mentors'. Not all the comments were positive. There was here, as well, some apparent confusion over roles at times and a plea for more preparation time - but overall AIR, like ITP, is clearly seen by students in these evaluation questionnaires, as an extremely valuable and productive introduction to the world of the classroom.

Conclusion

The first two concerns for this chapter were partnership and mentoring experiences in areas such as art and physical education and awareness of student views on partnership and mentoring experiences. The above discussion indicates the contribution that research at Cardiff Institute hopes to make to these areas of secondary ITT partnership study. The third concern was to explore the 'theory practice gap' debate in the context of a continuing role for HEI tutors in these experiences of AIR and ITP, which can be seen to be at variance with research and experience emanating from Cambridge and Oxford Universities.

In many respects it is possible to see the AIR and ITP projects at Cardiff as belonging to an earlier tradition of informal partnership developments with schools, involving collaboration between HEI tutors, students and teachers, which is perhaps best known in the context of IT-Inset work based at the University of Leicester (Everton and Impey 1989). It can be argued that more recent partnership research and experience has moved the debate on to one where the key factor in complementing the different forms of knowledge which tutors and teachers may deploy in their engagement with student teachers, is establishing the proper domains rather than collaboration which involves teacher educators in work in the classroom. Much of this is, of course, common sense and is accepted by all involved in the process of teacher education. However, it may be possible that a form of 'teacher-education political correctness' is in danger of developing here which is seen to frown upon examples of practices such as AIR and ITP which all involved in the Cardiff course, especially students, find so worthwhile.

In the examples looked at in the Cardiff research, teacher educators do bring skills and craft knowledge to their work in classrooms with teachers and students. As they are teachers in HEIs, so they remain teachers, in these instances, in schools. The robe is seamless and the quality of the garment is better. To maintain that 'teacher educators are not teachers' is an absurdity, in this context at least and one suspects in many others. There remains a commitment at Cardiff to procedures such as AIR and ITP as a way of tackling the 'theory practice gap' and within the constraints of the current scene in ITT to extending these practices - as an historian I look forward to working with students as 'historians-in-residence'.

In his critique of the Oxford University Internship Scheme, Professor Paul Hirst observes that one aspect of this pioneering development in teacher education which still needs working through is the role that tutors have in relation to students' practical school experience. He argues that tutors need to understand student individual practical professionalism if they are to help them critically reflect on the principles they currently accept in their own practice (Hirst in Benton 1990). This is a laudable aim as we all seek to overcome the 'theory practice gap'. Our initial research at Cardiff encourages us in our belief that at times we need to involve tutors in school teaching with students and mentors to achieve this.

Acknowledgements I wish to thank the students and the course teams of the PGCE art and design and physical education courses and in particular the subject leaders, Julia Longville and John O'Neil, for their assistance.

194

16 The mentoring process in initial teacher education: The respective roles of personnel in a pilot school-based scheme

Judith Dormer

Introduction

This chapter examines the progress of a school-based programme for training PGCE students as it has evolved in its pilot year in a large comprehensive school. My own experience in ITE has been first as a secondary teacher with responsibility for students in traditional teacher training schemes, secondly as the mentor of an articled teacher, and more recently as a principal subject tutor for the pilot scheme.

The aims of the research

My previous research into the nature of the mentoring roles and processes as developing in ITE has led me to argue that successful mentoring is encouraged where there is a framework or structure to support it, and to propose a possible framework for use in the continuum of teacher education (Dormer 1994). This framework (Figure 16.1) suggests that the mentoring role is defined by the needs of the protégé, and the position of the mentor in the institution. For example, a student in the first term of teaching practice will be challenged by discussion, ideas, and formative assessment. Newly qualified teachers nearing the end of their first year may need career advice, reference and preparation for possible appraisal.

Level One

SUPPORT	confidence; listening; developing trust; provision of a 'holding' environment (Daloz 1986: 212)
CHALLENGE	stimulation by provision of ideas and resources: assessment by negotiation as a form of continuous development; positive expectations
VISION	inspiration and motivation

Level Two

SUPPORT	providing structure and a sense of identity and place within it; enabling; the emergence of mutual benefit
CHALLENGE	providing professional development/career opportunities; assessment including possible appraisal/job references
VISION	the overview of the institution; awareness of developing initiative and current trends

Figure 16.1: An extended two level model of support, challenge and vision (Dormer 1994: 133).

The deliberate approach to learning to teach as used in the pilot scheme also provides a structure for mentoring. It defines the complementary roles of mentors within a scaffolding for training teachers. Within this context the intention of my research was:

1. to investigate the reaction of participants directly involved in the scheme in my own institution - mentors, students, and university personnel;

2. to examine the complementary nature of the mentoring roles, and the way in which the deliberate approach to learning defined a structure for these roles;

3. to determine whether this framework had been a useful tool in expediting the mentoring processes, the integration of theory with practice, and the development of professionals with critical reflective faculties.

The initial teacher training scheme

The scheme in question is based on a model for mentoring incorporated within 'the deliberate approach to learning to teach' (Harvard and Dunne 1992: 40). Teaching is presented as a complex activity as devised by nine dimensions of teaching.

The nine dimensions of teaching: a summary

Dimension 0: Ethos. Mutual respect between teacher and taught, a shared sense of purpose, a spirit of co-operation.

Dimension 1: Direct Instruction. Includes the ability to tell, describe, demonstrate and explain.

Dimension 2: Management of Materials. The preparation, provision, selection and design of consumable materials, hardware and visual aids.

Dimension 3: Guided Practice. The design and implementation of appropriate tasks to allow the memorisation of selected facts and practice of skills, processes and routines, which have utility or lead to the development of important concepts.

Dimension 4: Structured Conversation. The ability to elicit pupils' perspectives, enable them the listen to each other, and provide and draw attention to conflicting ideas.

Dimension 5: Monitoring. The active thoughtful role of the teacher in collecting information about pupils, sensitively interpreting this information, and using it to guide action.

Dimension 6: Management of Order. The development of a classroom which is orderly, busy and productive.

Dimension 7: Planning and Preparation. Planning to enable children to learn in a classroom with an appropriate ethos, paying attention to the variety of modes of teaching, to the management of order, and to the monitoring of children's work.

Dimension 8: Written Evaluation. The process of collection and interpretation of data to enable deliberate reflection on the student's progress.

Students are supported as they progress through increasing levels of competence in these dimensions by three mentors: the subject mentor known as the principal subject tutor, the co-tutor, primarily a colleague with an overview of the school context, and the university tutor(s).

Mentoring is seen as an organic process and the scheme encourages a model of teaching which:

> with its emphasis on the continuing development of performance, intellectual processes and schema, has pointed to some clearly defined complementary roles in mentoring... (Dunne and Harvard 1993: 128).

The instructional design (Figure 16.2) defines areas for examination by the student together with the co-tutor in a number of supervisory conferences. This model, together with an agenda compiled by the student and annotated by the principal subject tutor, is central to the development of the student during the school-based programme. The agenda consists of the student's intention within the classroom, and focuses on one or more of the dimensions. The principal subject tutor annotates the agenda making an accurate record of the episode of teaching as it takes place. The student then works on the agenda drawing on areas defined by the instructional design in preparation for a supervisory conference and assessment on the dimension(s) selected.

During the supervisory conference the co-tutor works on the cognitive development of the student, using the prepared agendas. Co-tutors are not subject based and exhibit 'professional naviety' during the process of challenging the student to examine and develop their performance. Emphasis is placed on the independence of the student as a self-directing professional with responsibility for their own development.

INSTRUCTIONAL DESIGN		
understanding of how children learn	nine dimensions of teaching	syntactic substantive subject-matter knowledge
	example of teaching	
research and theoretical work	National Curriculum and other statutory requirements	traditional lore of teachers (often in craft knowledge)

Figure 16.2: Instructional design

My own perceptions of the mentoring roles within the scheme in action are summarised as follows.

1.   The principal subject tutor is responsible for:

- inducting the students in their subject areas;

- arranging the 'nuts and bolts' of the teaching programme;

- seeing to the day to day needs (pastoral and resourcing) of the student;

- providing access to the craft skills of teaching;

- providing 'episodes' for modelling by the student;

- helping the student develop an 'annotated agenda' for later discussion and development;

- liaising with co-tutors, class teacher and university tutors;

- providing 'off the cuff' formative assessment through reflection

199

and ongoing discussion with the student;

- helping students prepare and apply for their first teaching posts.

2.   The co-tutor is responsible for:

- reflection of teaching episodes, through discussion of the 'annotated agenda';

- the formulation of action plans for the future;

- ensuring that formative and summative assessments of the school-based practice are carried out and fed back to the university;

- enabling - by providing resources for examination of whole school issues and an overview of the whole school context;

- liaising between the two institutions as well as individual personnel.

3.   The university tutor is responsible for:

- the construction of the course - definition of the theory upon which it is based, and the mechanics and devices by which it will proceed;

- the induction of the students into the university and the course;

- the practical arrangements necessary to match students with schools;

- oversight of the student through the progressive phases of the course;

- final assessment and moderation.

The data collection

Thirteen personnel, six PGCE students, four mentors and three university tutors, were interviewed. This is obviously a small sample of those taking part in the scheme in the South West and can only be seen as a 'school's eye view'. Respondents were working within three departments taking part in the pilot scheme. Departments A and B traditionally had close working relationships between the two institutions, but department C did not. The university personnel in the departments A and B were committed to the pilot scheme and had managerial responsibilities within it in addition to their tutoring roles. The university tutor for department C was on a temporary one-year contract with no previous experience as a university tutor. The relevant experience, commitment and attitudes of these departments was an important factor in the development of the students.

Semi-structured interviews took place in the final term of the academic year 1993-1994 when students had been formally assessed and were coming to the end of their main school experience. Interview schedules consisted of questions examining the relative importance and success of the mentoring roles and processes and the course structure in determining the following:

- the support, development and assessment of the students;

- the integration of theory and practice, with opportunities to critically reflect on both;

- outcomes in terms of perceptions of students' competence and the implications for future course developments including possible autonomy of schools in ITE.

The roles of personnel responsible for student support, development and assessment, and the effect of the course framework upon them

Respondents felt that the personnel responsible for students' progress were the principal subject tutor, the co-tutor, and the university tutor together with the staff of the school, especially other class teachers and the students themselves. Many felt that the responsibility was shared by a partnership of these participants, but the students from department C nominated only their peers and the subject department.

1.   *The role of the principal subject tutor*

The quality of the relationship with the principal subject tutor was felt to be crucial by everyone. Fortunately all students and subject tutors felt that they were good. Subject tutors were seen by the students as personal, specific within teaching, reservoirs of advice and support, and the main supervisors and assessors of their school experience. By the co-tutors they were seen as having a major role in assessment of classroom practice, but surprisingly second in responsibility for the quality of challenge and support. University tutors felt that subject tutors had a part to play in school-based competence and 'providing they are aware of the relevant issues and not all are'. The subject tutor from department C felt that his was by far the most important role in the students' development, but another subject tutor saw himself in a target-setting overview role and as a buffer between extreme activities within his department.

In general subject tutors found the structure imposed by the deliberate approach to learning helpful, but there were reservations. Conflicts arose in the expectation of their roles as defined by the course structure and the reality in practice. No formal time was allotted by the school for the role of subject tutor. University expectations were that they were not responsible for assessment, and that the majority of contact would be in the classroom, providing agendas for discussion with the co-tutor, modelling episodes for the student and ad hoc discussion. In reality the bulk of the organisation for induction, time-tabling and resources fell upon the subject tutor, together with gathering information for assessment and providing written assessments for use by the co-tutors. All subject tutors found it difficult to find time to induct other classroom teachers fully in the mechanisms of the scheme.

The gradual induction of students in the classroom was found to be beneficial despite some initial difficulty found by pupils, students and teachers inexperienced in sharing their classes in sometimes knowing who was in fact in control!

Reactions to the Nine Dimensions were mixed. They were found to be a useful framework by most participants if used flexibly.

2.   *The role of the co-tutor*

There were conflicting views from the students. Those from department C felt that the process with the co-tutor was a waste of time (and each had a different co-tutor). They saw it as bureaucratic, entailing unnecessary preparation. Both they and one of the other students were unable to see the value if the co-tutor did not see them in the classroom. The perception of the other three students was much clearer. They found the process valuable and were able to identify the contrasting roles of their school-based mentor, appreciating both the close involvement of the subject mentor and the more objective 'professional naivety' of the co-tutor. Both principal subject tutors felt the role of the co-tutors worked well within the scheme and one recognised the value of 'significant pressure' applied by the co-tutors, as did the university tutors. They felt that co-tutors, as did the university tutors. They felt that co-tutors should challenge the students 'forcing them to explain and justify'.

Co-tutors themselves were clear about their roles as defined by the course and felt that the Nine Dimensions were useful - particularly in the early part of the students' development. The attitude of the students together with their preparation was seen to be fundamental to success.

3.   *The role of the university tutors*

University tutors were generally felt to be vital, even when as often happened they were the focus of criticism, 'a useful scapegoat' as seen by one subject tutor. Those who were seen as good were greatly appreciated, and those who were seen as poor were resented for their lack of contribution both in terms of course structure and presence in school. They were not thought to be unnecessary. Students, even those who said that the school-based part of the course was overridingly important, seemed to see the university tutor as an umbilical cord. One co-tutor emphasised the role of the university in providing an external overview. University tutors' reactions to the course structure were mixed. The concept of professional naivety was felt to be useful as was the preparation of agendas if used flexibly. The Nine Dimensions came in for most criticism. It was felt that although they could provide a useful structure to analyse practice and feed into supervisory conferences they should not be used exclusively, and one tutor felt the criteria should be rewritten so as to be subject specific.

4.   *The role of the student*

The responsibility for the students in their overall development was stressed by two of the university students, and by a number of other respondents in particular areas - in particular subject knowledge and reorientation. The opportunity for peer support was highly valued. Cross-curricular support from students in other departments was appreciated and was felt to be an

203

alternative support if schools could not accept two students in the same subject area.

The role of the agenda in encouraging students to take responsibility for their own learning was felt to be crucial if used appropriately, and students from departments in the school and the university who facilitated this use fared better. It was clear that students from department C were ill-prepared by the university in its use, and were initially not encouraged to develop it by the subject department in the school. They saw little relevance or importance in any part of their course that did not relate directly to classroom practice.

In contrast the other students saw value in the structure as long as there was the flexibility in its use - especially as they became increasingly autonomous.

The roles of personnel and the effect of the course framework upon the integration of, and critical reflection upon, theory and practice

Three main elements appear to be key to these issues:

- partnership and communication in planning and implementation;

- timing of the elements within the structure of the course;

- finding the time (with all the implications for resourcing) necessary to ensure a deeper awareness of relevant theoretical and practical issues.

There was an attempt to broach all the relevant areas of the course theoretically by the university tutors in the first term. This was followed by two school-based terms with the emphasis on classroom practice. Attempts were made to link theory with practice in three main ways. First the students were given a number of written assignments. Secondly the instructional design encouraged them to draw on theory in preparation for the supervisory conferences and discussion with co-tutors. Thirdly they returned to the university for regular seminar days with university tutors. Although theoretical issues were still felt to be mainly the province of the university there has already been a blurring of roles. One very perceptive student nominated all three tutors as sharing in the development of a range of issues including the theory of learning and child development. She was also very clear about the relative value of the institutions involved and the importance of revisiting theory to support the practice.

Dunne and Jennings stress the importance of 'breaks with experience' (1994: 11). They emphasise that this model is dependent on students having sufficient time to think about teaching thus providing the opportunity for cognitive development. They draw attention to the need to challenge student-teachers' perspectives by providing conflicting ideas and fostering thoughtful consideration.

Respondents found that these aims had been partly met. Reflection was felt to have taken place in a number of ways. First, informal reflection took place alone, with peers and with subject tutors. Secondly, more formal opportunities were available in supervisory conferences and seminar days. However all participants felt that there was insufficient time in three main areas: firstly to plan the integration of theory with practice so that schools were fully aware of what was intended by the university; secondly to create opportunities for ongoing informal reflection with peers and principal subject tutors; thirdly to cover all the taught elements in the first term, and subsequently for students to adequately complete assignments whilst under the pressure of school-based practice.

Outcomes in terms of perceptions of students' competence and the implications for future course developments including possible autonomy of schools in ITE

1. *Student competence*

The majority of the respondents felt that the course had prepared the students as well if not better than traditional HEI based courses of ITE. There were, however, several provisos. First it was recognised that this is a pilot course. We have still to see what happens when the students take up full-time appointments, and when a wider range of schools is included. The pilot schools were selected and chose to participate. Secondly, one university tutor felt that although the course produced students who were more competent in the classroom he feared that they would have 'less rich and broader based practitioner skills'. Finally the students in department C felt that they succeeded 'despite the course rather than because of it'.

2. *The perceived strengths and weakness of the course*

The main strengths of the course were seen in terms of the quality of the school experience. The advantages were seen as the more gradual initiation of the student in the classroom, the eighteen / six week split of school-based practice which enabled a greater depth of school immersion and classroom experience, and the opportunity to have a second school experience. Most respondents saw it as a genuine attempt to improve on existing schemes - a good course structure with small flaws to be ironed out in the future.

The major weakness mentioned by more than half the respondents was the lack of personal contact with university tutors, and the fact that students, particularly those who were less aware, tended to divorce themselves from the theory once in schools. A university tutor feared a loss of objectivity with the declining role of the university.

The university tutor from department C felt the main weaknesses were a confusion about roles, and the geographical spread which made it difficult to visit schools as much as he would have liked.

3.   *Possible future developments in course design*

Positive developments suggested were:

- the inclusion of classroom teachers in the mentor training programme;

- increased contact at all stages between staff from both institutions;

- more information on assignments given by the university so that schools could assist the students in carrying them out;

- built in time for reflection, perhaps with more contact in clusters of schools.

It was recognised however that many of these depended on greater funding. Several school-based mentors recognised the need for the students to have a break from experience and felt that they had imposed too heavy a timetable.

When asked whether school could be autonomous in ITE the subject mentor from department C felt that schools could and should go it alone. However other respondents felt that, although there might be a blurring and transferring of responsibilities, the way forward at present was to develop the partnership.

Conclusion

The framework of the deliberate approach to learning provides a structure within which mentors feel they can operate successfully. Mentors felt that, although a degree of rigour should be used in assessing the students to prepare for supervisory conferences, a degree of flexibility and creativity should be used in two main areas. Firstly, whilst both agendas and the Nine Dimensions of teaching provided a useful structure for mentors to aid student development, their use should not exclude other rich areas for exploration. Secondly, as the practice progressed and students achieved greater autonomy in the classroom, their use in lessons and conferences was felt to be more limited.

It was thought important to critically challenge the students' perspective, and to allow them sufficient 'breaks with experience' as defined by Buchmann and Floden (1993). Perhaps by ensuring appropriate challenge and the opportunity for critical reflection we might avoid the possible narrowing effect of the 'sitting with Nellie' apprenticeship model.

The comparison of departments A and B with that of C indicates that commitment and preparation of participants is a key factor. This appeared to be more important than the personality of the co-tutor. Efforts made to break down any traditional conflict between institutions by involvement and 'ownership' of the scheme by all participants might be helpful. Mentor training which included preparation of classroom teachers would help in the delivery of the structure in school, although this training might be school-based.

Integration of theory and practice needs developing through communication between the course planners and the participants in school. In this way issues could be presented with relevance to both the immediate school environment and wider educational context. Resources are needed to allow the development of theory and practice, and space for critical reflection.

Whereas schools could 'go it alone', most participants are wholeheartedly in favour of a partnership between personnel from both school and HEIs. A clear definition of roles and responsibilities can be balanced by blurring and sharing knowledge and skills.

17 Managing time within the initial teacher training partnership: Chenderit's first year as an internship school

Trevor Arrowsmith

Context

Chenderit is an 11-18 mixed, comprehensive school, situated about three miles north-east of Banbury, and 23 miles north of Oxford. Rather confusingly, the school's Oxon post code conceals its allegiance to Northamptonshire LEA. Of the 960 pupils, around 165 constitute the Sixth form. The catchment consists of rural villages (70 per cent of pupils arrive by bus), and the suburbs of Banbury. The school caters for the full ability range in what is a truly comprehensive intake.

It is appropriate to mention the achievement of pupils, since one of the key reasons for our involvement in initial teacher training is central to it. If we take GCSE results as one indicator of successful learning, the development between 1986 and 1993 can be represented by the increase in Year 11 pupils gaining five A - C passes from 32 per cent to 51 per cent.

The key to this improvement has been the consistent and multifaceted focus on learning with staff and pupils. Central to this focus and improvement in learning is the constant regeneration of our diverse and flexible staff development provision. As horizontal staffing structures are as valued as vertical ones it is logical and effective for staff development to be managed by a mixed group of staff.

This provision has for six years included work with PGCE students, including input into courses at Warwick University, Oxford University and Westminster College, Oxford. Students from these institutions and Bedford College have also visited Chenderit for school experience. In this context, it was natural, despite the pressures of National Curriculum changes ('developments'), and other internally generated work, to consider entering into a partnership with an HE institution to manage initial teacher training.

Why get involved with initial teacher training?

A central motivation is the opportunity it presents to sharpen debate and critical reflection on good classroom practice and school improvement with a number of staff. We also value the curriculum input available from HE staff. In a time of increasing stratification of the education system, experience of effective comprehensive education is vital if new teachers are to appreciate its relevance.

Why enter into a partnership with Oxford University and Westminster College?

The Internship PGCE course reflects our values and approach to ITT. The scheme has been tried, tested and developed over the last six years. The increase in the number of partnership schools over this period is one indicator of success of the Internship Scheme. Geographically, the M40 provides direct access for students between Chenderit and Oxford.

Main elements within the Internship Scheme

The post-graduate Internship Scheme meets the requirements of Department for Education Circular 9/92. The distinctive features of Internship are:

- the uniting of Oxford University Department for Educational Studies with Westminster College, Oxford, as the HE side of the partnership;

- the use of college and school staff to support the intern - this consists of a college general tutor and curriculum tutor, a school professional tutor and subject mentor;

- the professional tutor co-ordinates all activities related to internship in his/her school;

- the students' incremental and protracted experience in one school (initially two days a week, later five days a week);

- this is complemented by an experience in another school towards the conclusion of the course in June;

- the division of the course into two phases: the first concerned with developing the intern's understanding and competence; the second is particularly concerned with development of self-analytical and reflective powers;

- the complementary arrangement of written projects and classroom experience which encourage interns to relate their own perceptions and teaching experience to the pedagogy and a specific school context; the focus is both subject-based and professional issue based;

- continuous assessment through profiling, with a structured emphasis on self-assessment and reflection; this is complemented by three assessment points (interviews akin to Individual Action Plan interviews) during the course.

The management of time at Chenderit School

When involvement in the Internship Scheme was initially explored with staff, the availability, creation, use and management of time were the issues most frequently raised and discussed. Using a school effectiveness approach to these issues, the following estimated data are of significance.

To summarise, these are the (rather alarming) hours required to service the Internship Scheme at Chenderit, assuming a 12 week term.

STAFF	WEEKLY (hrs)	TERMLY (hrs)
A Mentor	3.5	46.6 (incl. termly meetings etc)
A Professional Tutor	2.75	41.5 (incl. termly meetings etc)
A Form Tutor	1.0	15 (incl. termly meetings etc)
A Head of Year	-	1.0
A Subject Teacher	2.0	2.0 (incl. termly meetings etc)

Total Staff Hours: 69.75 (weekly) 697 (termly) - see Table 17.1 (p.206)

Note: these are maximum figures and apply particularly to the January - March term when the interns are in school five days a week, with the exception of weeks one and two. The Total Staff Hours reflects involvement of nine mentors, three professional tutors, ten form tutors, four year heads and ten other staff (discussed below). The weekly figures apply to 24 out of 39 school weeks annually; the figures exclude pre-course and other training time.

211

With these time requirements, how does the scheme run at Chenderit?

This section moves from the school effectiveness stance above to one focusing on school improvement. Clearly, if staff were to be released to compensate for time devoted to internship, the cost would be prohibitive to the school, the University, and the DFE. (Our annual ITT budget from the University is £6,000 with an additional £3,000 in curriculum services.) Further, discontinuity of teaching would render the scheme unworkable.

If, alternatively, staff were remunerated, say six staff each awarded a temporary increment of one point for additional responsibilities, then quality would surely suffer both for ITT and pupils taught by these six staff. Chenderit's solution is provided by the school's existing culture. It is characterised by an inclusive management approach in which horizontal staff structures encourage the involvement of a broad range of staff in leading and managing developments. Pressures on staff are reduced at Chenderit by devolving responsibilities as widely as possible.

Mentors and other staff are involved in every stage of the planning and development of the scheme, including agreed dates and formats for evaluation. Commitment to participation in Internship in 1994-1995 is dependent on agreement over the benefits of this year's scheme.

Internship and the style of its adoption is in keeping with Chenderit's values. For four of the five subject areas involved, we have two mentors for each pair of students. The exception is history, where one of the potential mentors is professional tutor. We are the only internship school, to our knowledge, to 'double-up' staff in this way. In addition to reducing work-load and ensuring wider participation of school staff, the arrangement ensures that intern students can benefit from a broad range of subject expertise. Similarly, we have three professional tutors who support specific intern students and mentors.

The involvement of form tutors as 'pastoral mentors' was a conscious decision to widen staff involvement in the scheme and Interns' involvement in the life of the school. Subject mentors are not pastoral mentors. Other staff were also recruited to provide interns with brief alternative form tutoring experiences prior to their main placement with a pastoral mentor.

Mentors are encouraged to make use of supply cover to compensate to a limited extent for the hour per week spent counselling each intern. They take this release time in a pattern which suits them. Several staff prefer to take five hours as a block per half term, others prefer a different hour each week to avoid discontinuity with a particular teaching group. The financial consequence is a saving; staff tend not to take their full entitlement of release time. Professional tutors and form tutors can make use of release time, but, again, tend only to do so at crisis points.

Another concern about time

How would you feel if you knew that your Year 7 daughter was being taught by a student during maths, English and German lessons between February and May. Mentors, year heads and professional tutors discussed this issue and agreed that an acceptable norm would involve a pupil encountering interns in no more than two subjects. As interns, for the majority of the time, work with or observe the regular teacher, this seems a reasonable expectation.

Staff agreed that a more realistic and positive view was that there are many benefits to pupils from this arrangement, including additional teacher intervention and the possibility of groups of pupils working independently of the main class. Careful planning is required since access to pupils tends to be concentrated on Years 7-10, with occasional Year 12 involvement.

An evaluation of time management within the 1993-1994 scheme including implications for the 1994-1995 scheme

This evaluation involved discussion of the seven points above which summarise Chenderit's approach to the management of time with the following: interns, mentors, professional tutors, form tutors, year heads, several other teachers and the university general tutor and three curriculum tutors. The following evaluation points were noted by more than one respondent.

1.   *Wide and sustained involvement of staff in the planning and development of the scheme*

All Chenderit staff commented on the helpful degree of consultation, both prior to the scheme and during the year. Several staff mentioned that the inclusion of previously agreed key internship dates in the school calendar from September had helped by allowing them to plan for demanding periods.

2.   *Participating staff see internship as aligned with Chenderit's model of good practice*

Staff commented that the flexibility of internship which allows students to

213

progress at their own pace was similar in conception to the school's belief that pupils have individual needs which we try to meet in a variety of ways. The management of the scheme reflected existing good practice in school. When problems were raised, solutions were agreed with staff and interns. Where appropriate, practices were not uniform across subject areas, but they did meet interns' needs and PGCE course requirements. The mix of frantic and less pressured times during the year was seen as an advantage by the majority of staff and interns.

3.   *The involvement of nine mentors with ten intern students*

This was well received by school and college staff. Only the lone history mentor felt he would not wish to work with two interns again. He was particularly unfortunate because one history intern was frequently absent through illness. This caused a considerable additional burden for the mentor who could only occasionally turn to his professional tutor history colleague for support. During 1994-1995 we may request one history student only. With the above exception, mentors tended to share duties with their pair of interns, thus ensuring the benefits to students outlined above.

4.   *The involvement of three professional tutors*

Although university staff and some mentors admitted that they had initially been a little concerned about the co-ordination of the scheme in school if three professional tutors were to be involved, they all agreed that it had worked well. This stemmed from a clearly communicated division of duties between the three professional tutors and one professional tutor with an overview of the entire scheme. On-going discussions between all staff involved in the scheme took place in addition to formally convened meetings. This is the 'intense interaction and communication' identified as central to school improvement by Fullan (cited in Hopkins 1986: 92).

5.   *The form tutor as pastoral mentor*

This was seen to work well by staff an interns, although the interns would have liked a freer hand in choosing their placements. We did sound them out initially, but would have had five interns attached to the same year group.

6.   *The flexible use of supply cover*

This was appreciated by mentors who said they would be unlikely to make greater use of the supply budget even though direct funding to schools for 1994-1995 is to be increased by 40 per cent because they would be concerned about leaving their classes.   Two mentors in different areas asked for a timetabled reduction of an hour per week in their 1994-1995 teaching allocation to avoid discontinuity; this is being explored.

   School staff were aware of the substantial amount of time that they invested in the interns, but did not usually resent this for one or all of the following reasons. They gained considerable satisfaction from the progress of the interns even when it had been slow.   Their involvement with the interns enhanced their own professional and personal self-regard.   They viewed as useful to their pupils the sharpening of their reflective powers.   The need to articulate descriptions of their own classroom practice and the reasons behind them was seen as professional development which directly improved their own teaching.   This point recalls research by Barbara Jaworski where she quotes a mentor:

> 'Needing to express my own analysis of an event and account for it to someone else, enabled me to be more critical of my own thinking. This put me in a better position for future action.' (Jaworski 1993: 41).

7.   *The allocation of interns to subject classes*

The maximum norm of two interns per pupil was generally felt to have been successful.   There had been some difficulty in monitoring this in Years 9 and 10, owing to non-tutor group grouping and the use of rotations in some subjects.   However, after studious completion of pupil year lists by mentors, only four pupils were identified as having worked with these, rather than two interns during the Spring term.   Staff, and the few pupils interviewed, confirmed that the presence of interns was stimulating and helpful to pupils' learning. This is a reflection of the appropriateness of mentoring strategies.

Conclusion

The research suggests that aligning approaches to ITT with the values and culture of the school is central to the success of the partnership.   One consequence of this at Chenderit is to reduce the significance of the financial arrangements for the success of the partnership in favour of a range of school improvement factors.

It may also suggest that hierarchical school structures, in which delegation and staff autonomy are more limited, would find difficulty in adopting the scheme for financial reasons and possibly in terms of effectiveness for interns, staff and pupils. Chenderit's approach to the management of time has ensured wide staff involvement, with consequent benefits for interns, staff and pupils.

Table 17.1: An estimate of teacher time used in the maintenance of ITT at Chenderit

Time Required For	Weekly Hours	Termly Hours
Each Teacher Mentor		
Meeting with Intern	1	
Pre and post lesson discussion	1.5	
Liaison with professional tutor	0.5	
Other liaison	0.5	
College curriculum meeting		1.5 (excl. travel)
Profiling point		0.5
School meeting with curriculum tutor		1.5
School mentor meeting		1
TOTAL (assume 12 wk term)	**3.5**	**46.5**
Each Professional Tutor		
Professional development session delivery	0.5	
Liaison with mentors	1	
Liaison with interns	1	
Liaison with general tutor	0.25	
Professional development session planning		5
School mentor meeting		1
College professional tutor meeting		1.5 (excl. travel)
Profiling point		1
TOTAL (assume 12 wk term)	**2.75**	**41.5**

Each Form Tutor		
Form tutor mentoring	1	
Liaison with HOY/professional tutors and other staff		3
TOTAL (assume 12 wk term)	**1**	**15**
Additional Support by Individual Teachers		
Delivery and planning of PDP sessions	2	
HOY liaison with form tutors and interns		1
TOTALS (assume 12 wk term)	**2***	**3***

Note: different staff are involved each week, in addition to professional tutors.

18 Comparing HEAPs with SAPs: Initial teacher education in the secondary sector

Rosalind Goodyear, Ian Abbot, Linda Evans and Alan Pritchard

Introduction

With Kenneth Clarke's announcement, in January 1992, that 80 per cent of initial teacher education should take place in schools, the government declared its commitment to shift initial teacher education from higher education into schools. This fuelled the debate over initial teacher education which is the key issue of the 1994 Education Act.

The debate over where, and how, teachers should be trained is not new. Its recent history may be traced back to several sources: to Professor David Hargreaves' advocacy of the use of 'teaching schools' in a role similar to teaching hospitals in medical training; to Baroness Warnock's (1985) suggestion of a role of teacher tutor to the pioneering teacher training partnership model of the Oxford Internship (see McIntyre and Hagger 1992), and the Articled Teacher Scheme, introduced after the 1988 Education Reform Act.

The government's commitment to much more school-based initial teacher education heralded by the Consultation Document 40/92 (DES 1992b), is reflected in the reforms stipulated in Circular 9/92 (DFE 1992), which require PGCE secondary students to be trained in higher education/school partnerships and to spend a minimum of 66% of their courses in schools.

The government's proposals for the reform of initial teacher training

The so called Blue Paper (DFE 1993b), which set out the government's proposals for the future administration and funding of initial teacher education, goes further down the path of removing teacher training from higher education. Focusing on choice and diversity, the Blue Paper proposed a reduction of the length of undergraduate initial teacher education courses from four to three years, with financial incentives to encourage higher education institutions to offer three year degrees.

More significantly, in relation to the PGCE for secondary school teaching, the government initiated a scheme for the establishment of school-administered, rather than higher education-administered, programmes:

> ... the government has proposed some specific new approaches; in particular, a scheme for encouraging consortia of schools to offer postgraduate courses. Groups of schools pioneering this approach will be recruiting students for September 1993 and January 1994. There is evident interest, particularly from secondary schools, in proposals to expand this scheme (DFE 1993b:4).

Government commitments to the promotion and funding of shorter, more intensive BEd courses and school-administered courses have been further underlined in Circular 14/93 (DFE 1993d paras 20,27).

It is on the comparative effectiveness of the new, school-administered, PGCE programmes that the research outlined in this paper focuses. The study which we describe and discuss below is funded by the Association of Teachers and Lecturers and is being carried out by a research team from the Teacher Development Research and Dissemination Unit at Warwick University's Institute of Education.

The research

What it aims to achieve

The justification for change to educational policy lies in the perceived improvements which its implementation will bring. The rationale for the changes to secondary PGCE training which are being implemented is predicated upon more effective and efficient teacher training than that which current approaches achieve. Our main research aim, therefore, is to assess the relative effectiveness of secondary PGCE training in consortia of schools which are responsible for administering the training, when compared with courses which represent partnerships between schools and higher education. We refer to these two models as SAPs (School Administered Programmes) and HEAPs (Higher Education Administered Programmes) respectively. Our choice of terminology (see Abbott and Evans 1994) was prompted by the evident confusion surrounding the interpretation of what is meant by 'school-based'. The term is an ambiguous description in the light of the increasingly school-based focus in response to the requirements of Circular 9/92 of many higher education-administered PGCE courses. Furlong et al. (1988) use the term in inverted commas and point out that, because of the disparity amongst the courses used in their study, '... what school-based training meant would vary significantly' (p. 13). Similarly, Edwards (1992) refers to 'school-based' as a 'slogan', about whose interpretation there remains uncertainty and which still needs to be defined and understood. Moreover, confusion over terminology has been exacerbated by considerable ignorance of the existence of the SAPs.

Clearly, making comparisons involves value judgements which determine criteria for appropriateness or effectiveness. If, as Edwards (1992) argues, the government's current stance on initial teacher education reflects the view that higher education-administered training promulgates 'outmoded egalitarian and progressive ideas', then the government's criteria for the effectiveness and appropriateness of its reforms would include the reduction of such ideological influence upon student teachers; an influence which, Edwards (1992) suggests, is exaggerated to the extent of being mythical.

We have included in our research agenda consideration of the extent to which specific models of initial teacher education evidently promote particular ideologies, attitudes and philosophies of education. For the most part, though, our research aims to focus upon the contribution made by initial teacher education to teachers' professional development. We interpret 'teachers' professional development' as the process by which teachers' professionalism and professionality (see Hoyle 1975) may be enhanced, and we apply it to our study in a wide sense, to include the professional development of the teachers being trained, those involved in providing the training, and the teaching profession as a whole. This wide interpretation and application incorporates the significance to teacher development of the formulation of professional-related ideologies, philosophies and attitudes.

The research design

Our basic research design is that of a two year, comparative study of two models of PGCE secondary initial teacher education, as represented by:

> The SAP model one of the five 1993-1994 pilot school-administered programmes. The SAP used in our study consists of two consortia of schools, each consortium being relatively autonomous but ultimately under one directorship.

The HEAP model two separate PGCE programmes, each a partnership scheme administered by a higher education institution.

For each of these models, the research sample comprises all students registered in September 1993 and a sample of teacher mentors and, in the case of the HEAP model, a sample of higher education tutors. A sub-sample of the original sample of students is to be followed up in the year following PGCE training, taking the study into its second year. During this second year the sample will also include members of the teaching staff from the schools at which the former students are employed, and who have responsibility for supervising the newly qualified teachers' first year of teaching.

Data collection includes self-completion questionnaires and semi structured interviews and is designed to elicit answers to the specific research questions presented below.

The research questions

1. What are (i) students', (ii) higher education tutors' and (iii) teachers' perceptions of students' needs, requirements and preferences in relation to initial teacher education, and how effectively do they consider that they are being met/satisfied by the courses examined?

2. What are (i) students', (ii) higher education tutors' and (iii) teachers' perceptions of the implications of perceived course effectiveness, and what, if any, remedial measures do they suggest?

3. To what extend does each course fulfil criteria for effectiveness identified by the DFE (DES 1992) and by HMI (OFSTED 1993c)?

4. What evidence is there of initial teacher education courses influencing (i) attitudes, (ii) educational philosophy and ideology, (iii) teachers' professionality and (iv) practice?

5. What factors do newly qualified teachers consider have been influential on their professional development?

6. To what extent, and in what distinct ways, does each course contribute to the professional development of serving teachers involved in supervisory and/or mentoring roles?

7. To what extent, and in what distinct ways, is each course (i) cost-effective and (ii) manageable?

8. In relation to research questions 1. - 7. above, what differences, if any, are identifiable within (i) the student sample, (ii) the higher education tutor sample and (iii) the teacher sample, and between (i), (ii) and (iii), and what factors account for these differences?

The study's progress

At the time of writing, data collection planned for the first year of the, stages 1 to 3 (see Table 18.1), has been completed.

Questionnaires were completed by the entire student sample during the first weeks of their PGCE courses. Biographical data were obtained, and students indicated reasons influencing their choice of course, expectations and early impressions of the course. Also elicited were views on, and attitudes to, issues, including the role of higher education in PGCE teacher training, streaming, and the characteristics of a good teacher. End-of-course questionnaires have been used to obtain evidence of attitudinal change in relation to the same topics, students' evaluations of their courses and data on success at finding jobs. During the last weeks of the courses interviews with sub-samples of students, higher education tutors and teacher mentors provided qualitative evidence of individual perspectives and attitudes and the factors which have influenced them. During the second year the influence on the former students, who will then be newly qualified teachers, of workplace-specific factors such as colleagues, pupils, school professional climate and school leadership will be assessed and compared with the evident influence of initial teacher training. Follow-up interviews with the original student interviewee sub-sample are scheduled to take place during their third term as newly qualified teachers. These will provide evidence of individual perspectives and attitudes, the extent to which these have changed, if at all, since earlier stages of data collection, and of the reasons for any change.

The findings so far

Student satisfaction with overall course programmes

In many areas where student and staff opinion to teacher education was sought, there was overlap in the finding from the higher education administered (HEAP) and school administered (SAP) approaches. The most striking of these concerns student-teacher course satisfaction. Students tended simply to think well of their courses if, at the end of the year, they had been treated well in schools, especially their final teaching practice schools. Their criteria for good treatment were: a welcoming department; a variety of teaching and classes; and, most of all, positive supportive and explicitly encouraging teachers and mentors.

The initial questionnaires had revealed a considerable degree of dissatisfaction with courses early in the autumn term; this was centred on organisation, or rather a perceived lack of it. The criticism extended across both SAPs and HEAPs and was voiced by both students and school-staff mentors. But, by the end of the PGCE year, follow-up questionnaires and interviews showed that most of the student disgruntlement had been superseded by feelings of satisfaction and loyalty to courses which individuals felt had served them well. However, the second questionnaire, upon which this finding is based, was administered immediately after final teaching practice, when students knew, or assumed, that they had passed the course. It will be interesting to see whether student satisfaction has been maintained as NQT satisfaction in the summer term of 1995.

However, satisfaction was not universal, and one student, within each of the four student interviewee subsamples, HEAPs 1 and 2 and SAPs 1 and 2, was categorised as 'dissatisfied'. Two of these students had jobs, at the time of interview, two had not.

Course aims, rationales and procedures

The aim of all courses was to produce highly skilled teachers, competent throughout the range of design and technology subjects. However, within this, SAP philosophy emerged as focused more sharply upon the production of a course programme to deliver to trainees and which was linked to the explicitly vocational purpose of contributing to the reversal of the decline in British manufacturing industry. That of HEAPs was, by contrast, person-centred, focused on student-teachers and their initiation into a life of continuing, broad professional development.

Both types of course were supported by clearly written sets of management structures and course procedures, but those of HEAPs were the more comprehensive, detailed and reading available to students. SAPs, by their very devolved nature, were one or two degrees removed from their HEI administrative centre and that, combined with their relative lack of familiarity and with its formal procedures and administrative structure and practices, put the course participants and organisers at some disadvantage. SAPs were also subject to two different sets of administration, firstly from the HEI, outlined above, and secondly from their associated Trust steering committee.

Course structures and course programmes

All four courses had similar basic course components, covering knowledge and practical skills in a wide range of design and technology related subjects; skills and knowledge of teaching and learning in those subjects; knowledge of the National Curriculum, especially at Key Stages 3 and 4; issues associated with teaching at secondary level and within the current education system; and practical experience of teaching in at least two schools.

Neither of the two school administrated courses gave student teachers the most time in school on practical teaching. A higher education administrated course - HEAP 2 - did that. HEAPs also spent more time on broad-based issues than SAPs and both planned and taught their courses in three relatively separate and distinct components. The SAP structure, on the other hand, led to a much more integrated, developmental, five phase programme, which was very complex and extremely difficult to comprehend.

Assessment of the taught components of each of the four courses was similar; by means of sets of assignments associated with individual course components, or themes, but which could require students to make cross component, or phase, links. Assignments were spread through the courses, but continued closer to the end of the SAP than either of the HEAPs. Almost all written work linked taught with practical course elements. Only one, single assignment, in HEAP 2, was wholly literature-based. Booklists and journal reference lists were infrequent overall and non-existent in the material supplied from SAPs for this report.

Assessment of practical teaching was formally undertaken during the final, summer practice in all three course patterns. The first practice was, in all cases, diagnostic. There was a noticeable difference amongst courses in relation to the explicit setting out for students or school staffs, of information about the roles of teachers and mentors supporting and judging student competence; the role of the external examiner and detailed procedures, in the case of potential and actual student failure. Only one course, HEAP 2, had comprehensive, clear, concise, common guidelines for everyone concerned with the assessed practice. Other courses were less explicit and comprehensive. Both SAPs lacked detailed operational procedures for the monitoring of student assessed practice overall, or week-by-week and for warning of possible failure.

Students choices of course

There was a distinction between HEAP and SAP students in their preferred choices of PGCE course. The choices of HEAP students were influenced by such factors as personal, domestic circumstances and the geographical location of the HEI administrating the course. SAP students, on the other hand, based their applications for courses more on employment prospects; the financial incentive of the additional grant paid by the organisation which had initiated the course and was administrating it; course content and specifically school-centred focus.

Knowledge of other PGCE models

Students held widespread misconceptions about models of teacher training other than their own. SAP students typically underestimated the proportion of course time spent in schools by HEAP students and were unaware of Circular 9/92, which had affected those HEAP courses, as much as they had influenced the setting up of their own training programmes. This ignorance was not confined to students in training; many school-staff knew nothing of them either.

Students' perceptions of their courses

By the end of their courses most students displayed loyalty to the course model and particular programmes in which they had participated. The course advantage most frequently identified by SAP students was the high degree of immersion in school life and culture. However, many of the HEAP student interviewees made the same sorts of comments about the school experiences provided by their traditional courses. The evidence, so far, is that SAPs do not have any great advantage in respect of students' perceptions of having been immersed in school environments and cultures.

Students from all four courses displayed anxiety about and some dissatisfaction with the organisation and content of workshop skills components. It is clear from interviews with staff in schools and HEIs that there is a widespread and longstanding problem in enabling PGCE students, from a wide variety of backgrounds, to attain the broad range of craft and high technology skills required to teach Design and Technology. One HEAP has taken the step of launching a two year PGCE in 1994-1995 to overcome the problem.

226

Students from both HEAPs and SAPs experienced some difficulties in getting access to library resources, but these difficulties were more keenly felt by the two sets of SAP students. SAP students also highlighted the lack of peergroup socialisation, support and relationships.

Involvement in higher education

There was broad and persistent support amongst both HEAP and SAP participants for the involvement of higher education in teacher training. Support for the principle of that involvement was almost universal, as it was for the continued inclusion in PGCE courses of components which incorporated educational theory and professional studies. Student interviewees from all four subgroups agreed that higher education institutions provided a valuable focal point, physical location and setting for the development of student group identity, culture and support, on the one hand, and, on the other, an environment where they were able to step back and reflect upon their school experiences.

The SAP consortium which had brought-in expertise from higher education for their 1993-1994 programme, intended to continue with it in 1994-1995. The other SAP consortium which had not brought-in the regular services of a single higher education institution was negotiating to buy-in such provision in 1994-1995. SAP mentors generally favoured greater higher education involvement in courses that had occurred in 1993-1994.

Support from mentors and other staff

A general picture of satisfaction with support given by staff in all areas of courses emerged from interviews. There were variations concerning the degree of satisfaction expressed, but these constituted a second area of individual, school-specific or personality difference, not one related to course. Reports of support in school, ranging from excellent to poor, were provided within each subsample of interviewees. Individual personality clashes were the most commonly quoted cause for dissatisfaction, but it is quite clear that the structure of SAPs leaves them the more vulnerable to this influence, because the potential range of staff support is narrower in wholly school-based courses than where and HEI is also involved. The most extreme examples occurred where the designated mentor was also the head of department, and the only teacher whose classes an individual student took.

Mentors' views of courses

Mentors from all four subgroups interviewed were positive about their greater degree of involvement in initial teacher education as a result of Circular 9/92. HEAP mentors all declared their support for a school and higher education partnership; none was in favour of a wholly school-administered course. There was also consensus amongst SAP mentors for higher education involvement, and for a greater degree of involvement, in future programmes.

Remediation of course deficiencies

The directors and mentors involved in the SAP initiative were aware of and acknowledged organisational problems which had occurred during 1993-1994, and attributed them, at least in part, to the short, six week, period available for planning before the course commenced. An example cited by both SAP consortia directors was lack of co-ordination between professional studies and brought-in educational theory with the practically-orientated mentoring in schools.

With the exception of one mentor, whose dissatisfaction with the organisation of the consortium to which he belonged prompted him to withdraw his school's participation half-way through the year, the SAP mentors were committed to continued involvement in the initiative. They were also committed to improving the PGCE programme and reported plans for considerable remedial changes in the 1994-1995 programmes.

Enchanced professional development of mentors

Involvement in teacher training was reported by designated mentors in schools as beneficial for their own professional development, for the development of colleagues who had taken on student mentoring in an unofficial capacity and, in many cases, for entire departments. Support for the mentoring role and the greater involvement of serving teachers in initial training was almost universal.

Time for mentoring

The greatest constraint on mentoring was the time required to do it effectively. There was universal agreement that the time needed for mentoring was considerable. All mentors reported having had insufficient time in which to carry out their mentoring responsibilities. Mentors involved in the SAP initia-

228

tives reported greater demands on their time than those working in HEAPs, who shared responsibilities for organising and implementing the new, post 9/92, programmes in their schools. The problem of insufficient non-teaching time for mentoring was seen as insurmountable, since all conceivable solutions were perceived as threatening to the quality of mentors' teaching. All mentors ranked their commitments to pupils as of higher priority than that to student teachers and their training.

There was disquiet, within the subsample of SAP mentors interviewed, about the lack of mentor training for these demanding school-based programmes.

Counting the cost

Staff from HEAPs and SAPs were aware that the introduction of school-based initial teacher education had not been fully costed. As a result there was general agreement that schools in HEAPs and SAPs had not received sufficient funds to compensate for the amount of staff time involved.

At this stage in the research there is no evidence that a SAP is more cost effective than a HEAP. The transfer of resources to schools participating in a HEAP or SAP has not been a significant factor in encouraging participation. Financial details were difficult to obtain from either HEAPs or SAPs and more data are required to answer the key questions relating to costs and benefits.

Note

Full details of this research, together with an analytical commentary on the findings set out here, are to be found in: Evans, L., Abbot, I., Goodyear, R. and Pritchard, A., *Hammer and Tongue: the Training of Technology Teachers* (Interim report of the preliminary findings of the first year of a comparative study of school-administered and high education-administered secondary PGCE initial teacher training), published in 1995 by the Association of Teachers and Lecturers, who funded it.

Table 18.1: Data collection

	Method of Data Collection	Sample	
		HEAPs 1 & 2	SAPs 1 & 2
Stage 1	Questionnaire	All students	All students
Stage 2	Interview	Sub-sample of students corresponding mentors course tutors	Sub-sample of students SAP mentor in each school 3 SAP directors
Stage 3	Questionnaire	All students	All students
Stage 4	Interview	Sub-sample of former students, now NQTs supervising colleagues	Sub-sample of former students, now NQTs supervising colleagues
Stage 5	Questionnaire	All former students, now NQTs	All former students, now NQTs

230

19 An evaluation of Nene College's PGCE pilot project 1993–94

Joanna Moxham

Introduction

The concept of partnership has traditionally underpinned Nene College's teacher education courses. Schools' active participation in the planning and delivery of courses and in the selection and assessment of students has been welcomed. During the autumn term of 1993 in response to DFE circular 14/93 a pilot project, involving the year's cohort of 98 primary PGCE students, designed to reflect a more balanced partnership was implemented. There were several components of this project, the most notable being the transfer of funding to participant schools to finance their supervision of the school-based training. Other innovative elements of the course, all of which were conceived to strengthen the school/college interface, were the pairing of students within a particular classroom, the structuring of college directed classroom-based assignments within the core curriculum areas and the introduction of serial school experience.

Clearly such innovations were likely to be of less significance to a group of students embarking on a one year training course who were both oblivious and indifferent to the previous course structure. However, for college staff and teachers in the partnership schools the project implied a considerable change of roles and responsibilities and a significant redrafting of the course structure. In an endeavour to monitor the impact of these changes and to assess the extent of their success an evaluative exercise was undertaken within the School of Education.

It was the expectation that this exercise would yield information and insights which would inform subsequent course design and enhance the prospects of the partnership programme. The initial evaluation programme was, in its embryonic stage in the spring term of 1993, rather more ambitious than that which was ultimately implemented. Restrictions in internal funding

231

resulted in severe pruning of the personnel attached to the project. However, whilst the scale of the exercise was reduced, the design in essence remained the same insofar as it involved gathering quantitative and qualitative data from college tutors, teacher tutors and students. These data were gleaned from course documentation, unstructured interviews, fieldwork notes and questionnaires on the following time scale.

Summer term 1993

All headteachers who had previous involvement with the PGCE course were invited by the course leader to participate in the pilot project, with the transfer of funding being conditional on designated teacher tutors attending a half day training session. There were at this stage 40 positive responses to this invitation.

The project evaluator interviewed the PGCE course leader about the proposed changes in the course structure.

Autumn term 1993

Prior to the PGCE students' arrival, teacher tutors attended a training session during which the structure of the course was outlined and their and the college's respective roles and responsibilities clarified. At the conclusion of the session the project evaluator briefly explained her role and administered a questionnaire which was designed to elicit a range of professional biographical details. Thirty-one out of the 35 teacher tutors completed questionnaires and all but one indicated that they were prepared to be interviewed by the project evaluation. The refusal was on the basis of an impending inspection.

By the end of the first week of the course immediately prior to their first week of school experience the students were paired within their education groups, of which there were two each representing the 4-7 and 7-12 age phases. Given the constraints of time, geographical and alphabetical considerations provided the only basis for the pairing. At this junction, four pairs of students, selected from each of the four education groups, were interviewed by the project evaluator on an individual basis. The interviews with the students were brief and unstructured, designed chiefly to establish some sort of relationship with the individuals concerned, elicit some biographical details and ascertain their views on their forthcoming school experience. There was no intention to view these students as a representative sample of their peers, rather they were targeted because their placements

232

appeared broadly to represent the range of schools and teacher tutors students would encounter during the autumn term. Between them they were placed in an urban middle school, an urban lower school, a three teacher rural primary school and the largest primary school in the county whose grant maintained status added an extra dimension to the programme. The students' tutors promised similar representative variety insofar as one was a college tutor, one was a young PGCE trained deputy head with less than ten years' teaching experience, one was a teacher with less than five years' experience who had recently embarked on an MBA course and one was a teacher with more than 20 years' experience. All of them had previous experience, albeit varied, of working with students.

Serial school experience was undertaken on Mondays and Tuesdays for a seven week period in October and November. Thirty-five pairs of students were receiving teacher tutor supervision whilst School of Education staff tutored the remaining 14 pairs of students who were each visited a minimum of three times. In addition the group receiving teacher tutoring were visited once by their education tutor. The project evaluator's visits to the eight selected students in order to interview them and their teacher tutor/class teacher were scheduled to coincide with one of these visits. The evaluator also visited two other schools where the unfolding pattern of teacher tuition appeared to be deviating from the predetermined plan.

In early December all students were invited to complete a questionnaire devised by the project evaluator; 92 per cent responded. Teacher tutors were similarly asked to complete a questionnaire; 80 per cent did so. Teacher and student questionnaires focused on their views of the success or otherwise of the pairing, the time spent discussing student progress and writing reports, the extent to which schools were able to accommodate college directed activities, the allocation of free time for teacher tutors and instances where the student presence freed teacher tutors to cover for absent colleagues. In addition teacher tutors were asked if they would be prepared to undertake the role in future.

Spring term 1994

The traditional pattern of the course continued namely college-based sessions followed by block school experience with college tutor supervision. The project evaluator analysed the previous term's data and prepared a provisional report on the autumn term project.

The students completed the college-based element of the course and spent seven weeks on final school experience, again being supervised by college tutors. The project evaluator continued to collect data and during the final week of the course, when the students had returned to college, asked them to complete another questionnaire informing her of their perceptions and experiences of the course as a whole.

Findings

As has already been indicated, the students' experience during the first term of the course comprised four distinct elements which were designed to promote the partnership model and enhance the students' learning consequent upon which would be increased professional effectiveness. The argument in favour of teacher tutors is that unlike college tutors they are 'on the spot' and therefore more readily able to make valid assessments of and give appropriate assistance to students undertaking school experience.

The serial nature of the school experience allied with college directed core curriculum activities had been designed to increase students' confidence and enable them to engage in an ongoing exchange about their classroom practice between teacher tutors on the one hand and college tutors on the other. It was argued by the PGCE course team that in previous years the autumn term's period of school experience involving students for four days a week had resulted in excessive numbers of them engaging in coping strategies which in too many instances had escalated into bad habits. The argument would appear to be endorsed by McIntyre and Hagger's (1992) account of the Oxford Internship model in which they assert that '...traditional teaching practices have overwhelmed (the students) with their stressfulness and have led them to aim simply at coping or surviving rather than learning to teach.' Additionally, the previous course format appeared to inhibit students' capacity to make connections between college lectures and classroom practice. Again, McIntyre and Hagger highlight the benefit to students when on a week by week basis, the same issues are discussed, investigated and explored in university and school contexts.

The pairing of students was similarly introduced to enhance their initial experience of school via shared planning and mutual observation. Again, the likely increase in professional confidence and effectiveness formed the basis of the course team's rationale. Stephenson's (1994) account of Bedford

College's Primary PGCE pairing policy underlines the team's belief that by having another colleague in the situation, there would be a natural forum for mutual help, and most importantly, a culture of discussion leading to analysis.

Whilst these four constituents of the partnership project were obviously interwoven, it is possible for monitoring purposes to evaluate them as discrete elements. Given the innovative nature of the project, teacher tutor preparation for their role was arguably one of the key issues. The course leader's stipulation that the transfer of funding was conditional on attendance at the training session reinforces its status.

Preparation and training of teacher tutors

1.   *Teachers' responses and perceptions*

Two obvious measures of the success or otherwise of this preparation were teachers' responses to both the course documentation and the training session. There were initial difficulties over the training session. Despite clear written information stressing that student placements with teacher tutors were conditional on attendance at this session, three schools rang immediately prior to the meeting to tender apologies and one teacher withdrew from the scheme having attended the meeting. In all of these cases a college tutor was substituted for the teacher tutor. In one case a headteacher attended the training session rather than the two teacher tutors whom he had nominated. In this case the teachers were not withdrawn from their role but one pair of the students affected belonged to the group of eight interviewed and visited by the project evaluator. Subsequent interviews with the two teachers who had not attended the training session revealed that little information about it had been passed on to them. In fact they had not been aware of their entitlement to attend the session. Lack of knowledge about their precise role had appeared to contribute to one student in this school misleading her teacher tutor about the purpose of the school experience file. The teacher had consequently felt uneasy about looking at the student's file and had not insisted on doing so. It was not until November when the student's education tutor visited the school that the teacher tutor finally received accurate information about this aspect of her role.

There were additionally several instances of teachers, who having attended the training session and received all the relevant documentation, misinterpreted the procedures. Two pairs of students were split up and placed in separate classrooms. In one of these cases the tutor immediately intervened and the pair was rejoined but the other pair continued to work in separate classrooms throughout the term because what the college perceived to be a team teaching situation proved not to be so.

There was one isolated case of a small infant school whose headteacher had attended the training course as she, rather than the class teacher, intended to act as teacher tutor. This decision proved not to be too problematic in a small, apparently tightly knit, school where the head was a frequent visitor to all classrooms. An interview with the head revealed her strong sense of responsibility to training issues. She emphasised her belief that teacher supervision should be undertaken by a member of staff in a position of seniority and in possession of considerable practical experience. Certainly she appeared sensitive to the personal and professional needs of the two students who felt their school-based training was very valuable. The headteacher concerned has been consistently supportive of training initiatives and it seems likely that this factor combined with the particular organisation of the school contributed to the positive impact of her personal response to the task of teacher supervision. Headteacher supervision would be less likely to succeed in a large school or indeed one where the head was less committed to the value of a school/college partnership permeating initial teacher training courses.

Apart from these initial difficulties and apparent misunderstandings 61 per cent of the teacher tutors responding to the questionnaire considered that the course documentation relating to their tutoring role was clear and 68 per cent felt that they had been adequately prepared for their role. Generally, respondents who did feel that they had been adequately prepared for the teacher tutor role failed to add qualifying comments in contrast to those teachers who felt negative about their preparation who were vociferous with their qualifications. One apparently positive respondent said that she only felt prepared because she had previously undergone mentor training with another institution and commented 'reassurance would have been nice'. Several teachers who indicated that they felt ill prepared expressed a wish for a set of guidelines and knowledge of the work which students were pursing in college. In fact this information had already been provided in course documentation relating to the students' activities which 89 per cent of teachers acknowledged to be clear.

There were no clearly discernible trends amongst the respondents about their future training needs, indeed the greatest consensus came from the 32 per cent who considered that they had no further need for training that in the words of one of them 'the experience has proved enough'. The only other clear level of agreement came from the 18 per cent of teacher tutors who indi-

236

cated that they would welcome clear guidance on the content and structure of the student file.

2. Students' responses and experiences

Analysis of the students' post school experience questionnaires suggested that there was wide interpretation of the clearly stated expectation that they should receive three interim reports from their teacher tutor. Responses from 13 per cent of the students who received teacher tuition indicated that they had only received two reports whilst 9 per cent received only one report. More positively, 24 per cent of student received the required three reports, 10 per cent seven reports and one individual, nine written reports!

Whilst the mechanics of gaining access to the transferred funding or indeed its application were in the majority of cases of little or no relevance to the teacher tutors, confusion over this issues in some instances clouded the partnership. Given the fact that funding issues featured in the correspondence which went out to schools and were raised in the training session then they are pertinent to the whole issue of preparation. Several schools queried the logistics of invoicing the college and the headteacher of one school, which undertook tutoring responsibility for three pairs of students, wrote a critical letter to the course leader outlining a variety of reasons why he and his staff felt unable to support future initiatives of this type. The concluding sentences of the letter are perhaps significant in the context of this paragraph. 'When we were first approached to accept students we were informed that there would be a financial consideration involved. However, two months after the initial meeting our school has received nothing, moreover the teachers who travelled to Nene College ...have received no travelling expenses. We feel we have been working under a misapprehension. Is this training on the cheap?'

It is worth noting at this point that schools were given written instructions about the logistics of applying for funding, and that it was made clear in these instructions that the funding was to pay for teacher tutor release to attend the training session and from classroom duties in order to facilitate student supervision. The course leader emphasised that the specific allocation of these funds was left to the discretion of individual headteachers. Seventy one per cent of teacher tutors who responded to the questionnaire were given cover to facilitate their tutoring role. Whilst the amount of time ranged from one hour to seven hours it averaged out to 3.6 hours per teacher tutor.

Student and teacher perceptions of the school experience

1. *Timing*

The nature and timing of the school experience was apparently acceptable to 68 per cent of the teacher tutors and 60 per cent of students said that they had been able to accomplish college directed curriculum assignments relatively easily in contrast to the 40 per cent who had undertaken these tasks 'with some difficulty'. The college received two strong letters of complaint from headteachers about the term's school-based activities. Both letters included criticisms endorsed, albeit less forcefully, by many questionnaire respondents. Weekly, timetabled swimming lessons, staff meetings and INSET courses were amongst the reasons cited by schools as undermining their ability to accommodate students and their assignments. One member of the college staff who was heavily timetabled on Mondays and Tuesdays found it difficult to arrange visits to schools. Similarly, some students, particularly those in middle schools which are traditionally more tightly timetabled, experienced difficulties in undertaking certain college directed classroom activities. Nonetheless, these problems should not be exaggerated and schools were generally able to accommodate student tasks. Arguably, there would be organisational inconveniences associated with any permutation of days. On balance it seems that the structure and timing of the school experience did enhance the student experience and provided them with a framework which minimised the 'theory versus practice' schism which too often polarises the teacher education debate. Moreover, staff, teachers and student benefited from increased understanding of the pattern of the course.

2. *Pairing*

Such a level of consensus was not apparent in responses to the issue of pairing. Whilst 85 per cent of the teacher tutors expressed a feeling that the pairing of students had been advantageous, the responses from students were less clear cult. Twenty four per cent of the students commented that working within pairs was not generally beneficial. What is particularly interesting about teacher and student reactions to this issue is the lack of agreement between the three individuals involved. There was only one documented incident of both members of the pair and the class teacher agreeing that the pairing had been problematic. In six of the 11 apparently incompatible pairs one of the pair voiced no concerns.

The most common complaint though was not concerned with compatibility but with overcrowding. Several teachers and students felt that the pupils were confused by the presence of so many adults. One student commented that this situation increased the teachers' 'work load and stress and the children suffered'. Interestingly, it might be anticipated that this problem of overcrowding would be more apparent in a junior rather than infant context given the traditionally more flexible and 'open' organisation of the latter. However, adverse comments about overcrowding by adults were more or less equally divided between students in Key Stage 1 classrooms and those operating in a Key Stage 2 context.

The perceived element of competition also gave some concerns to both teachers and students - although more to the latter. One teaching head commented, 'At times there was a feeling of competition between the two', also though neither of the students involved appeared to share his concerns. One student's reaction to being paired was, 'I do not feel I gained anything from working in pairs as I could not easily talk to my partner without feeling that I was not doing well. He was not very encouraging and I did not feel I could be honest with him'. Another student's recorded response to being paired was, 'I was nervous and he cramped my style. I hated it!' Subsequent information about this particular student has revealed that she frequently experienced problems when working with her peers and was at her happiest when placed in a rural school with no peer contact. Conversely, the individual about whom she complained so vehemently worked quite happily in a school with another student during his final placement and generally it seems that these problems should not be overstated. The evidence suggests that the majority of students exploited the opportunity to engage in mutually constructive planning and observation. Certainly the pairing instilled the students with an initial feeling of confidence which encouraged them to show more initiative in terms of classroom practice than might otherwise have been possible. One teacher tutor remarked how valuable it had been for a marginally over-confident student to view the quiet, but nonetheless effective, resolve of her partner when they undertook shared responsibility for the class fairly early on in the term. Both students, when interviewed individually, commented on this early experience in the classroom - one on how it increased her confidence, the other on how it encouraged her to be less 'boisterous' as a teacher and more self critical. They spoke positively on the advantages of pairing. One or two pairs of students who had uneasy relationships with teacher tutors appreciated the support that the pairing offered in this situation. Indeed, even in the last week of the course one student commented that had it not been for the support of her peer she would probably have withdrawn from the course. It might be argued, though, that the very presence of two students in a classroom was instrumental in contributing to the stress which led to an uneasy student/teacher relationship. One student in such a situation did make this observation.

Only two out of 28 students being supervised by college tutors saw no advantages to working within a pair. Although this issue has not been explored, it could be that the presence of an outsider with comparatively less personal investment in the classroom had a moderating effect. It might also be argued that in cases where competition might have developed there was not the constant pressure of an ever present presence to impress. Whatever the reasons, comparisons between the two groups would be odious as the four college tutors involved were all experienced members of staff who, as group tutors, had a higher personal and professional investment in their students.

Conclusions and implications for course development

The nature of this pilot project makes definitive comparisons with earlier cohorts or predictions about its efficacy fraught with difficulties. Such is the spectrum of variables involved that they defy experimental validity. Specific evaluation of the teacher tutor role is particularly problematic. Moreover, firm conclusions at a point when the students have barely completed the course suggest undue haste. That said, the data gathered from all participants in the project can enable tentative observations to be made and subsequently used to inform course design. Eighty-two per cent of the students who responded to the questionnaire prior to being tutored by a teacher tutor were happy with the arrangement. There was a similar level of satisfaction amongst the 14 pairs of students scheduled for college tutor supervision. However, whilst the latter group remained contented as a result of their experience in school, 15 per cent of the other group changed their minds. Six of these students were placed in a school where there was obviously discontent on both sides. One of the students expressed it thus, 'My workload increased and stress increased. The teacher's stress increased and the children suffered'. Such mutual disillusion in the context of the school was already discussed where there were concerns over funding issues and questions about so called 'education on the cheap'. It is worth noting that whilst all three teachers had volunteered to undertake teacher tutoring, they expressed uncertainty about why they had done so. The majority of teacher tutors questioned anticipated that the role would be mutually beneficial to them and their students and they welcomed the reflective opportunities which it was likely to bring. In another case two students had a severe problem over an un-

240

communicative, relatively newly qualified teacher tutor which necessitated intervention by the PGCE course leader. Both the teacher and students involved were critical of each other and expressed unhappiness about their interpretation of their respective roles. In half of the cases where the partnership did not appear to be beneficial the teachers commented on the fact that they received no allocation of either time or money to support them in their role.

Once again it is worth striking a note of caution and avoiding over reaction to a minority of forcefully articulated complaints. The majority of students appreciated the support mechanisms implemented by their teacher tutors and exploited the constant availability of professional advice. The students recorded an average input of three-and-a-half hours per week from their teacher tutors which in these financially driven days must be deemed value for money.

There are drawbacks to every course. Given the current pace and extent of educational change there are likely to be conflicts of interest and misunderstandings in any partnership. Tensions will be heightened in a context where students are undergoing a concentrated and pressurised professional training. The innovative implications of the autumn term programme for college tutors and schools should not be underestimated and the entire project should be viewed in this context. Although it seems likely that the tutor visit to every school in the partnership involved probably ameliorated everyone's sense of being cast adrift. Nonetheless, the overwhelming impression is that the partnership succeeded in preparing and supporting students in the preliminary stages of their training. Sixty-three per cent of the students felt that one of the course's main aims for the term, to enable them to understand the role of the primary school teacher and to gain some experience of taking on that role, had been wholly met. The remaining 37 per cent felt that it had been partially met. Despite the cited adverse reactions from some schools, 78 per cent of teacher tutors indicated that they would be prepared to undertake the role again - although only 59 per cent of these positive responses were unqualified. Qualifications included, inter alia, requests for payment and more supply cover.

Clearly in a climate of transferred funding on an increasingly ambitious scale there are pressing training and development issues arising from the pilot project. For whilst the accumulated evidence suggests that given the innovative nature of the partnership in a context of severe financial and time constraints the preparation of teacher tutors was generally successful, complacency in this area would be misplaced. Certainly the course leader's insistence on teacher tutors' attendance at the training session appears to have

241

been vindicated. It is entirely impractical to suggest that the course team could ever achieve total success in terms of all teacher tutors reading and adhering to the appropriate course documentation. However it would seem desirable for the documentation relating to teacher tutors' roles and responsibilities to be clarified via the adoption of the following strategies to supplement existing training sessions and course documentation.

1.   In order to make the financial arrangements absolutely clear, and to minimise the likelihood of funding anxieties clouding teacher tutor training sessions, it would seem appropriate to preface them with specific meetings for headteachers of participant schools. Transfer of funding might be conditional on the head (or delegate) attending such a meeting which would detail the structure of the course, the mechanics of the transfer of funding, an outline of the respective responsibilities of the elements of the partnership and the timetable of teacher tutor training.

2.   The inclusion of specific guidance on the structure and content of the student file in the teacher tutors' training session.

3.   The provision of opportunities for intending teacher tutors to work alongside a college tutor observing a student teacher.

4.   The distribution of an additional written synopsis summarising the main teacher tutor responsibilities and incorporating a timetable which indicates clearly at which point in a particular school experience students should be receiving written teacher tutor reports.

5.   The scheduling of an interim meeting between teacher tutors and college tutors half way through each period of school experience. Such meetings would be likely to reap additional dividends in terms of alleviating anxieties and providing a forum for the sharing of responsibilities allied to which would be an increase in teacher tutors' confidence.

6.   A commitment from the college to respond to any emergencies which might arise particularly in terms of a breakdown in the relationship between teacher tutor and student.

242

Schools' appreciation of the necessity to offer incentives in terms of time or money to teacher tutors might be attendant on these enhanced training opportunities, as would headteachers' sensitivity to the process of selecting teacher tutors. The most successful partnerships are likely to be symbiotic. The fact that 64 per cent of students being tutored by schools were asked to undertake supply cover, albeit willingly, in their first term of training indicates that despite the drawbacks there are identifiable benefits to be accrued for all participants in the partnership. It would, however, be misguided to judge the pilot project merely in the context of the autumn term. It was the intention that the initial term should provide the foundation for the rest of the course. During the penultimate week of the PGCE course the external examiner commented that in her view the students had attained an even higher standard than last year's cohort. Whilst it would be a massive oversimplification to attribute this to the course structure, all elements of the partnership must derive some comfort from these observations. Similarly encouraging is the absence of any failures for the first time in three years combined with the lowest non completion rate in five years - 5 per cent compared with an average of 12 per cent - statistics which will probably offer greater comfort when the students have all been successful in their applications for first teaching posts.

20 Externally enforced change: The experience of students and mentors during the pilot year of a post 9/92 school-based course

Jean Howard

Introduction

> It is one thing to say that student teachers should be learning their craft from experienced teachers; it is quite another to be clear about *what* they should learn and *how* that learning may be most effectively accomplished (Brown and McIntyre 1993: 12).

This is an interim report on a study in progress into professional responses to externally imposed change in initial teacher training. Previous studies of school-based teacher education have focused on institutions which negotiated, planned and established courses reflecting their own professional growth and understanding. The Oxford Internship Scheme is possibly the best documented. For instance in the early stages of that particular scheme 12 senior members of staff were seconded from secondary schools to work with the course team for a year to plan course development. In contrast, the compulsory reform of all postgraduate secondary training to a school-based model involved colleges such as my own setting up a model that neither they nor their associated schools had previously considered in any depth, within a two year planning and implementation period.

In 1991 the HMI report on school-based teacher training had concluded that 'school-based training could not sensibly be increased without appropriate provision of time reosurces and training for those who could be expected to provide it' (HMI 1991: 35). The provision of transitional funding for the short period of transfer to the new school-based PGCE courses enabled planning and some training to take place, but in very different circumstances and on a very different timescale to the Oxford model. The aim of this study is to investigate the experience of those concerned in implementing school-based training as a result of central government guidelines in Circular 9/92.

Evidence

The evidence for this study was gathered in a number of ways. Firstly all the people involved in the study were involved in full-time jobs or study, so information had to be gathered in the normal course of busy working lives. One of the most important forums in which school and college staff were able to exchange views was during the mentor training programme. A series of 12 hour basic introductory courses were run throughout 1992 and 1993 involving a total of 120 teachers.

Secondly, working in school with students, there was an opportunity for informal interviews to take place with the staff concerned. However this method alone would not enable all the staff with students to feedback their concerns, since schools are busy places and teachers seldom had time to speak at length. For this reason questionnaires were also used in the six schools, with which I worked most closely. These schools were a varied group, single sex and co-educational, denominational and non-denominational, comprehensive and selective. One school was involved also in school-centred training.

Thirdly, working in college with staff both individually and in formal meetings or informal groups, views were sought from tutors concerned. Again a questionnaire was also employed to enable people to express views that they had either had insufficient time to discuss at length or did not wish to discuss in public forum.

Fourthly, the experience of the students concerned was also sought, through questionnaires, informal interviews and group discussions with tutors. Students were informed from the start that their experience would be written up in this paper, and consequently they made sure that I was kept well-informed of their feelings. The use of questionnaires was particularly important in this respect, to ensure that not only the views of a vocal minority were being represented.

Fifthly, I looked at outcomes. As a Scottish presbyterian by upbringing, working in a Roman Catholic college by choice, I was guided by the principle 'by their deeds shall ye know them'. I looked at what people, both staff and students, actually did.

The study was begun during the planning year 1992-93 in an informal manner through discussion, and the recording of work in progress through the normal procedures of minuting meetings, responding to training needs through the production of materials and dealing with queries and concerns of school and college colleagues.

During the pilot year of the school-based course 1993-1994, questionnaires were employed, schools and college colleagues were also asked to formally register their response in writing where they had particular issues to which they wished attention to be drawn. A final questionnaire was also sent out in June 1994 to all schools who indicated they did not wish to be involved with the college during 1994-1995 to discover their reasons for rejecting a formal partnership arrangement.

Previous PGCE provision

The changes enforced by government had been in no way sought by the practitioners involved in PGCE training at St. Mary's, although the need was generally recognised for a more formally organised partnership with schools in terms to student selection, support and assessment.

The previous PGCE course worked on a goodwill basis. Paperwork for the school was minimal. Negotiation between school and college was personal, mostly face to face and spoken. Assessment of practical teaching by the school involved writing a short report on the student at the end of a block practice. The nature of the college, a small denominational college working often with denominational schools and with staff who had themselves trained at the college, encouraged a family atmosphere. This had both advantages and disadvantages. Family rows as well as compassionate support were evidenced. Procedures grew up through custom and practice, and on occasion were insufficiently challenged. Much depended on the professional integrity of individuals.

Nevertheless, the nature of the college was summed up by HMI when they inspected the humanities provision in 1989; 'Accommodation is mediocre in quality and appearances are generally shabby. However the college is a civilised and harmonious place in which to work and relationships are excellent' (HMI 1990).

This excellence of relationships is also noted in external examiners' reports on the PGCE course with regard to professional co-operation with schools and in relationships between staff and students. The PGCE had been a college-based course with two blocks of school experience in different schools, four weeks prior to Christmas and nine weeks arranged to span the schools Easter holidays. This combined with two weeks initial observation and five individual days of pre-TP visits to arrange timetables gave a total of 16 weeks in school. School placements were organised by a lecturer with responsibility for this area, usually by means of telephoning schools and asking, until the number of students increased to such an extent that letters had to be sent well in advance.

To thank schools for their involvement in training, every second year a formal buffet dinner was arranged by the College in the historic setting of the Walpole House and the Waldegrave Drawing Room. The Principal and college staff acted as hosts for the evening. It was a splendid occasion, the college having a long tradition of entertaining professional colleagues. This old-fashioned gentlemanly collegiate approach to the education of teachers was still largely in place when the reforms of 1992 were introduced.

Initial reactions to government proposals

How then did professional colleagues in school respond initially to the proposed changes in the college PGCE provision? As befitted the informal family nature of college/school relationships, we started by arguing over money.

Our local situation was very much complicated by the Institute of Education launching their new school-based PGCE throughout the whole Greater London area to coincide with Kenneth Clarke's address to the North of England Conference in January 1992. Schools were being offered what seemed at the time a large sum of money for what other colleges were apparently asking them to do for nothing. At least this was how it appeared superficially to a number of schools who contacted us during the earliest stage of the dissemination of information from the Institute. Not surprisingly, many school and college staff were angry, confused and aggrieved.

However, it had been my experience in school and LEA of similar funding disputes related to central government policy, that honesty was the best approach in discussions about money. If the available funding was being wisely and justly spent, then it did no harm to give others the detail of spending or planning in order to let them comment on it. If it was fair and sensible, then the others who had access to the facts on which the allocation of resources was based, would in all likelihood reach the same conclusions. If they did manage to come up with a better idea then everybody would benefit.

Consequently we invited any school which was interested to come to an initial conference and to subsequent mentor training courses. We did not limit our training programme to those already closely linked in the past, nor did we exclude particular sectors, such as independent schools or schools considering school-centred training. We welcomed whoever wished to come. Our aim was to develop professionally together to meet the demands of the new situa-

248

tion

The early part of mentor training was devoted to studying the government's plans (to whatever stage they had then reached) and to provide details on the funding of teacher education and how the college spent the fees which the students brought with them. The outcome of this approach was constructive. The most common response was righteous professional indignation on discovering the actual financial conditions under which HEI staff worked.

Most teachers had until then simply based their views on their own nostalgic, hostile or indifferent reminiscences of their own training, and before we could move forward we had to establish accurate, informed common ground. The subsequent areas covered in the mentor training sessions dealt with the practical aspects of implementing training in the workplace, with a particular focus on providing feedback, target setting and assessment.

Responses from teachers

The responses which emerged from the mentor training courses were initially positive, looking towards developing a greater involvement at all levels between schools and college, and there was a growing willingness to acknowledge the particular contribution higher education made to the process. These feelings were echoed in the questionnaires, as the following examples illustrate:

I do not have the academic depth to assess written work. I don't have time to research the reading required. (This from a teacher with only two years' experience in one school yet responsible for tutoring students on training.)

Supporting students is only an enjoyable experience if they have been well prepared by the college and are au fait with current thinking on methodology.

I feel we have a duty to have students in our schools. However to carry this responsibility we need support.

I am concerned about issues of monitoring the evenness of student assessment between schools.

My less than enthusiastic response is due entirely to lack of time and the fact that I would not wish to encourage this ghastly government to create yet another agency. I'd rather see institutions like St Mary's doing what their expertise qualifies them to do.

The overwhelming concern of school staff was their lack of time to carry out training responsibilities and their lack of awareness of what was expected or was taking place in other schools. They were worried that their judgement related to their own experience of a small number of students in limited number of settings. It was generally acknowledged that college staff had an overview of practice and research that could not easily be acquired in the school setting.

Assessment was another area of concern. Even a respondent who stressed that time spent in school was the most essential part of training was not happy 'about being responsible for affecting a student's future by writing a report on him on the basis of a few lessons. Experience can radically alter anyone's performance as a teacher.' This reluctance to fail a student was later also evidenced in the grades awarded to a very weak student by school mentors.

School staff, students and college tutors were all very aware of the differences which existed between schools both in attitudes to teachers on training and in the practical provision made for them. Of the 48 teachers who responded by questionnaire, only eight had any time allocated on their timetable for the support of students. Of these, six were involved in school-centred training. However even three of these six felt strongly that they did not have enough time to give to their students.

Responses from students

Student responses on the support they received in school were surprisingly positive considering the concerns experienced by school and college staff. Sixty of the 82 completed questionnaires received from a cohort of 96 stated that they strongly or mildly agreed that the support they had received had been adequate for their professional development. However when this was followed up by more detailed questioning, only 19 students strongly agreed that they had been systematically observed in class, and only 15 that they had received clear guidelines for professional development in the form of written feedback on observed lessons.

Thirty-eight students remained neutral or disagreed with the statement that the written feedback provided in school had given them clear guidelines for professional development. In 18 cases no written feedback at all had been given. On the other hand 60 students strongly or mildly agreed that spoken feedback had provided them with this advice. Sixty-one also felt that the spoken feedback had given them encouragement. Thirty students strongly agreed that they had been encouraged by the spoken feedback they received in school. This was the largest group of very positive responses to any question.

This would match the concerns of school staff that they had insufficient time to provide feedback and it would seem that the majority are simply speaking to their students when they can find a moment.

However, within the group who felt encouraged and supported by spoken feedback in school 22 added their own comments to explain their experience further. Only three of these comments actually reinforced their positive feelings in what they said. The others had the following negative points which they wished to register:

I found it disheartening speaking to someone [the teacher in charge of students] who showed very little interest and treated the teaching practice as unimportant.

Clearer guidelines are needed for schools to enable them to support students adequately.

I found it demoralising to have constant negative feedback.

Within the staffroom individual teachers were helpful, but there was no cohesion within the department, which made getting a straight answer or specific help sometimes very difficult/awkward to get.

Nobody available when head of department was away, which was often.

The school had no concept of 'team teaching' so observation carried on too long and I became restive.

I would have appreciated teachers giving me feedback, without having to ask for this.

I got no feedback at all from my head of department, but it didn't bother me ... I thought he would complain fast enough if he was concerned.

Since these were comments from the students who felt encouraged by spoken feedback in school, some doubt has to be cast on what the students interpreted as adequate professional support. Judging from the discussions held with tutors to debrief following school experience, the majority of students felt supported if individual staff were civil and welcoming to them. Most telling perhaps was the comment from a very appreciative student: 'I could ask anyone for help. Everyone was very friendly'.

In discussion it emerged that students were very conscious that they were a nuisance to staff, who had little time to deal with them. Mature students with plenty of experience of the work environment were particularly reluctant to bother staff.

Students also felt isolated in their schools, a problem exacerbated by the traditional placement pattern of the college, with very small groups or even individual students all over the London and home counties area. Student recommendations for change in future course organisation included mechanisms for getting people together in college during their school experience and also that efforts should be made to persuade schools to accept larger groups of students, so that they could support each other. This latter recommendation is likely to prove extremely hard to implement. What an increasing number of schools are doing with regard to school-based training is to reject entering into a formal contract to be involved.

Withdrawal from involvement in school-based training

The 111 schools taking this course of action were asked in a questionnaire why they had come to this decision. Of the 76 replies received so far, 24 are only prepared to accept students as and when their situation allows (the old 'goodwill' model). Others do not wish to be involved because they have a large number of NQTs or an OFSTED inspection, which amounts to a similar response, in that they will only accept students when the general work of the school allows. Twenty-two say they are worried about the effect on pupil progress and wish to avoid additional pressure on staff. The money side of things is mentioned as a concern, but not as central to their reasons to withdraw. Only 25 say they prefer to be involved with another college.

This year we were unable to place three well-qualified science students, until in desperation members of college staff approached personal contacts in school, and literally begged them to take these students. All went in to Roman Catholic schools who had a particular connection with the college, but who really were not able to accept a student at that time. One school would only take the student if they did not have to do any paperwork. The college tutor had to undertake to go in and do all the necessary feedback and assessment. Before we reached this desperate stage, 16 schools had been approached on behalf of a physics graduate for a science placement within travelling distance of the East End of London

What schools seem to be doing is refusing the additional responsibility imposed on them by school-based training. Most worrying to government should be the particular lack of enthusiasm for this model amongst high achieving academic schools. One local school has written regretfully to sever its long association with the college, on the grounds that teachers must give priority to pupils' learning not to the training of students. Another has expressed its concern along similar lines, though has retained a link of possibly accepting one student if circumstances allow. A third states 'we have high academic standards and we do not wish the pupils' learning to suffer'.

At a conference for the independent sector at which the possibility of undertaking school-centred training was raised by the Minister of State, the participants expressed their willingness to be involved in training only as and when their situation allowed. Only 35 of the 126 schools approached wished or were able to attend, some 15 registering that they had no interest in teacher training, while 46 made no response.

School staff involved in the early stages of planning the school-based PGCE have indicated they do not wish to continue unless support and funding for their efforts is provided by their senior management. After the end of transitional funding, courses and meetings will increasingly be planned as twilight sessions, to avoid the cost of cover. Few teachers seem prepared to continue on this basis. One wrote in an essay on her MA course:

> The job of the teacher is to teach pupils. The weight of responsibility for doing so, coupled with the demands of the new initiatives for ITT pose the greatest threat to the success of school-based training, in spite of the assurances of partnership.... I am aware of the sheer under resourcing of the initiative .... The staff of the school where I work are deciding against it. (Harrison 1994).

253

Emerging trends in response to the government's reforms of ITT

This is an interim report on a study in progress. Already there are trends which seem to be emerging. Responsible and high achieving schools may be withdrawing their goodwill, on the grounds of pressure on staff and pupils. Nor does there seem to be any great enthusiasm for school-centred training at present. There are indications that ordinary teaching staff are unhappy with this particular initiative .

Only in one school where staff had worked closely over the years with a local HEI and followed a well-organised training programme, and where the deputy head had been seconded for a term to the HEI, were the responses to school-based training largely positive. However that school had chosen to be involved in school-based training, even before 9/92.

At this early stage in my own study it seems that staff in both college and school are carrying out a large part of their training work while they should strictly speaking be doing something else. Because college staff are called upon to provide support for schools, well above the contact hours allotted to them for this purpose, they have to cut back on their research, preparation and publication work. Because staff in schools have no time allocated to them specifically for students they are supporting them in the non-contact time which they have for marking, administration and lesson planning.

In July 1994 the external examiner reported to the examination board his concerns that 'the gap between schools which do provide an appropriate environment for student teachers to develop in and those which merely accept students appears to have grown wider'. He pointed out that 'with the new balance of responsibilities a poor host school now has a much more detrimental effect on a student teacher's development'.

One of the students spoke very clearly and maturely of her own experience which reflects the justice of such concerns:

> On a personal level the staff were very friendly towards me and made me feel welcome in the staffroom. I did not however receive adequate professional support. I felt I was floundering around and was left to decide lesson content, schemes of work etc without help or advice from subject teachers. I received very little feedback despite asking for advice on lessons observed. The subject teachers themselves were under a lot of pressure and a student teacher was foisted on them without consultation. This was a difficult situation for teachers and myself and resulted in very little professional support for me as a trainee teacher.

It is my own concern that where teachers are not consulted adequately with regard to their own involvement in training, this effective self-detachment from the task is another form of professional response to externally imposed change. Thirty of the school staff who responded felt in practice that supporting students was extra to the work they expected to do as teachers, although in principle most recognised that helping students was a part of a teacher's professional responsibility. Seventeen teachers also felt they had not been consulted adequately about their own involvement in training.

These responses come from schools who have worked with students and with the college for years. The fact that they were willing to help in this research and were interested enough to write their comments in some detail, indicates that these responses may not be representative of less positive or supportive schools, or those which do not enjoy a constructive, developing relationship with their HEI.

Twenty-six of the respondents were heads of department, two were deputy heads, seven were subject teachers, seven were teachers involved in co-ordinating ITT work in school and six were mentors involved in school-centred training. The majority had over five years' experience and had worked in two or three schools. The schools themselves were in large, mixed catchment areas in West London. They had stable staff and enjoyed popularity with their parents and the communities they served.

If a significant number of staff are finding the demands of school-based training unmanageable in such schools, we need to know whether this is a temporary transitional situation, 'teething troubles' as our HMI hopefully put it, or whether imposing a particular training format on schools and colleges will actually achieve an improvement in the quality of teacher education in the long term.

21 Stringing along: Untying the knots in a college-school PGCE teacher training network

Derek Glover and George Hudson

Introduction

The chapter is based upon the evaluation of one of the largest secondary PGCE courses in the country. Its concern is not about describing, defining or prescribing mentor roles but rather about role identity and relationships between ITT tutors, school mentors and students. Our comments are based upon the experience of subject mentors, professional mentors, students and the associated college link tutors in ten schools and one college of further education. The evaluation, by an internal and an external evaluator, has been by interview and the completion of a student questionnaire which is currently being analysed. The comments in this chapter are drawn from the interview data.

The findings so far have highlighted the tensions between the change in roles which are the products of a changing culture, a change of a PGCE course based in a college to one based in a school. Similar findings on the training of teachers have been outlined by earlier researchers (Benton 1990, Wilkin 1992a). Such tensions arise from the differential interpretation of teacher and tutor roles and role relationships. Further, there has been a continuing expectation from the PGCE students that the college input will continue to be at the same level as in the previous course. It could be said that this expectation is specified by the folklore of traditional teacher training courses.

Although now termed 'school-based' it could be argued that initial teacher training (ITT) has always been school-based because all such courses have had a teaching practice as the major element for the preparation of students for their professional role. However, Circular 9/92 (DFE 1992) set out the minimum time requirement for the school-based experience of student teachers together with seven skill areas and competences that a newly qualiified teacher should acquire. The requirements of 9/92 have moved much of the content of ITT courses out of the higher education institutions into the school together with the responsibility of assessing student performance.

The interest and research in the changes that have followed 9/92 have been mainly focused on the emergence of the role of the school based 'mentor', the teacher(s) given the new responsibility for inducting a student into the school, acquiring professional and subject skills and knowledge, and the assessment of student's performance (Williams 1993). This transfer of training and assessment functions has been paralleled by a transfer of funds to the schools to support the additional work undertaken by the mentors.

An important facet of school-based teacher training is the transfer of funds, a fact that is currently under research by a group of universities and the Esmee Fairbairn Foundation (reporting November 1994). In this chapter we are not concerned with the value of the money transferred but with the impact of its distribution and perceived work demands made upon the staff in the schools. Our evidence suggests that there is a range of arrangements made by the management of schools for the distribution of funding but the more money is returned either directly or indirectly to the staff undertaking the additional work, the less the tension and the greater the feeling that the additional work is being recognised. Money colours attitudes.

The former PGCE course

In order to understand the status of the changes now taking place it is necessary to understand the culture, the beliefs, values and roles, of the 'old' college based course. This course was characterised by general professional and subject knowledge teaching to graduates encompassed within a validated framework. However, the boundaries of professional tutors, the subject tutor and the teachers dealing with students in the school were relatively loosely defined. The role of the teacher helping a student with professional and subject knowledge was in support of that provided by college tutors. The nature of the role relationship between teachers and tutors, particularly subject tutors responsible for the main assessment of a student's classroom performance, was always negotiable at the level of individual schools. Subject tutors from the college were pivotal to the course and role network of its 'team' professional tutor, the school teachers and the students.

Role relationships within the college were defined by the organisation of the PGCE course. Professional tutors contributed to a general course while individual students were also attached to a student subject group and a subject tutor. This division of labour recognised that there was a distinction between professional and subject knowledge. The division of labour was negotiated between professional and subject tutors in finer detail. The drawing up of lesson plans and the management of classroom resources are two examples of areas negotiated by professional and subject tutors. These arrangements produced a tailored content for each student subject group, and like bespoke suits, fitted the various interests and expertise of tutors. The negotiation removed any ambivalence in tutors' roles yet covered the requirements of the course.

The professional tutor's role in supervising a student in a school was a relatively minor one, monitoring and affirming the validity of the subject tutor's assessment. In the few cases of disagreement the final assessment of a student's performance would be made by an external examiner. These arrangements again emphasised the pivotal nature of a subject tutor.

Schools made a formal decision over the number of students and the subject areas they would accept on to teaching practice. Most schools had a teacher responsible for students and in co-operation with the head of a department and other teachers provided an arena, timetable and classes, for the performance of the student's teacher role. But, as with the relationship between the college tutors, subject tutors' relationships with other teachers was agreed through negotiation. The only bureaucracy required from teachers was a written evaluation of their students on the completion of teaching practice. The teachers' roles and their relationship with students was to advise, assist, comment and assess. These roles were negotiated by teachers and the individual supervising college subject tutors. Over a number of years and with stability of staffing, this enabled a strong bond to be established between subject teacher and subject tutor.

The culture of the 'old' course could be described as collegiate in the very real sense of community, as the roles were developed through negotiation and their voluntary nature produced for individual members a professional identity and a moral commitment to a shared set of norms (Vonk 1993, Livingston and Borko 1989).

The new PGCE course

In the new school-based course the college has followed the model adopted in many ITT institutions. The college has entered into a contractual arrangement with a number of partnership schools who receive funding according to the number of students they will accept for training. In addition to providing the arena for a student's teaching practice, teaching staff now undertake the supervision of the development of their professional and subject knowledge and skills in partnership with the college. In the school this responsibility is managed by the professional mentor. Schools also designate subject mentors who have responsibility for development of a student's teaching within the subject area. The partnership schools are organised into clusters of about six schools whose main contact with the college is through a professional link tutor. College subject tutors no longer have responsibility of observing, advising and assessing the students' teaching performance although they are responsible for the background courses offered during the college attendance periods. The organisational arrangements for this new course are radically different from the old PGCE course but our work suggests that many schools and indeed, college staff have not assimilated the changed roles. For example, the official communication from a school to college about a student is now from the subject mentor in the school to the professional mentor, to the link tutor. The link tutor will decide whether this will involve action on the part of the subject tutor.

Findings

It is clear that in the first year of a new arrangement much depends upon the ability of the college to negotiate with the partner schools. This may have been in terms of the financial arrangements, the development of contractual statements and the understanding of roles and responsibilities, but it also required the rapid training of subject mentors and professional mentors within establishments in a very short period of time. For all the efforts made by the college to ensure understanding, tensions have developed and as the response of schools to the college evolves it would seem necessary that some common practice should be developed.

In the ten schools considered in detail, seven had staff who did not understand that the move of training into the schools was a government requirement and not undertaken by the college to save money. Five schools had staff who resented 'the additional work which we have to do', and three produced comments about 'the failure of the college staff to undertake their work'. There were, however, college-based meetings between subject tutors and subject mentors, and link tutors and professional mentors to ensure consistency of content, approach and assessment of student experience. These meetings have been successful in building bridges and extending understanding of the new roles, especially where support has been given to school staff who feel the work of assessment to be both onerous, and worrying because 'our decision on a teaching practice could ruin a student's life'.

Management

The comments made by participants when questioned about all aspects of the management of the new partnership indicate that there is a spectrum. This ranges between placement - seen as the traditional opportunity for students to develop within a school but 'boarded out' by the college; and partnership - seen as a joint activity between school and college but with an understanding that a student is part of school organisation and develops an experience supervised by a mentor. Where there is a whole school appreciation of the partnership, often linked to in-service and professional development opportunities, ITT takes place within a positive and supportive environment.

At a basic level the contractual arrangements require that a student should be given supervision and professional development opportunities whilst within a school. In return a fee is paid to the school to be used as a school's management decides to recompense the organisation and individuals for the additional work undertaken. Our evidence shows a wide range of practice - at the placement end the money has passed to the school central funds and the student works with a variety of staff although with a notional 'mentor' who may or may not get an honorarium, whilst at the partnership end of the spectrum all the fee is returned to the staff who will be working with the student, either as payment or as a time allocation. The tendency is for mentoring under the latter scheme to be very much 'one to one' with clearly defined responsibilities and highly supportive relationships.

Mentoring

The allocations of additional mentoring responsibilities appears to have been developed according to the way in which the revised scheme was 'sold' to the staff. Where a school has maintained an old pattern of working shown in three of the ten schools, the tendency is for the professional mentor to be a deputy head, and for the subject mentors to be heads of department although students indicate that these are usually staff who are heavily burdened with administration and for whom the student mentoring is seen as a bolt on activity. Two other schools have sought mentors who have demonstrated a

261

willingness to supervise, who have a background of successful teaching and interpersonal relationships and who see mentoring as a means of self-development. Not all these are totally altruistic in their motivation - we heard mention of the potential for promotion, and of additional payment because of the activity, but all have been selected because of the joint qualities of willingness and competence. The process of interview and selection with an annual review has done much to enhance the status, and the commitment, of the mentor in two schools.

The role of the professional mentor has changed considerably but in only seven of the ten schools does this appear to have been realised with evidence of regular counselling and support sessions for students, a prescribed course of meetings leading to a greater understanding of educational issues, and, in two schools, the use of appraisal processes for students. In the other schools there has been a change of nomenclature but the role is still seen as being that of an organiser for the students, frequently as an adjunct to a heavy administrative load.

Expectations

This variety of practice then leads to a range of expectations of the revised arrangements. There is still a view in four of the ten schools that the college staff should be taking a much greater part in the supervision and assessment of students than the time allocation under the contract allows. One or two observation visits by the subject tutors during the main practice are seen as inadequate by school staff both because of the hit and miss nature of a single visit and also because of the belief that assessment should be both developmental and continuous. These tend to be the schools where there is concern that the professional development profile is either inadequate or not usable as a basis for student evaluation and target setting in competence development. Five schools which have developed the arrangements to greatest advantage recognise that the college is there to assist if things are going wrong and to add a view at the evaluation stage so that there is some consistency in approach and in the determination of pass-fail standards, but have developed their own system of teaching, supervision and assessment. Best practice, seen in two of the ten schools, is based upon appraisal techniques and the constructive use of college professional development competence-based profiles. Indeed, one of these schools is actively seeking a partnership which can build upon the professional development potential of the college link for the good of all staff (Shaw 1992).

262

Funding

The funding of the schools to enable them to undertake this work is, in effect, an export of tutor labour time with a consequent, and radical, pruning of the hours allocated to tutors for work on the PGCE course within college. This has not been realised within the schools and we found considerable evidence of 'sleight of hand' in the way in which the funding was passed on to subject mentors. Although schools had been given a figure of five hours for one to one supervision of a student during the second term practice, 'the reality was that we were spending that time every week - especially where there were weaknesses'. In over half the schools there was no payment to the staff concerned but an additional sum for the departmental budget. Even where the funding has been passed on to the staff concerned it is seen as an honorarium and not as a payment for the additional hours worked. The expectations of staff are that the degree of support previously enjoyed will continue and they find it difficult to appreciate the way in which devolved funding requires the school to make realistic arrangements for time, reward or both.

Students and the college

Under the old course the students were clearly college student teachers. It might have been supposed that the formal arrangements of the new PGCE with the division of responsibilities are biased more towards school mentors and that this would have weakened the nexus of the student tutor relationship. The evaluation findings show that students have become even more attached to the college asking for 'a wee umbilical cord to the college' during a term's teaching practice. Unlike tutors and mentors, PGCE students are novices to the course and renewed each year, so their wish to be attached to a college tutor can only be explained by the structure of the course. Their attachment would appear to be the product of fragmented experiences and the ambivalence of the roles played by mentors within schools. In the words of one student, 'we need something of an anchor within the college set-up - we came to expect that that was the way things were done and with three practices we need a stable element somewhere'. In only two of the ten schools, however, had relationships between mentor and student become poor to the extent that some college intervention was required. If the wish for continued support by the college is widespread then it shows that students have an anticipated identity with the college which is exacerbated where student, subject mentor and subject tutor roles are poorly understood (Ryan

263

1986). The difficulty with the student's wish for reassuring contact, with tutors during their weeks in schools is that this time no longer exists. But to continue tutor contact in addition to the mentors' contact would inhibit change by maintaining the relics of former roles and the sediments of organisation of the old course. This has left some school staff with the feeling that they have 'an ineffective base upon which to build our understanding of the way in which we should support students' (see also Leithwood 1992).

The link tutor

There are potential problems in the way in which the professional development of a student who will have two, and may have three, school experiences is managed. The role of the college link tutor is fundamental to this and three of the schools were critical of both the inadequate time the link tutor had for visits, and the degree of involvement in the training and general education process. This is seen to be more of a problem if a student is either unsuited to the environment of the school, has poor interpersonal skills when working with school staff, or is patently unsuited to the profession. The schools which have developed a confidence in handling such problems have a strategy for coping with minimum initial involvement of the link tutor - except to keep him or her informed. At the other end of the scale there is no agreed process, and 'return to college' is seen as the only possible course of action. There is evidence that a student with problems who made headway in one school was persuaded to leave a placement, and the professional training, because of the immediate action taken within a department supported by senior management against the wishes of the professional mentor.

The subject tutor

Because a link tutor liaises with the professional mentors from a cluster of schools (or post-16 colleges) he or she teaches professional studies within the college elements to a mixed subject student group, a student group all of whom will have teaching experience within the tutor's cluster. Whether this mixed subject group of students is 'good' at promoting cross fertilisation of ideas or preventing group cohesion, is a question yet to be answered. However, such an arrangement does limit opportunity for the negotiation of link and subject tutors' tasks for the link tutor must now liaise with several subject tutors, just as subject tutors can only approach their students' 'place-

264

ment' schools through several link tutors. The change for the subject tutors has meant the loss of their pivotal role and for some this has not simply been the loss of tasks and responsibilities but also the undermining of their identities as teacher trainers. The pivotal role of the subject tutor has been taken by that of the professional link tutors who have been required to learn new tasks and acquire a new identity. Perversely, our evidence suggests that students are not prepared to assign a role to the link tutors which they had previously accorded to the subject tutors and it may need a longer period of course development within college before the new role is accepted - and used. Continuing our earlier suit metaphor, negotiation is now at the level of the PGCE team producing an 'off the peg' model for link and tutor role, universal in its cover but not fitting everyone's taste, 'it is OK but not quite me'.

Management of change

The fundamental problem appears to be that, because many school staffs have failed to assimilate the changed philosophy of student training and not changed their roles, the school is still not perceived as the focus of training. As a result there are examples of school staffs engineering an adverse view of college support and opposition to the new responsibilities within school. This was demonstrated as we built up a picture of the way in which change was introduced. At best the senior management team of the school had outlined the advantages and disadvantages in time, cost and commitment for the staff concerned and the school as a whole before seeking staff approval of participation in the scheme outlined by the college. This scheme had then been put to governors and in one instance, to parents, before acceptance was agreed. Three of the ten schools then used an in-service day to explore the administrative and pedagogic issues with the whole staff. The students then began their course with staff showing a high level of awareness of the nature of change and with some common consent as to the purpose of the exercise. At worst, in two of the schools, staff understanding of changed arrangements has been affected by the micro-political grapevine with talk of who is getting the money, the failure of the college to do its work, and the way in which some staff are involved in a new empire, scarcely conducive to a happy relationship for the students.

Although there is much talk about partnerships, ostensibly the government has created a market place for the training of teachers where the institutions responsible for their recruitment and quality of training purchase a major part of their courses from the schools. But it is not a market where perfect competition prevails and the institutions, as customers, cannot exercise the choice of the sovereign consumer and cannot control the quality and cost of that provided. The institutions have been compelled to purchase but the schools do not have to provide. Indeed, nationally there is evidence that some schools are reluctant providers or have declined to be part of teacher training courses. In a highly competitive arena it is difficult for teacher training institutions to negotiate change or move to new schools if costs rise or the quality of provision deteriorates.

Features of successful training schools

We have looked at the ten schools to see whether there are any common characteristics which might indicate potential success as a training school. We looked for evidence of the renegotiation and clear understanding of roles and a shift of philosophy from placement to partnership. The schools and one college of further education are drawn from: a range of sizes, including a school of 520 pupils which has taken ten students very successfully; a range of organisations including an independent grammar school, and schools which have become semi-selective since the operation of parental choice; a range of former association with the college, including schools which helped to formulate the present arrangements and 'newcomers', and a range of socio-economic backgrounds. On our spectrum of partnership there are good and bad within each grouping. The characteristics of those schools which have successfully adapted to change do have some similarities in style and culture.

It appears that we are able to see the constituents of a school experience which is valued by the student. It is mentored by a selected member of staff with wide experience of the subject and willingness to think deeply about the mentoring process. He or she receives a fair reward in time or payment for the effort involved. It is supervised by a professional mentor who not only coordinates and assesses but also fosters a full and challenging professional studies programme and maintains positive links with the college. It is staffed within the school by people who understand and apply professional assessment in a way which supports individual development, and above all it takes place within a welcoming and confident environment where the training role is seen as a positive contribution to whole school life. The tension free situation reflects the open management style and positive culture of co-operation which marks success in so many other aspects of school organisation.

266

The future

The way forward appears to us to lie not simply in the development of college-based training courses for subject and professional mentors but in the funding of opportunities for the college to work within individual schools to develop some shared view of the training role, its philosophy and demands, and the procedures necessary to ensure consistency in standards and approach. The difficulty is that schools at the placement end of the continuum fail to recognise that a change of culture is required.

No doubt time might bring about the further assimilation of the new mentor and tutor roles, and this, together with new and changing staff,will facilitate the realisation of the planned change to a school-based PGCE. In the meantime the sediments of the old culture,the adherence to past procedures and the playing out of lost role identities, will inhibit and divert the direction of the change. This is the well known phenomenon of the difference between intended and unintended consequences of change. The PGCE management team can insist on observing the new procedures that govern mentor, tutor and student relationships but it is these procedures that have either not been assimilated by teachers or changed the roles of tutors. To cut this knot it will be necessary to utilise old culture to found the new. This can be done by identifying and using teachers who approximated to mentors to train their colleagues. In the college it means recognising and affirming the expertise of the subject tutors in mentor training and in the production of course materials. With this positive orientation all involved might be persuaded to try on a new suit.

Part 4
CONCLUSION

22   Policy, market and school-based training

Vincent Hanley

The work reported in the preceding chapters reveals many of the complexities and dilemmas of school-based training. As a collection, it adds to the accumulating evidence for rational debate and helps to redress the balance against dogmatism and sloganising. The assumption in this chapter is that the different sets of findings speak for themselves and, in a number of cases, make clear links or follow familiar themes. The purpose of this chapter, therefore, is not to subsume links and themes in broad, unifying conclusions. The preferred approach is to concentrate on a small number of issues and, where appropriate, to consider implications.

The imposition of school-based training with clear, prescriptive elements and the opening up of new routes into teaching are part of a market approach. Tensions and changes attendant on the embryonic market are recurring, underlying themes in this book; there is concern to understand the market, the rationale behind it and the ways in which it is displacing familiar, valued models and practices. Other concerns identified by contributors cluster round partnership and competences. The basis and operation of partnership is still being explored; there is a noticeable convergence on the interpretation of new, professional roles in the school and in the HEI as another important issue. The whole question of resources, as indicated by many researchers, remains problematical. The positioning of competences as the core of the student-experience, and the consistency of the experience itself, are matters of continuing interest.

The market in teacher training, like others in the public services, is founded on consumer choice and ubiquitous competition. Choice lies in the hands of the student who, depending on individual circumstances, can choose a route into teaching e.g. Licensed Teacher Scheme, School Centred Teacher Training and school-based, conventional courses (BEd, PGCE). Choice may be limited but, there is competition for the student and for the funding that

271

follows him/her. A further competitive element is the transfer of funding to the school, via the HEI, for each placement; in the present climate, the placement yields income and it is reasonable to assume that the school will wish to go into partnership with the highest paying HEI in its area. This may not always be the case; other factors may affect the school's choice. Nevertheless, recognisable elements of the market are in place; with consumer choice on one hand and competition on the other, it is anticipated that market forces will decide eventually a future for initial teacher training in which successful partnership schemes oust the unsuccessful. Success may be measured by compliance with a notional, regulatory model of partnership and conformity to approved models of teaching.

Evidence in preceding chapters suggests an increasing awareness of market approaches but, for participants, choice and competition are still uncomfortable notions. For the government, the notions are being translated into guiding principles essential to a new, pervasive vision for re-constructing society. Teacher training, argue ideologues, must be reconstructed because it, too, has manifestly failed; success can be achieved by defining it in terms of market processes and outcomes, objectified in the apparent neutrality of commonsense business arrangements - i.e. partnership - or occupational skills - i.e. competences. The apparent neutrality lends a political gloss to reconstructed training, endows it with a sense of 'naturalness' and removes it to a safer, less contestable distance. In reality, the government is pursuing its policy through its creation, the market; training is commodified and products are available. The market is a socio-politico framework for training, established without recourse to empirical research findings and interpreted in detail in the technical-rationalist language of DFE circulars. In these circulars, the technicist model of the teacher is broken down - some might say atomised - under broad categories of competences, redolent with values and purposes that are difficult to reconcile with those of the reflective practitioner. The important point here is that Circulars 9/92 and 14/93, like all DFE circulars, mediate policy and set the parameters for relations with, and within, the education system. DFE circulars are not politically neutral.

Within present parameters, teacher training is being devolved and dispersed; the impression given is that, in a move to redress imbalances between student experience in school and HEI and between theory and practice, more training has been transferred to school. The commonsense justification, derived from New Right thinking has populist appeal. School-based training is often portrayed as liberation from previous well-intentioned but misguided courses in HEIs and, it is alleged, responsible for failure in education. Ironically, the change from school-based training in France repor-

272

ted by Cotton (Chapter 9) is a thought-provoking contrast. Yet, while liberation proceeded apace, many powers, formerly dispersed, were gathered and centralised under new legislation which the Secretary for State, both directly and through quangos, now holds.

In this situation, centralising and liberating tendencies may seem paradoxical but, in terms of Realpolitik, perhaps the paradox can be explained. The market in initial teacher training allows the government to withdraw - or to be seen to withdraw - from the close exercise of power; as a result, teacher training is then seen to be regulated and managed from centres of influence at lower levels, in accordance with policy. The market and its ramifications, therefore, help to convey an impression of government withdrawal; in terms of political rhetoric, it might be described as 'rolling back the frontiers of the state'. Control is less overt and is exercised through what Kickert (1991) calls 'steering at a distance' and Ball (1994) elaborates as 'a new paradigm of public governance'. The governance, Ball suggests, deflects resistance and adopts a top-down style in managing its centres of influence. According to Kickert, there is '... no negotiated way of protest, complaint or formal appeal'. These dimensions of context and control will be recognised, no doubt, by many teacher educators.

As the work of contributors shows, the new terrain of initial teacher training is still being explored. The complexities and dilemmas they report reveal an unsettled state of affairs in a new system based on different values and about which there was little real consultation. The themes, processes and case studies discussed by researchers cover a wide spectrum but, as indicated at the outset, we will concentrate on a limited number; they are partnership, professional roles, competences and student experience.

Partnership between school and HEI is not entirely the invention of the market; partnership had been evolving in different forms. What has changed is the formalising of new partnership arrangements and professional roles to sustain it as a market entity. It is within these contexts that contributors reported. The processes through which partnership might be interpreted and planned is central to work by Ellis (Chapter 11); consensus and benefits to both partners are essential. Under new formalised arrangements, however, even consensus must be translated into accountability in the form of written agreements (in the first instance) as noted by Dann (Chapter 5) and Kerr (Chapter 8). Yet, despite agreements, partnerships need to allow for adjustment (Glover, Chapter 21) and the wide approval afforded to principles of partnership should be acknowledged. In espousing partnership, Lambert and Totterdell (Chapter 2) see opportunities for genuine bridge-building between the school and HEI. Dormer's findings (Chapter 16) confirm a school's ability to 'go it alone' - i.e. single proprietorship, not partnership - and, at the same time, an unwillingness to do so. Respondents were whole-heartedly in favour of partnership. In this and other studies, the issue of resources - their distribution, loss and gain - within partnership surfaces frequently and is subtly exposed, for example, in work by Constable, Hubbard and Norton (Chapter 6). The work suggests a need for more detailed probing of the impact of school based training on schools and HEI. It may serve also as a reminder of a general reluctance to discuss resources.

The ways in which teachers and tutors are interpreting and realising new roles emerge in several studies. For some teachers, Dann (Chapter 5) explains, the transition from supervision to mentoring 'carries mixed emotions'; similar effects of change are reported by Blake, Hanley, Jennings and Lloyd (Chapter 14). Martin (Chapter 7) likens the loss of former roles to bereavement; the short timescale for change - and speed of implementation - disorientate tutors and teachers. At the operational level, time is a major issue; the responsibilities, tasks and demands are heavy and, in toto, there are inadequate time allowances. The issue here is the hidden subsidising of teacher-training, with attendant human cost in stress and possible loss in course quality because of overloading. Some might see the solution in developing better time management skills. The need for training and development in this and other areas is confirmed by Kerr (Chapter 8) and Dormer (Chapter 16). Underlying many of the findings on this topic, of course, are tensions arising from conflict between incumbents' long held values and professional attitudes and the new, market emphasis on totalising, competence and performance.

Cain and Kickham (Chapter 13) detail the careful, collaborative processes through which competences were agreed in 'teacherly terms' and the benefits that accrued from the exercise. Baumfield and Leat (Chapter 3) trace the emergence of five broad areas to replace the atomising of teaching into 27 competences. The usefulness of the competences as foci for discussion with students is universally acknowledged and, interestingly, Baumfield and Leat found little discrepancy between teachers' and tutors' perceptions of qualities to be developed in students (for effective teaching). What is clear, of course, is that competences are wide open to interpretation. Constable, Hubbard and Norton (Chapter 6) remark on the emphasis on different competences in different schools. There are also concerns - in the absence of guidelines from the DFE - about levels of competence and the way that some may be more highly rated that others. The findings here also cast doubt on how performance might be judged in a holistic way.

Research into the student experience produced mixed findings. Kerr

(Chapter 8) found that students' school experiences were satisfactory or better, as did Blake, Hanley, Jennings and Lloyd (Chapter 14) However, the major issue in this area is differential school experience. The differences in experience were most noticeable in the levels of support afforded in schools and in the variety of local practices. Kerr (Chapter 8) comments on the different cultures between schools in the same partnership scheme and, indeed, between departments in the same school. Opportunities for further interpretation of theory and practice through school-based training are noted by Dormer (Chapter 16) and Egan (Chapter 15) but findings from ChIHE's project (Chapter 14) suggest that theory was being seriously displaced. Students were very keen to demonstrate competence through 'hands on' experience from an early stage.

The effects of the market can be detected in many areas of initial teacher training but, at the present time, its inroads are uneven. The 'old' has not yet been removed; the 'new' is not yet firmly established. When judged by what some professionals say and feel (Martin, Chapter 7), the speed and depth of change is revolutionary; when measured by the findings of others, change seems evolutionary. Whatever the case, the likelihood is that developments set in train by Circulars 9/92 and 14/93 will continue; since there is no going back, teacher-training must find a modus vivendi with market principles. This speculation is a vantage point from which to glance beyond the current school-based context. We cannot be sure what the long-term consequences might be but present trends are one kind of augury. For example, the shifting of more training into school - with increasing resources and funding to follow as years go by - will inevitably force the HEI to re-consider its position; with reducing participation and funding, the ability of the institution to hold a position in teacher-training will be severely tested. Contrary to the wishes of many schools, therefore, the HEI may be forced to abandon its role. At the moment, there are no substantial findings from research into SCITT schemes so we do not know how schools would - or could - cope.

The increasing sense of mis-match between the government's implied definition of professionalism in its circulars and those held by teachers and tutors will need to be brought into the open. Here, we might expect some polarisations - e.g. competent technicist v reflective practitioner; the accompanying tensions and conceptual difficulties affecting the quality of training will warrant researchers' attention.

Research at the deeper interfaces between the state and its education system also may be needed. The government controls the market and makes claims about freedom of choice and competition. These claims should be explored in order to test the view that school-based and customised approaches are being developed to neutralise educational problems and remove the government from front-line blame.

References

Abbott, I. D. and Evans, L. (1994) 'Separating the HEAP from the SAP: Initial Teacher Education in the Secondary PGCE Sector', *Mentoring*, 1(3).

Alexander, R. (1992) *Policy and Practice in Primary Education*, London: Routledge.

Applebee, A. (1989) 'The Enterprise We are a Part of: Learning to Teach' in Moon, B. and Murphy, P. (eds) *Developments in Learning and Assessment*, London: Hodder and Stoughton.

Ashcroft, K. and Griffiths, M. (1989) 'Reflective Teachers and Reflective Tutors: School Experience in an Initial Teacher Education Course', *Journal of Education for Teaching*, 15 (1).

Ashton, P., Henderson, E. and Peacock, A. (1989) *Teacher Education through Classroom Evaluation: the principles and practice of IT-INSET*, London: Routledge.

Assessment of Performance Unit (APU) (1991) *The Assessment of Performance in Design and Technology*, London: School Examinations and Assessment Council.

Avis, J. (1994) 'Teacher Professionalism: One More Time', *Educational Review*, 46 (1).

Bailey, A. and Oldroyd, D. (1993) 'School Managed Training: A Re-Examination of School Management Task Force Policy', *British Journal of In-Service Education*, 19 (2).

Ball, S. J. (1994) *Education Reform: A Critical and Post-Structural Approach*, Buckingham: Open University Press.

Bancel, D. (1989) *Créer une Nouvelle Dynamique de la Formation des Maîtres*, Rapport du Recteur Daniel Bancel à Lionel Jospin, Ministère de l'Education Nationale: Paris.

Banks, F. (ed.) (1994) *Teaching Technology*, London: Routledge.

Barnes, H. (1989) 'Structuring Knowledge for Beginning Teaching' in Reynolds, M. C. (ed.) *Knowledge Base for the Beginning Teacher*, Oxford: Pergamon Press.

Barnett, R. (1992) 'The Learning Society', *Reflections on Higher Education*, 4.

Barrett, E., Barton, L., Furlong, J., Galvin, C., Miles, S. and Whitty, G. (1992) *Initial Teacher Education in England and Wales: a Topography*, Interim Report by the Modes of Teacher Education Research Project.

Barrow, R. and Milburn, G. (1990) *A Critical Dictionary of Educational Concepts*, (second edition) London: Harvester Wheatsheaf.

Barth, R. (1990) *Improving Schools From Within*, San Francisco: Jossey-Bass.

Benton, P. (ed.) (1990) *The Oxford Internship Scheme: Integration and Partnership in Initial Teacher Education*, London: Calouste Gulbenkian Foundation.

Berliner, D. (1993) *Implications of Studies of Expertise in Pedagogy for Teacher Education and Evaluation*, Education Testing Service.

Bines, H. (1992) 'Issues in Course Design' in Bines H. and Watson D. (eds) *Developing Professional Education*, Buckingham: Society for Research into Higher Education and Open University Press.

Bines H. and Watson D. (eds) (1992) *Developing Professional Education*, Buckingham: Society for Research into Higher Education and Open University Press.

Booth, M. (1993) 'The Effectiveness and Role of the Mentor in School: the Students' View', *Cambridge Journal of Education*, 23 (2).

Booth, M., Furlong, J. and Wilkin, M. (eds) (1990) *Partnership in Initial Teacher Training*, London: Cassell.

Broadfoot, P. and Osborn, M. with Gilly, M. and Bûcher, A. (1993) *Perceptions of Teaching: Primary School Teachers in England and France*, London: Cassell.

Brown, S. and McIntyre, D. (1993) *Making Sense of Teaching*, Buckingham: Open University Press.

Buchmann, M. and Floden, R. E. (1993) *Detachment and Concern: Conversations in the Philosophy of Teacher Education*, London, Cassell.

Burke, J. B., Hansen, W. R. and Johnson, C. (1975) *Criteria for Describing and Assessing Competency Programs*, Syracuse University, New York: National Consortium of Competency Based Education Centres.

Burke, J. W. (ed.) (1989) *Competency Based Education and Training*, London: Falmer Press.

278

Burn, K. (1992) 'Collaborative Teaching' in Wilkin, M. (ed.) *Mentoring in Schools*, London: Kogan Page.

Busher, H. and Simmons, C. (1992) 'Living with CATE: the Case of Reflective Student Teachers', *Educational Studies*, 18, (1).

Calderhead, J. (ed.) (1988) *Teachers' Professional Learning*, London: Falmer Press.

Calderhead, J. (1989) 'Reflective Teaching and Teacher Education', *Teaching and Teacher Education*, 5 (1).

Calderhead, J. (1994) 'The Reform of Initial Teacher Education and Research on Learning to Teach: Contrasting Ideas' in John, P. and Lucas, P (eds) *Partnership and Progress: New Developments in History Teacher Education and History Teaching*, Sheffield: Standing Conference of History Teacher Educators in the United Kingdom (SCHTE) in association with The Division of Education, University of Sheffield.

Calderhead, J. and Gates, P. (1993) *Conceptualising Reflection in Teacher Development*, London: Falmer Press.

Chandler, P., Robinson, W. P. and Noyes, P. (1991) 'Is a Proactive Student Teacher a Better Student Teacher?', *Research in Education*, 45.

Chi, M. T. H., Glaser, R. and Rees, E. (1982) 'Experience and Problem Solving' in Sternberg R. J. (ed.) *Advances in the Psychology of Human Intelligence, Volume 1*, Hillsdale, New Jersey: Lawrence Erlbaum Associates.

Cohen, L. and Manion, L. (1994) *Research Methods in Education*, (fourth edition) London: Routledge.

Constable, H. and Norton, J. (1994) 'Student Teachers and their Professional Encounters' in Reid, I., Constable, H. and Griffiths, R. (eds) *Teacher Education Reform: Current Research*, London: Paul Chapman Publishing.

Cotton, P. and Dexter, S. (1985) *Observations on the French Education System*, Centre d'Etudes Pedagogiques de Sèvres.

Crozier, G., Menter, I. and Pollard, A. (1990) 'Changing Partnership' in Booth, M., Furlong, J. and Wilkin, M. (eds) *Partnership in Initial Teacher Training*, London: Cassell.

Cullingford C. (1994) 'Steps in Training Must be Sound', *Times Educational Supplement*, 10 June.

Daloz, L. A. (1986) *Effective Teaching and Mentoring*, San Francisco: Jossey-Bass.

Dart, L. and Drake, P. (1993) 'School-Based Teacher Training: a Conservative Practice?', *Journal of Education for Teaching*, 19 (2).

DeJong, T. and Ferguson Hessler, M. (1986), 'Cognitive Structures of Good and Poor Novice Problem Solvers in Physics', *Journal of Educational Psychology*, 78.

Department of Education and Science (DES) (1972) *Teacher Education and Training* (The James Report), London: HMSO.

Department of Education and Science (DES) (1983) *Teaching Quality*, London: HMSO.

Department of Education and Science (DES) (1984) *Initial Teacher Training: Approval of Courses. Circular No. 3/84*, London: HMSO.

Department of Education and Science (DES) (1989a) *The Education (Teachers) Regulations 1989 Circular No. 18 89*, London: HMSO.

Department of Education and Science (DES) (1989b) *Initial Teacher Training: Approval of Courses. Circular No. 24/89*, London: HMSO.

Department of Education and Science (DES) (1989c) *Initial Teacher Training in France*, London: HMSO.

Department of Education and Science (DES) (1992a) *Speech of the Secretary of State for Education and Science to the North of England Education Conference*, Southport, 4 January.

Department of Education and Science (DES) (1992b) *Reform of Initial Teacher Training, A Consultation Document*, London: HMSO.

Department of Education and Science (DES) (1992c) *Curriculum Organisation and Classroom Practice in Primary Schools, A discussion paper* (Robin Alexander, Jim Rose and Chris Woodhead), London: HMSO.

Department of Education and Science (DES) (1992d) *Curriculum Organisation and Classroom Practice in Primary School*, London: HMSO.

Department of Education and Science (DES)/Welsh Office (WO) (1990) *Technology in the National Curriculum*, London: HMSO.

Department of Education Northern Ireland (DENI) (1993) *Review of Teacher Training in Northern Ireland.*

Department for Education (DFE) (1992) *Initial Teacher Training (Secondary Phase). Circular No. 9/92*, London: HMSO.

Department for Education (DFE) (1993a) *The Initial Teacher Training of Primary School Teachers: New Criteria for Course Approval Draft Circular*, London: HMSO.

Department for Education (DFE) (1993b) *The Government's Proposals for the Reform of Initial Teacher Training*, London: HMSO.

Department for Education (DFE) (1993c) *Letter on the Second Round of the School-Centred Initial Teacher Training Scheme (SCITT)*, 29 September.

Department for Education (DFE) (1993d) *The Initial Training of Primary School Teachers: New Criteria for Courses. Circular No. 14/93,* London: HMSO.

Department for Education (DFE) (1993e) *The Education Bill: An Act to Make Provision About Teacher Training and Related Matters,* 23 November, London: HMSO.

Dormer, J. (1994) 'The Role of the Mentor in Secondary Schools' in Wilkin, M. and Sankey, D. (eds) *Collaboration and Transition in Initial Teacher Training,* London: Kogan Page.

Dunne, R. and Harvard, G. (1993) 'A Model of Teaching and its Implications for Mentoring' in McIntyre, D., Hagger, H. and Wilkin, M. (eds) *Mentoring: Perspectives on School-Based Teacher Education,* London: Kogan Page.

Dunne, R. and Jennings, S. (1994) *The Model of Student Teacher Learning,* Unit 4 Module P45 Mentor Training, University of Exeter.

Earley, P. (1992) *Standards for School Management, The School Management Competences Project,* London: HMSO.

Earley, P. and Kinder, K. (1993) *Initiation Rights: Effective Induction Practice for New Teachers,* Slough: National Foundation for Educational Research (NFER).

Education Nationale: Écoles (1985) *Arrêté du 22 Janvier 1985,* Paris: Ministère de l'Education Nationale.

Edwards, D. and Mercer, N. (1987) *Common Knowledge,* London: Methuen.

Edwards, G. (1992) 'A Strategy for the Curriculum', *Journal of Curriculum Studies,* 24 (5).

Edwards, T. (1992) 'Issues and Challenges in Initial Teacher Education', *Cambridge Journal of Education,* 22 (3).

Elliott, B. and Calderhead, J. (1993) 'Mentoring for Teacher Development: Possibilities and Caveats' in McIntyre, D., Hagger, H. and Wilkin, M. (eds) *Mentoring: Perspectives on School-Based Teacher Education,* London: Kogan Page.

Elliott, J. (1988) 'Why Put the Case Study at the Heart of the Police Training Curriculum?' in Southgate, P. (ed.) *New Directions in Police Training,* London: HMSO.

Elliott, J. (1991), 'A Model of Professionalism and its Implications for Teacher Education', *British Educational Research Journal,* 17, (4).

Ellis, P. D. (1988) 'Developing a Policy for Teaching Practice Supervision' in Terrell, C. and Coles, D. (eds) *Recent Innovations in Initial Teacher Education for Intending Primary School Teachers,* Cheltenham College of St. Paul and St. Mary.

281

Eurydice (1991) *Initial Teacher Training in the Member States of the European Community*, Brussels: Eurydice, European Unit.

Everton, T. and Impey, G. (1989) *IT-INSET: Partnership in Training - the Leicestershire Experience*, London: Fulton.

Everton, T. and White, S. (1992) 'Partnership in Training: the University of Leicester's New Model of School-Based Teacher Education', *Cambridge Journal of Education*, 22 (2).

Figueroa, P. (1991) *Education and the Social Construction of 'Race'*, London: Routledge.

Flanagan, J. C. (1954) 'The Critical Incident Technique', *Psychological Bulletin*, 51.

Follain, M. (1994) 'In and Out of the Classroom', *Education*, 28 January.

Fullan, M. (1991) *The New Meaning of Educational Change*, London: Cassell.

Fullan, M. (1992) *Successful School Improvement: the Implementation Perspective and Beyond*, Milton Keynes: Open University Press.

Furlong, J. (1990) 'School-Based Training: the Students' Views' in Booth, M., Furlong, J. and Wilkin, M. (eds) *Partnership in Initial Teacher Training*, London: Cassell.

Furlong, J. (1994) 'The Rise and Rise of the Mentor in British Initial Teacher Training' in Yeomans, R. and Sampson, J. (eds) *Mentorship in the Primary School*, London: Falmer Press.

Furlong, J., Hirst, P., Pocklington, K. and Miles, S. (1988) *Initial Teacher Training and the Role of the Schools*, Milton Keynes: Open University Press.

Gitlin, A. and Smyth, J. (1989) *Teacher Evaluations: Educative Alternatives*, Lewes: Falmer Press.

Grace, G. (1972) *Role Conflict and The Teacher*, London: Routledge and Kegan Paul.

Grace, G. (1993) *London Institute of Education PGCE: Visiting Examiner's Reports for 1992/93*, Durham: University of Durham School of Education.

Greaves, T. and Shaw, K. (1992) 'A New Look in French Teacher Education?', *Cambridge Journal of Education*, 22, (2).

Grieve, E. (unpublished) *Project Work in Technology at Key Stage 4*, (Research in Progress) The Open University.

Grossman, P. L., Wilson, S. M. and Shulman, L. S. (1989) 'Teachers of Substance: Subject Matter Knowledge for Teaching' in Reynolds, M. C. (ed.) *Knowledge Base for the Beginning Teacher*, Oxford: Pergamon Press.

Haggarty, L. (1990) 'Learning to Teach: Discussing and Running Two Curriculum Programmes' in Benton, P. (ed.) *The Oxford Internship Scheme: Integration and Partnership in Initial Teacher Education*, London: Calouste Gulbenkian Foundation.

Hagger, H., Burn, K. and McIntyre, D. (1993) *The School Mentor Handbook*, London: Kogan Page.

Hake, C. (1993) *Partnership in Initial Teacher Training: Talk and Chalk*, Institute of Education, London: Tuffnell Press.

Hammersley, M. (1993) 'On the Teacher as Researcher', *Educational Action Research*, 1 (3).

Handy, C. (1985) *Understanding Organisations*, Harmondsworth: Penguin.

Hargreaves, D. H. (1994) 'The New Professionalism: The Synthesis of Professional and Institutional Development', *Teaching and Teacher Education*, 10 (4).

Harland, J. (1992) *PGCE Camden Area Based Scheme 1991-1992: An Evaluation*, London: University of London Institute of Education (ULIE).

Harrison, E. (1994) *What is Professional Performance: Some Considerations Arising from the Practice of being a Teacher-Mentor*, Unpublished M.A. dissertation, St. Mary's University College, Twickenham.

Harrison, M. E. (1993) 'Halfway There: Reflections on Introducing Design and Technology into the Secondary Phase' in McCormick, R., Murphy, P. and Harrison M. (eds) *Teaching and Learning Technology*, Wokingham: Addison-Wesley.

Harrison, M. E. (1994) 'Science and Technology: Partnership or Divorce?' in Banks, F. (ed.) *Teaching Technology*, London: Routledge.

Harvard, G. and Dunne, R. (1992) 'The Mentor in Developing Teacher Competence' in *Introductory Course for Subject-Tutors and Co-Tutors: Readings*, University of Exeter.

Haylock, D. (1994) 'The Extra Pair of Hands Comes with a Free Brain' in Reid, I., Constable, H. and Griffiths, R. (eds) *Teacher Education Reform: Current Research*, London: Paul Chapman Publishing.

Hennessy, S. and McCormick, R. (1994) 'The General Problem-Solving Process in Technology Education: Myth or Reality?' in Banks, F. (ed.) *Teaching Technology*, London: Routledge.

Her Majesty's Inspectorate (HMI) (1983) *Teaching in Schools: the Context of Initial Teacher Training*, London: HMSO.

Her Majesty's Inspectorate (HMI) (1990) *Aspects of Humanities Provision*, London: HMSO.

Her Majesty's Inspectorate (HMI) (1991) *School-based Initial Teacher Training in England and Wales. A Report by HM Inspectorate*, London: HMSO.

Her Majesty's Inspectorate (HMI) (1994) *HMI Report on Initial Teacher Training at the University of Leicester*, London: HMSO.

Hill, D. (1989) 'Teachers' Education, Teachers and that Attack on Equality', *National Union of Teachers (NUT) Education Review*, 3, (2).

Hillgate Group (1989) *Learning to Teach*, London: Claridge Press.

Hillman and Stoll (1994) *SIN Research Matters No. 1: Understanding School Improvement*, London: University of London Institute of Education (ULIE).

Holden, C. (1994) 'Unwanted Burden', *Education*, 184 (8).

Hollis, M. and Loukes, S. (eds) (1982) *Rationality and Relativism*, Oxford: Basil Blackwell.

Hopkins, D. (1986) 'The Change Process and Leadership in Schools', *School Organisation*, 6 (1).

Houghton, V., McHugh, R. and Morgan, C. (eds) (1975) *Management in Education: The Management of Organisations and Individuals*, London: Ward Lock Educational in association with The Open University Press.

Hoyle, E. (1969) *The Role of the Teacher*, London: Routledge and Kegan Paul.

Hoyle, E. (1975) 'Professionality, Professionalism and Control in Teaching' in Houghton, V., McHugh, R. and Morgan, C. (eds) *Management in Education: The Management of Organisations and Individuals*, London: Ward Lock Educational in association with The Open University Press.

Hyland, T. (1994) 'Silk Purses and Sows' Ears: NVQs, GNVQs and Experiential Learning', *Cambridge Journal of Education*, 24 (2).

IUFM - Douai (1991) 'A Propos du Role du Terrain Professional dans la Formation des Maîtres-formateurs Affectes dans les Écoles Annexe et d'application', *Unité de Formation de la Porte d'Arras, Douai*, Douai: IUFM.

Jaworski, B. (1993) 'The Professional Development of Teachers - The Potential of Critical Reflection', *British Journal of In-Service Education*, 19 (3).

Jeffrey, J. R. (1990) 'Design Methods in CDT', *Journal of Art and Design Education*, 9 (1).

John, P. D. (1991) 'A Qualitative Study of British Student Teachers' Lesson Planning Perspectives', *Journal of Education for Teaching*, 17 (3).

John, P. and Lucas, P. (1994) 'Putting the Agenda into Practice' in John, P. and Lucas, P. (eds) *Partnership and Progress: New Developments in History Teacher Education and History Teaching*, Sheffield: Standing Conference of History Teacher Educators in the United Kingdom (SCHTE) in association with The Division of Education, University of Sheffield.

Jospin, L. (1989), *Loi d'Orientation sur l'Education No. 89-486*, Paris: Ministère de l'Education Nationale.

Kerr, D. (1994) 'The Changing Relationship with Schools in Teacher Education: the Leicester Partnership Scheme' in John, P. and Lucas, P. (eds) *Partnership and Progress: New Developments in History Teacher Education and History Teaching*, Sheffield: Standing Conference of History Teacher Educators in the United Kingdom (SCHTE) in association with The Division of Education, University of Sheffield.

Kickert, W. (1991) *Steering at a Distance: A New Paradigm of Public Governance in Dutch Higher Education*, paper for the European Consortium for Political Research, University of Essex, March.

Kolb, D. A. (1984) *Experiential Learning*, Englewood Cliffs, New Jersey: Prentice Hall.

La Boskey, V. (1988) 'A Conceptual Framework for Reflection in Pre-Service Teacher Education' in Calderhead, J. (ed.) *Teachers' Professional Learning*, London: Falmer Press.

Lacey, C. and Lamont, W. (1976) *Partnership with Schools: An Experiment in Teacher Education*, Falmer: University of Sussex Education Area Occasional Paper No. 5.

Lambert, D. and Sankey, D. (1994) 'Classrooms as Ecosystems', *Journal of Teacher Development*, 3 (3).

Lambert, D. and Totterdell, M. (1993) *Professional Studies and the Post-graduate Beginning Teacher*, Occasional Papers in Teacher Education and Training, 3, London: University of London Institute of Education (ULIE).

Lambert, D. and Totterdell, M. (1995 forthcoming) *Training Tomorrow's Teachers Today: A Professional Studies Model for the Developing Partnership in Teacher Education*, Occasional Papers in Teacher Education and Training: Perspectives, London: University of London Institute of Education (ULIE).

Lawes, J. S. (1987) 'Student Teachers' Awareness of Pupils' Nonverbal Responses', *Journal of Education for Teaching*, 13 (3).

Lawlor, S. (1990) *Teachers Mistaught: Training in Theories or Education in Subjects?*, London: Centre for Policy Studies.

Leinhardt, G. (1988) 'Situated Knowledge and Expertise in Teaching' in Calderhead, J. (ed.) *Teachers' Professional Learning*, London: Falmer Press.

Leithwood, K. A. (1992) *Teacher Development and Educational Change*, Lewes: Falmer Press.

Livingston, C. and Borko, H. (1989) 'Expert-Novice Differences in Teaching: A Cognitive Analysis and Implications for Teacher Education', *Journal of Teacher Education*, 40 (4).

Lucas, P. and Watts, R. (eds) (1992) *Meeting the Challenge: Preparing Tomorrow's History Teachers*, Sheffield: Standing Conference of History Teacher Educators in the United Kingdom (SCHTE) in association with The Division of Education, University of Sheffield.

Marris, P. (1986) *Loss and Change*, London: Routledge and Kegan Paul.

Maynard, T. and Furlong, J. (1993) 'Learning to Teach and Models of Mentoring' in McIntyre, D., Hagger, H. and Wilkin, M. (eds) *Mentoring: Perspectives on School-Based Teacher Education*, London: Kogan Page.

McClelland, D. C. and Dailey, C. (1973) *Evaluating New Methods of Measuring the Qualities needed in Superior Foreign Service Information Officers*, Boston: McBer and Co.

McCormick, R. (1990) 'Technology and the National Curriculum: the Creation of a "Subject" by Committee?', *The Curriculum Journal*, 1 (1).

McCormick, R., Murphy, P. and Harrison M. (eds) (1993) *Teaching and Learning Technology*, Wokingham: Addison-Wesley.

McCulloch, M. and Lock, N. (1994) 'Mentorship Developments in the Primary Phase of Initial Teacher Education at the University of Reading', *Mentoring*, 1 (3).

McDiarmid, G., Ball, D. L. and Anderson, C. W. (1989) 'Why Staying One Chapter Ahead Doesn't Really Work: Subject-Specific Pedagogy' in Reynolds, M. C. (ed.) *Knowledge Base for the Beginning Teacher*, Oxford: Pergamon Press.

McIntyre, D. (1990) 'Ideas and Principles Guiding the Internship Scheme' in Benton, P. (ed.) *The Oxford Internship Scheme: Integration and Partnership in Initial Teacher Education*, London: Calouste Gulbenkian Foundation.

McIntyre, D. and Hagger, H. (1992) 'Professional Development through the Oxford Internship Model', *British Journal of Educational Studies*, 40 (3).

McIntyre, D. and Hagger, H. (1993) 'Teachers' Expertise and Models of Mentoring' in McIntyre, D., Hagger, H. and Wilkin, M. (eds) *Mentoring: Perspectives on School-Based Teacher Education*, London: Kogan Page.

McIntyre, D., Hagger, H. and Wilkin, M. (eds) (1993) *Mentoring: Perspectives on School-Based Teacher Education*, London: Kogan Page.

McNamara, D. (1991) 'Subject Knowledge and its Application: Problems and Possibilities for Teacher Educators', *Journal of Education for Teaching*, 17 (2).

Miller, S. and Taylor, P. (1993) *The Teacher Education Curriculum in the Member States of the European Community*, Brussels: ATEE Cahiers 3.

Ministère de l'Education Nationale (1991) *Les Cycles à l'École Primaire*, Paris: Hachette.

Moon, B. and Murphy, P. (eds) (1989) *Developments in Learning and Assessment*, London: Hodder and Stoughton.

Munro, R. (1989) *A Case Study of School-Based Innovation in Secondary Teacher Training*, Unpublished Ph.D. thesis, University of Auckland, New Zealand.

National Curriculum Council (NCC) (1991) *The National Curriculum and the Initial Training of Student, Articled and Licensed Teachers*, York: National Curriculum Council.

Naughton, J. (1988) 'What is "technology"?' from *T102 Living with Technology, Unit 1, Introduction*, Milton Keynes: Open University.

Neather, E. J. (1993) 'Teacher Education and the Role of the University: European Perspectives', *Research Papers in Education: Policy and Practice*, 8 (1).

Neil, S. R. St. J. (1989) 'The Predictive Value of Assessments of the Non-verbal Skills of Applicants to Postgraduate Teacher Training', *Journal of Education for Teaching*, 15 (2).

Némo, P. (1991) *Porquoi Ont-ils Tué Jules Ferry?*, Paris: Grasset.

Norris, N. (1991) 'The Trouble with Competence', *Cambridge Journal of Education*, 21 (3).

Office for Standards in Education (OFSTED) (1993a) *Working Papers for the Inspection of Secondary Initial Training*, London: HMSO.

Office for Standards in Education (OFSTED) (1993b) *Handbook for the Inspection of Schools*, London: HMSO.

Office for Standards in Education (OFSTED) (1993c) *The New Teacher in School*, London: HMSO.

Office for Standards in Education (OFSTED) (1993d) *Curriculum Organisation and Classroom Practice in Primary Schools. A follow up report*, London: HMSO.

Office for Standards in Education (OFSTED) (1993e) *The Training of Primary School Teachers. March 1991-March 1992. A report from the Office of Her Majesty's Chief Inspector of Schools*, London: HMSO.

Office for Standards in Education (OFSTED) (1994) *Primary Matters. A discussion on teaching and learning in primary schools*, London: HMSO.

O'Hear, A. (1988) *Who Teaches the Teachers?*, London: Social Affairs Unit.

O'Keeffe, D. (1990) *The Wayward Elite*, London: Adam Smith Institute.

Open University (1983) *T263 Design: Process and Products*, Milton Keynes: Open University.

Owens, R. (1981) *Organisational Behaviour in Education*, Englewood Cliffs, New Jersey: Prentice-Hall.

Pendry, A. (1992) 'Mentoring in Teacher Education' in Lucas, P. and Watts, R. (eds) *Meeting the Challenge: Preparing Tomorrow's History Teachers*, Sheffield: Standing Conference of History Teacher Educators in the United Kingdom (SCHTE) in association with The Division of Education, University of Sheffield.

Pollard, A. and Tann, S. (1993) *Reflective Teaching in the Primary School: A Handbook for the Classroom*, (second edition) London: Cassell.

Pring, R. (1994) 'The Year 2000' in Wilkin, M. and Sankey, D. (eds) *Collaboration and Transition in Initial Teacher Training*, London: Kogan Page.

Pyke, N. (1994a) 'At Odds Over Self-Centred Consortia', *Times Educational Supplement*, 3 June.

Pyke, N. (1994b) 'In Training for Armageddon?', *Times Educational Supplement*, 3 June.

Reid, I., Constable, H. and Griffiths, R. (eds) (1994) *Teacher Education Reform: Current Research*, London: Paul Chapman Publishing.

Reynolds, M. C. (ed.) (1989) *Knowledge Base for the Beginning Teacher*, Oxford: Pergamon Press.

Rudduck, J. (1991) 'The Language of Consciousness and the Landscape of Action: Tensions in Teacher Education', *British Education Research Journal*, 17 (4).

Ryan, K. (1986) *The Induction of New Teachers*, Bloomington: Phi Delta Kappa.

Ryle, G. (1966) *The Concept of Mind*, Harmondsworth: Penguin Books.

Sands, M. and Bishop, P. (1993) 'Interpreting National Criteria for Initial Teacher Education: Creative Curriculum Development', *Cambridge Journal of Education*, 23 (2).

Schon, D. A. (1983) *The Reflective Practitioner: How Professionals Think in Action*, New York: Basic Books.

Schon, D. A. (1987) *Educating the Reflective Practitioner*, San Francisco: Jossey-Bass.

Senchuk, D. M. (1984) 'The Polymorphous Character of Teacher', *Educational Theory*, 34 (2).

Senge, P. (1990) *The Fifth Discipline*, London: Century Business.

Shaw, R. (1992) *Teacher Training in Secondary Schools*, London: Kogan Page.

Shulman, L. S. (1986) 'Those Who Understand: Knowledge Growth in Teaching', *Educational Research Review*, 57 (1).

Shulman, L. S. and Sykes, G. (1986) *A National Board for Teaching? In Search of a Bold Standard. A report for the task force on teaching as a profession*, New York: Carnegie Corporation.

Smith, R. (1992) 'Theory: an Entitlement to Understanding', *Cambridge Journal of Education*, 22 (3).

Smithers, A. and Robinson, P. (1992) *Technology in the National Curriculum: Getting it Right*, London: The Engineering Council.

Southgate, P. (ed.) (1988) *New Directions in Police Training*, London: HMSO.

Spencer, L. M. (1983) *Soft Skill Competencies*, Edinburgh: Scottish Council for Research in Education.

Stark, R. (1994) 'Supervising Teachers and Student Teachers: Roles and Relationships in Primary Initial Teacher Education', *Scottish Educational Review*, 26, (1).

Stephenson, J. (1994) 'The Anatomy of a Development' in Yeomans, R. and Sampson, J. (eds) *Mentorship in the Primary School*, London: Falmer Press.

Sternberg R. J. (ed.) (1982) *Advances in the Psychology of Human Intelligence, Volume 1*, Hillsdale, New Jersey: Lawrence Erlbaum Associates.

Talbert, J. et al. (1993) 'Understanding Context Effects on Secondary-School Teaching', *Teachers College Record*, 95 (1).

Taylor, C. (1982) 'Rationality' in Hollis, M. and Loukes, S. (eds) *Rationality and Relativism*, Oxford: Basil Blackwell.

Teaching as a Career (TASC) (1994) *School-Centred Initial Teacher Training Scheme. Information 5/94*.

Terrell, C. and Coles, D. (eds) (1988) *Recent Innovations in Initial Teacher Education for Intending Primary School Teachers*, Cheltenham College of St. Paul and St. Mary.

Tickle, L. (1992) 'Professional Skills Assessment in Classroom Teaching', *Cambridge Journal of Education*, 22 (1).

Tobin, K. and Fraser, B. J. (1988) 'Investigations of Exemplary Practice in High School Science and Mathematics', *Australian Journal of Education*, 32.

Tom, A. (1985) 'Inquiry into Inquiry-Oriented Teacher Education', *Journal of Teacher Education*, 35 (5).

Tomley, D. (1993) 'Individual Action Planning in Initial Teacher Training', *British Journal of In-Service Education*, 19 (2).

Turner, M. (1993) 'The Role of Mentors and Teacher Tutors in School-Based Teacher Education and Induction', *British Journal of In-Service Education*, 19 (1).

Tuxworth, E. (1989) 'Competence Based Education and Training: Background and Origins' in Burke, J. W. (ed.) *Competency Based Education and Training*, London: Falmer Press.

United Kingdom Central Council for Nursing, Midwifery and Health Visiting (UKCC) (1986) *Project 2000, A New Preparation for Practice*.

University of London Institute of Education (ULIE) (1994a) *Partnership in Training: the Secondary PGCE Course*, London: University of London Institute of Education.

University of London Institute of Education (ULIE) (1994b) *Initial Teacher Training: Secondary PGCE Handbook*, London: University of London Institute of Education.

Vonk, J. H. C. (1993) 'Mentoring Beginning Teachers: Mentor Knowledge and Skills', *Mentoring*, 1 (1).

Warnock, M. (1985) 'Teacher Teach Thyself', *The Listener*, 28 March.

Watkins, C. and Whalley, C. (1995 forthcoming) *Frameworks for Teacher Development*.

Welsh Office (1992) *Initial Teacher Training (Secondary Phase), Circular No. 35/92*, Cardiff: Welsh Office.

Welsh Office (1993) *Initial Teacher Training (Primary Phase), Circular No. 62/93*, Cardiff: Welsh Office.

Welton, J. (1906) *Principles and Methods of Teaching*, London: University Tutorial Press.

Whitty, G. (1991) *Next in Line for the Treatment? Education Reform and Teacher Education in the 1990s*, Inaugural lecture at Goldsmith's College, 14 May.

Whitty, G. and Willmott, E. (1991) 'Competence-Based Teacher Education: Approaches and Issues', *Cambridge Journal of Education*, 21 (3).

Wilkin, M. (1992a) 'On the Cusp: from Supervision to Mentoring in Initial Teacher Training', *Cambridge Journal of Education*, 22 (1).

Wilkin, M. (ed.) (1992b) *Mentoring in Schools*, London: Kogan Page.

Wilkin, M. (1994) *An Alternative Perspective on Initial Teacher Training: the Dialogue of Ideology and Culture*, Unpublished paper presented at the conference on 'Researching School-Based Teacher Education' held at the Chichester Institute of Higher Education (formerly West Sussex Institute of Higher Education), 15 July.

Wilkin, M. and Sankey, D. (eds) (1994) *Collaboration and Transition in Initial Teacher Training*, London: Kogan Page.

Williams, E. A. (1993) 'Teacher Perceptions of their Needs as Mentors in the Context of Developing School-Based Initial Teacher Education', *British Educational Research Journal*, 19 (4).

Williams, E. A., Butt, G. and Soares, A. (1992) 'Student Perceptions of a Secondary Postgraduate Certificate in Education Course', *Journal of Education for Teaching*, 18 (3).

Wilson, B. (1962) 'The Teacher's Role: A Sociological Analysis', *British Journal of Sociology*, 13, (1).

Wolf, A. (1994) 'Assessing the Broad Skills within Occupational Competence', *Competence and Assessment*, 25, produced by the Department of Employment.

Woods, P. (1987) 'Ethnography at the Crossroads: A Reply to Hammersley', *British Educational Research Journal*, 13 (3).

Yeomans, R. and Sampson, J. (eds) (1994) *Mentorship in the Primary School*, London: Falmer Press.

Zeichner, K. (1983) 'Alternative Paradigms of Teacher Education', *Journal of Teacher Education*, 34 (3).

Zeichner, K. (1990) 'Changing Directions in the Practicum: Looking Ahead to the 1990s', *Journal of Education for Teaching*, 16 (2).

Contributors

Ian Abbott co-directs the Teacher Development Research and Dissemination Unit at Warwick University. He has researched and published in the areas of the City Technology College initiative, vocational education, teaching and learning in higher education, and initial teacher education.

Trevor Arrowsmith is currently Deputy Head with responsibility for staff development/curriculum at Chenderit School, Northants.

Frank Banks graduated from the University of York, and holds a higher degree from the Open University. He taught in schools in England and Wales, worked as an Advisory Teacher and as a Lecturer in Education at the University of Wales. He is currently working for the Open University PGCE team and his research interests are in distance-learning and the development of pedagogical content knowledge in beginning teachers.

Vivienne Baumfield until recently held a dual role as a teacher supervising students in school and a Visiting Lecturer in Religious Education in the Department of Education, University of Newcastle. She has now been appointed to a full time post as a Lecturer in the Department of Education where she has been involved in the Mentor Development programme.

David Blake taught in primary schools and has a continuing interest in the primary school curriculum. Specific interests include school reviews, curriculum evaluation, classroom research and staff development. His research interests lie in the area of teacher education policy and practice. Current responsibilities are those of primary tutor and Head of Section.

Tim Cain is Senior Lecturer in music at LSU College of Higher Education in Southampton and a member of the department of Teaching Studies. He is the Director of the Southern Centre for Music Education and editor of the termly magazine 'Music in the Curriculum'.

Hilary Constable is coordinator of research in the School of Education, University of Sunderland. She has a continuing research interest in professional and organisational development.

Penni Cotton is a senior lecturer in the School of Education at Kingston University. Her specific interests focus on the implications of teacher education for children's language and literacy development within Europe. She is currently developing a European children's literature project in conjunction with HE colleagues from other member states.

Ruth Dann. Following research in the University of Wales on teacher professionalism and teacher appraisal Ruth was part of the Assessment and Evaluation Unit at Southampton University. She then taught at Highfield First and Middle School (Southampton) before taking up her current post of lecturer in Primary Education at Keele University.

Judith Dormer taught in comprehensive schools for 24 years and is currently second in charge of the Mathematics department at Exmouth Community College. Her experience in ITE is as a teacher in charge of students within traditional schemes of training and is a mentor of an Articled teacher and within a pilot school-based scheme.

David Egan is Head of the School of Secondary and Continuing Education in the Faculty Education and Sport at Cardiff Institute of Education. He has worked previously as a history teacher, lecturer and teacher-educator.

David Ellis taught for 12 years in primary schools in the north of England and the west country, including two years as a headteacher of a small school. For the last 14 years he has worked in teacher education at Edge Hill College in Lancashire and at Swansea and Cardiff Institutes of Higher Education in Wales, as well as spending three years at Ohio State University in the USA, where he took his Ph.D.

Linda Evans co-directs the Teacher Development and Dissemination Unit at Warwick University. She has researched and published in the areas of teacher morale and job satisfaction, teaching and learning in higher education, and initial teacher education.

Derek Glover was a headteacher in a secondary school. He has been an external examiner to PGCE courses and now works as a consultant and evaluator to a number of higher education institutions.

Rosalind Goodyear writes on government education policy, particularly as it relates to the initial education and continuing professional development of teachers, and has researched and evaluated local authority INSET.

Vincent Hanley teaches on PGCE, B.Ed., and MA (Ed.) courses. He has taught in primary and secondary schools and his specific interests are the teaching of English and practitioner-research.

Jean Howard, a philosophy graduate registered childminder and unqualified nursery assistant, entered teaching as a mature student in the early 70s by means of a one year shortened Teachers' Certificate course. She taught in secondary schools in Sunderland, Hounslow and Berkshire, becoming involved in Berkshire's pioneering work in multicultural/antiracist education under Robin Richardson. She then moved on to the Section II post of Teacher Adviser in Multicultural Education with Merton LEA before entering teacher education at St. Mary's University College, Strawberry Hill in 1987. She has a particular interest in denominational education.

Gill Hubbard is a research student in the School of Education, University of Sunderland. She is investigating the means by which beginning teachers acquire strategies in class management.

George Hudson is a senior lecturer in Professional and Education Studies at Worcester College of Higher Education. He has carried out educational research and evaluations in the primary, secondary sectors and into vocational education.

Mike Jennings taught mathematics and geography at a secondary school and worked as a teacher of English in a large language school in London before becoming a primary teacher. He spent ten years teaching in three ILEA primary schools, working from nursery through to fourth year juniors before becoming a member of a research group on assessment and an Advisory Teacher for Primary Mathematics. He is the coordinator of primary education across the B.Ed./BA (QTS), PGCE and Articled Teacher programmes, and his research interests are in school-based teacher training, induction, mentorship and local history studies.

David Kerr is a Lecturer in Education at the School of Education, University of Leicester with responsibility for the History PGCE (Secondary and Primary) courses and GEST primary history course. Prior to that he was project co-ordinator on the curriculum development project 'Economic Change and Society' based at the University of Leeds, and prior to that taught history in a school in Buckinghamshire. His research interests include history education, changes in teacher education and 16-19 education and training.

Catherine Kickham is currently the Programmes Director for Initial Teacher Education at LSU College of Higher Education in Southampton, and lectures in Primary Science at the college. Before joining LSU in 1990, Catherine had been deputy head teacher at Otterbourne Primary school in Hampshire. She retains a keen interest in children's learning in the classroom.

David Lambert is a Lecturer in Geography Education at the University of London, Institute of Education, and formerly head of geography and acting deputy headteacher at a comprehensive school in Hertfordshire. He has published numerous articles, particularly on geography in the national curriculum and its assessment, and his Key Stage 3 textbooks won the 1992 TES schoolbooks award. He is currently the co-ordinator for the eastern area of the Institute's Secondary Area-based PGCE.

David Leat is the Director of the Mentor Development programme in the Department of Education, University of Newcastle. He is involved in research into teachers' attitudes to teaching and learning and the need to develop a model of competence which links knowledge, feeling and behaviour.

Michele Lloyd is a researcher at the Chichester Institute of Higher Education. Her interests include feminist social research and she is currently investigating the professional socialisation of women and men secondary PGCE students.

Jane Maloney has been teaching at Kingston University since 1992. She previously taught in schools since 1976.

Terry Martin is a Lecturer in Education in the School of Education at the University of Southampton where he has been responsible for mentor training for the new partnership scheme. He has research and teaching interests in management in education, and counselling.

Joanna Moxham is a Senior Lecturer within Nene College's School of Education where her specific responsibilities are for Humanities within ITT and INSET courses. She has taught extensively on the Primary B.Ed. and PGCE courses and is currently involved in extending her PGCE focused research to engage in a collaborative exercise with colleagues from several other HE institutions on the benefits accrued by schools from student teacher placements.

Jerry Norton is a senior lecturer in education in the School of Education, University of Sunderland. He has published work on teachers' professional development and is especially interested in biography studies.

Andrew Powell has been teaching at Kingston University since 1988. Previously he taught in schools and colleges of further education.

Alan Pritchard is researching the role of teachers in the initial training of student teachers as well as working on a project investigating the role of IT in learning in the primary school.

Michael Totterdell is a Lecturer in Religious Education at the University of London, Institute of Education, and formerly head of religious education and senior teacher at a London school. For the past three years he has been the course leader for the PGCE in Religious Education and is currently the coordinator for the northern area of the Institute's Secondary Area-based PGCE. His research interests lie in the interrelationships between religion, culture and education, and he has recently been a Churchill Fellow.